IF FOUND, please notify and arrange return to owner. This flight manual is important for the owner's flight lessons. Thank you.

Pilot's Name _Bev Burt_

Address _61254 SR 15_

City/State/Zip _Goshen, In. 46526_

Telephone _(219) 533-4440_

Additional copies of *Recreational Pilot Flight Maneuvers* are available from

Aviation Publications, Inc.
P.O. Box 12848 • University Station
Gainesville, Florida 32604
(904) 375-0772

The price is $9.95. Orders must be prepaid and are shipped postpaid; i.e., we pay the postage. Florida residents must add 6% sales tax.

Aviation Publications, Inc. guarantees an immediate, complete refund on all mail orders if a resalable book is returned within 30 days.

ALSO AVAILABLE FROM AVIATION PUBLICATIONS, INC.
See pages 274-276 for additional information and an order form.

<u>Handbooks and Flight Maneuvers</u>

PRIVATE PILOT HANDBOOK
PRIVATE PILOT FLIGHT MANEUVERS
INSTRUMENT PILOT FLIGHT MANEUVERS & HANDBOOK
MULTIENGINE AND SEAPLANE FLIGHT MANEUVERS & HANDBOOK
COMMERCIAL PILOT AND FLIGHT INSTRUCTOR FLIGHT MANEUVERS & HANDBOOK

<u>Written Exam Books</u>

RECREATIONAL PILOT FAA WRITTEN EXAM
PRIVATE PILOT FAA WRITTEN EXAM
INSTRUMENT PILOT FAA WRITTEN EXAM
COMMERCIAL PILOT FAA WRITTEN EXAM
FLIGHT INSTRUCTOR/GROUND INSTRUCTOR FAA WRITTEN EXAM
FUNDAMENTALS OF INSTRUCTING FAA WRITTEN EXAM

REVIEWERS AND CONTRIBUTORS

Craig Delgato, CFI, B.S. in aviation management, Florida Institute of Technology, is a flight instructor and charter pilot at Gulf Atlantic Airways in Gainesville, Florida. He is a commercial pilot with instrument and multiengine ratings. Mr. Delgato reviewed the entire text, contributing to its technical accuracy.

Windy A. Kemp, B.S.Acc., University of Florida, assisted in the coordination of proofreading and production staffs. She will be joining a national public accounting firm in January 1990.

Paul E. McDuffee, CFII, is Chairman of the Flight Technology Department and Chief Flight Instructor at Embry Riddle Aeronautical University in Daytona Beach, Florida. He reviewed the majority of the text and provided many useful suggestions, some of which will be reflected in the Second Edition.

Patricia L. McGhee, B.A. University of Wisconsin-Madison, has 19 years of editing and production experience in scientific and technical publications. She assisted with the coordination of its production.

John F. Rebstock, CIA, is a graduate of the School of Accounting at the University of Florida. He has passed the CPA exam and is a CMA candidate. Mr. Rebstock prepared the page layout, reviewed the entire text, and coordinated its production.

Douglas E. Sims, CFI, is a flight instructor in single-engine and multi-engine airplanes. He reviewed the entire text, contributing to its technical accuracy.

The many FAA employees who helped, in person or by telephone, primarily in Gainesville, Florida; Orlando, Florida; Oklahoma City, Oklahoma; and Washington, DC.

The many CFIs, pilots, and student pilots who have provided comments and suggestions about all of my books during the past 8 years.

A PERSONAL THANKS

This manual would not have been possible without the extraordinary efforts and dedication of Ann Finnicum and Susan Young Burnett, who typed the entire manuscript and all revisions, as well as prepared the camera-ready pages. Ms. Burnett is also responsible for developing the typographic design utilized in this book.

The author also appreciates the proofreading assistance of Sandra Beasley, Debbie Durkin, Robert Francis, Appie Graham, Michael Kohl, Andrew Mason, Michael McLamb, Marcia Miller, Joan Millett, Leslie O'Donnell, Ketan Patel, Deanna Sanchez, Cristina Shaw, Mary Ann Vorce, Marie Wilker, Tina Wilson, and Chris Yost, and the production assistance of Debbie Durkin, Andy Mason, Joan Millett, Deanna Sanchez and Lori L. Stephens.

Finally, I appreciate the encouragement, support, and tolerance of my family throughout this project.

FIRST EDITION

RECREATIONAL PILOT

FLIGHT MANEUVERS

by Irvin N. Gleim, Ph.D., CFII

ABOUT THE AUTHOR

Irvin N. Gleim earned his private pilot certificate in 1965 from the Institute of Aviation at the University of Illinois, where he subsequently received his Ph.D. He is a commercial pilot and flight instructor (instrument) with instrument, multiengine, and seaplane ratings, and is a member of the Aircraft Owners and Pilots Association, American Bonanza Society, Civil Air Patrol, Experimental Aircraft Association, and Seaplane Pilots Association. He is also author of flight maneuvers and handbooks for the private, instrument, commercial, and flight instructor certificates/ratings, and study guides for the FAA written tests for the recreational, private, instrument, and commercial pilot.

Dr. Gleim has also written articles for professional accounting and business law journals, and is the author of the most widely used review manuals for the CIA exam (Certified Internal Auditor), the CMA exam (Certificate in Management Accounting), and the CPA exam (Certified Public Accountant). He is Professor Emeritus, Fisher School of Accounting at the University of Florida, and is a CIA, CMA, and CPA.

iv

Aviation Publications, Inc.
P.O. Box 12848 • University Station
Gainesville, Florida 32604
(904) 375-0772

Library of Congress Catalog Card No. 89-85119
ISBN 0-917539-22-2

The author is indebted to Beechcraft for permission to reprint various checklists, diagrams, and charts from the Beechcraft Skipper Pilot Operative Handbook, © 1980. These are reprinted **for academic illustration/training purposes only.** FOR FLIGHT, use your Pilot's Operating Handbook and FAA Approved Airplane Flight Manual.

The author is indebted to Cessna Aircraft Corporation for permission to reprint various checklists, diagrams, and charts from the C-152 Pilot Operating Handbook, © 1980. These are reprinted **for academic illustration/training purposes only.** FOR FLIGHT, use your Pilot's Operating Handbook and FAA Approved Airplane Flight Manual.

The author is indebted to Piper Aircraft Corporation for permission to reprint various checklists, diagrams, and charts from the Tomahawk Pilot's Operating Handbook, © 1978. These are reprinted **for academic illustration/training purposes only.** FOR FLIGHT, use your Pilot's Operating Handbook and FAA Approved Airplane Flight Manual.

CAUTION: This book is an academic presentation for training purposes only. Under **NO** circumstances can it be used as a substitute for your *Pilot's Operating Handbook* and *FAA Approved Airplane Flight Manual.* **You must fly and operate your airplane in accordance with your *Pilot's Operating Handbook* and *FAA Approved Airplane Flight Manual.***

HELP !!

This is one of two books of a new series designed specifically for recreational pilots. Please send any corrections and suggestions for subsequent editions to the author, c/o Aviation Publications, Inc. The last page in this book has been reserved for you to make comments and suggestions. It can be photocopied and mailed to Aviation Publications, Inc.

Also, please bring this book to the attention of flight instructors, fixed base operators, and others interested in flying. Wide distribution of this series of books and increased interest in flying depend on your assistance and good word. Thank you.

TABLE OF CONTENTS

PREFACE

The primary purpose of this FLIGHT MANEUVERS book is to provide you with the easiest, fastest, and least expensive means of successfully completing the Recreational Pilot (airplane) Practical Test. This has been accomplished by reorganizing and integrating the relevant FAA flight manuals and documents. We also have written the text to orient you completely with the FAA's new Practical Test Standards, which provide detailed specification of acceptable performance as a pilot.

To save you time, money, and frustration, we have listed the common errors made by student pilots in executing each flight maneuver or operation. Thus, you will be aware of what "not to do." We all learn by our mistakes, but this list provides you an opportunity to learn from the mistakes of others.

Most books create additional work for the user. In contrast, this FLIGHT MANEUVERS book facilitates your effort; i.e., it is easy to use. The outline format, numerous illustrations and diagrams, type styles, and spacing are designed to improve readability. Concepts are often presented as phrases rather than as complete sentences.

Read Chapter 1, "Learning to Fly," carefully. Also, recognize that this study manual is concerned with airplane flight training, rather than balloon, glider, or helicopter training. I am confident this manual will facilitate speedy completion of your practical test. I also wish you the very best as you complete your recreational pilot certificate, in subsequent flying, and in obtaining additional ratings and certificates.

I encourage your suggestions, comments, and corrections for future editions. The last page of this book has been designed to help you note corrections and suggestions throughout your study process. Please tear it out and mail it to me. Thank you.

Enjoy Flying -- Safely!

Irvin N. Gleim
September 15, 1989

CHAPTER ONE
LEARNING TO FLY

Learning to fly is both challenging and fun. This book tells you "how to" use airplane flight controls "to fly" single-engine airplanes. It is one of two books to assist you in earning a recreational pilot certificate. The other is

RECREATIONAL PILOT FAA WRITTEN EXAM, which is a carefully organized compendium of current actual FAA written test questions in a programmed learning format. Innovations for easy use include:

* Answer explanations provided to the immediate right of each question.

* Brief outlines preceding each series of questions explain exactly what you need to know.

* Questions presented in a logical order by topic.

* The deletion of all nonairplane questions, i.e., questions not applicable to your recreational pilot FAA written test.

The step above a recreational pilot certificate is a private pilot certificate. We offer the following books for the private pilot.

PRIVATE PILOT FAA WRITTEN EXAM
PRIVATE PILOT FLIGHT MANEUVERS
PRIVATE PILOT HANDBOOK

These books are similar in format to the recreational pilot books, except PRIVATE PILOT HANDBOOK is a helpful 432-page reference book that recreational pilots should probably obtain. The table of contents is presented on the next page.

We have summarized the basic information required for the recreational pilot certificate in PRIVATE PILOT HANDBOOK. It contains amplification of most topics. It will also assist you in gaining knowledge of

1. Night flight,
2. ATC clearances, and
3. Cross-country navigation.

These are subject areas that you are omitting by obtaining a recreational pilot certificate rather than a private pilot certificate.

See the order form on page 276 to receive a copy.

WHAT IS A RECREATIONAL PILOT CERTIFICATE?

A recreational pilot certificate is much like an ordinary driver's license. A recreational pilot certificate will allow the pilot to fly an airplane and carry one passenger and baggage, although not for compensation or hire. However, operating expenses may be shared with your passenger. The certificate, which is a piece of paper similar to a driver's license, is sent to you by the Federal Aviation Administration (FAA) upon satisfactory completion of

1.   Your training program,
2.   A written test, and
3.   A practical (flight) test.

A sample certificate is reproduced below.

Front   Back

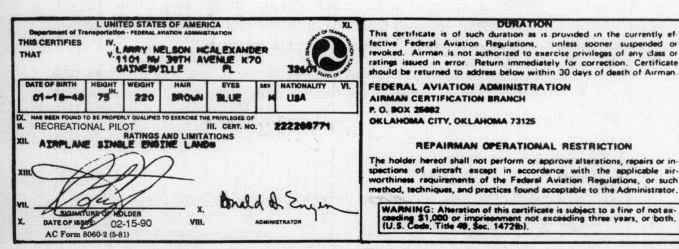

REQUIREMENTS TO OBTAIN A RECREATIONAL PILOT CERTIFICATE

1. **Obtain an FAA medical certificate.**

   a. You must undergo a routine medical examination which may only be administered by FAA-designated doctors called FAA medical examiners.

   b. To obtain this medical certificate, the applicant must be at least 16 years of age and be able to read, speak, and understand the English language.

   c. The medical certificate necessary for a recreational pilot certificate is called a third class medical. It is valid for 2 years and is good through the last day of the month issued (another medical examination is then required).

   d. Even if you have a physical handicap, medical certificates can be issued in many cases. Operating limitations may be imposed depending on the nature of the disability.

   e. Your flight instructor or fixed base operator (FBO) will be able to recommend an aviation medical examiner.

      1) FBO is an airport business that gives flight lessons, sells aviation fuel, repairs and rents airplanes, etc.

      2) Also, the FAA publishes a directory that lists all authorized aviation medical examiners by name and address. Copies of this directory are kept at all FAA District Offices, Air Traffic Control (ATC) facilities, and Flight Service Stations (FSSs).

   f. The front and back of a sample FAA medical certificate/student pilot certificate are reproduced below.

Front   **Back**

1)   The medical certificate will function as your student pilot certificate once it is signed by you and the medical examiner.

2)   Note that the back of the student pilot certificate must be signed by your flight instructor prior to solo flight (flying by yourself).

3)   The only substantive difference between a regular medical certificate and a medical certificate/student pilot certificate is that the back of the medical certificate/student pilot certificate provides for flight instructor signatures (called *endorsements*).

4)   It expires at the end of the 24th month after issuance.

2.   **Pass a written test with a score of 70% or better.** This test is administered at most Flight Standard District Offices (FSDOs) and at some airport FBOs. The test consists of 50 multiple-choice questions selected from the 445 airplane-related questions among the 500 questions in the official FAA Recreational Pilot Question Book (the balance of questions is for helicopters and rotorcraft). All 445 airplane-related questions are reproduced, answered, and explained in *RECREATIONAL PILOT FAA WRITTEN EXAM* (order form on page 276). The questions test the following topics:

a.   Introduction to Airplanes and Aerodynamics
b.   Airplane Performance
c.   Airplane Instruments, Engines, and Systems
d.   Airports and Air Traffic Control
e.   Weight and Balance
f.   Weather
g.   Federal Aviation Regulations
h.   Navigational Publications and Sectional Charts
i.   Flight Physiology and Flight Operations

You are required to satisfactorily complete a ground instruction or home study course prior to taking the written test. Page 272 contains a standard authorization form to take the written test which can be completed and signed by a flight or ground instructor, torn out, and taken to the examination site.

3.   **Obtain at least 30 hours of flight instruction and solo flight time.** The required FAA flight maneuvers are thoroughly discussed in this book. The requirements include

a.   15 hours of flight instruction from an authorized flight instructor, including at least
1)   Two hours away from the vicinity of the airport with at least three landings at an airport at least 25 nautical miles (NM) from the departure airport.
2)   Two hours in airplanes in preparation for the private pilot flight test within 60 days prior to that test.
b.   15 hours of solo flight time.

4.   **Successfully complete a practical test which will be given as a "final exam" by an FAA inspector or designated examiner.** See Chapter 14, "FAA Practical Test," which begins on page 235.

a.   FAA inspectors are FAA employees and do not charge for their services.

b.   FAA-designated examiners are proficient, experienced flight instructors and pilots who are authorized by the FAA to conduct flight tests and administer FAA written tests. They do charge a fee.

COSTS TO OBTAIN YOUR RECREATIONAL PILOT CERTIFICATE

The price of instruction varies across the country and also from FBO to FBO. Fuel, maintenance, and airplane costs play a major role in determining airplane rental rates. Just as with any sizable purchase, you should "shop around" to make sure you are buying what you want at a fair price.

Listed below is an example cost estimate totaling $2,000. Your total cost will depend on the FBO, equipment, local cost factors, competition, and the amount of training in excess of 30 hours. Fortunately, most flight schools require that cash outlays be made as time progresses, lesson by lesson, instead of all at once.

Medical exam	$ 35
Books and supplies (assuming self-study)	50 (a)
Written test fee	20 (b)
15 hours of dual	825 (c)
15 hours of solo	600 (d)
Rental of aircraft for flight test	60
Examiner's fee	100
Other	310
TOTAL	$2,000

a. **Books and Supplies, $50.** Assuming a course of self-study, *RECREATIONAL PILOT FAA WRITTEN EXAM, RECREATIONAL PILOT FLIGHT MANEUVERS, PRIVATE PILOT HANDBOOK*, a FAR/AIM book, a sectional chart, and a plotter will cost about $50. A plotter is used to navigate. FAR refers to the Federal Aviation Regulations, and *AIM* refers to the *Airman's Information Manual*. You may purchase these books as well as a sectional chart (an aviation map) at an FBO.

b. **Written Test Fee, $20.** This fee is the typical charge by most FBOs to administer the FAA written test. There is no charge if you take the test at an FAA Flight Standards District Office (FSDO). However, you may spend more than $20 in gas and time getting to and from the nearest FSDO.

c. **15 Hours of Dual, $825.** This is based on $40 per hour for the aircraft and $15 per hour for your instructor.

d. **15 hours of Solo, $600.** This is based on $40 per hour for airplane rental.

Many FBOs sell blocks of time, e.g., 10 or 20 hours at a discount of perhaps 10% if paid in advance.

Do not be upset if you have to fly more than 30 hours prior to your flight test. Most students will require about 40 hours of flight time. Thus, you should be prepared to spend several hundred dollars more than your original minimum estimate. Conversely, there are probably a few flight schools at which you can obtain a recreational certificate for less than $1,500.

STEPS TO TAKE

1. **Read this chapter.** Obtain copies of *RECREATIONAL PILOT FAA WRITTEN EXAM* and, as a supplement, *PRIVATE PILOT HANDBOOK.*

2. **Visit several FBOs, if more than one is available, to talk to flight instructors about flying lessons.** Look in the Yellow Pages under aircraft schools, airplane instruction, aircraft sales, airports, etc. Indicate that you are interested in taking flying lessons and want to choose a flight instructor you will feel comfortable with. Plan to speak to several instructors. Questions to ask prospective flight instructors include:

    a. *How long have they been instructing?* There is no preferable level of experience. Old timers may be the most competent or merely complacent. New instructors may be the most enthusiastic, thorough, diligent, current, etc.

    b. *Do they instruct full- or part-time?*

    c. *Are they familiar with* **Recreational Pilot FAA Written Exam** *and* **Recreational Pilot Flight Maneuvers**?

    d. *How long does their average student take to solo?* Note that the CFI who solos his/her students in the least amount of time may not be the best instructor. The objective of these questions is to gain insight into the personality of the CFI you are speaking with.

    e. *How many total hours of solo and dual flight do their typical students require?*

    f. Most students will require more than 30 total hours. Your question is *how much more?*

    g. *What is the rental cost for their training aircraft, solo and dual?*

    h. *Where do they recommend you take your flight test and how much will it cost?*

    i. *Where do they recommend you take your medical examination?*

    j. *Does the flight instructor's schedule and available aircraft fit your schedule?*

    k. *Do they have an "orientation flight" program for a nominal fee, e.g., $10 or $20?* If so, take it with the understanding of having no further obligation.

3. **Once you have made a preliminary choice of flight instructor and/or FBO, you need to sit down with your flight instructor and map out a schedule:**

    a. When and how often you will fly.
    b. When you will take the FAA written test.
    c. When you should plan to have your recreational pilot certificate.
    d. When and how payments will be made for your instruction.
    e. Review, revise, and update the total cost to obtain your certificate as outlined on page 5.

4. **Schedule and take your flight physical** to receive your combined medical certificate/student pilot certificate.

5. **Consider purchasing an airplane** (by yourself or through joint ownership) **or joining a flying club.** Frequently, sharing expenses through joint ownership can reduce the cost of flying. Note, however, that insurance for student pilots and flight instruction is very expensive. Thus, unless there are other student pilots already using the plane, the incremental insurance costs may be prohibitive.

a.   Inquire about local flying clubs. Call a participant and learn about their services, costs, etc.

b.   Take several lessons prior to investing in any aircraft. You may find that you do not like flying. (You would certainly be in a minority!)

6. **Pass the written test and the practical test.**

7. **Enjoy flying -- safely!**

LEARNING FLIGHT MANEUVERS

The purpose of Chapters 2 through 14 of *RECREATIONAL PILOT FLIGHT MANEUVERS* is to carefully explain each phase of your flight training program for the recreational pilot certificate (i.e., your in-the-airplane training). The main objective is to think and plan ahead. Accordingly, this text will help you anticipate the various conditions you may encounter while flying, and the resulting required actions on your part.

Each chapter is designed to be short and to the point to encourage you to study each topic before you practice it in the airplane and to study it again immediately after your flight training. You should make notes in the margins throughout this chapter and all other chapters and appendices of this text.

Prior to your first flight, read Chapters 2, 3, 4, and 5. This will permit you to get off to a good start toward developing your pilot skills. The primary purpose of all flight training is to develop safe and proficient pilots. The FAA flight proficiency requirements for a recreational pilot license (certificate) are

1. Executing tasks within the airplane's performance capabilities and limitations, including use of the airplane's systems.

2. Executing emergency procedures and maneuvers appropriate to the airplane.

3. Piloting the airplane with smoothness and accuracy.

4. Exercising good judgment.

5. Applying aeronautical knowledge.

6. Showing mastery of the airplane within the range of the Practical Test Standards (PTSs), and with the successful outcome of a procedure or maneuver never seriously in doubt.

Chapters 2 through 14 of this book follow a logical sequence of flight topics.

Chapter 2 - Airplanes and Aerodynamics
Chapter 3 - Learning Your Airplane
Chapter 4 - Preflight Procedures
Chapter 5 - Taxiing
Chapter 6 - Takeoffs
Chapter 7 - Basic Flight Maneuvers
Chapter 8 - Landings
Chapter 9 - Slowflight, Stalls, and Spins
Chapter 10 - Ground Reference Maneuvers
Chapter 11 - Solo Flight
Chapter 12 - Navigation
Chapter 13 - Emergencies
Chapter 14 - FAA Practical Test

You should feel free to skip around from chapter to chapter, however, to suit your interests and the suggestions of your flight instructor. For each flight maneuver, the following should be understood:

1.   What should be done.
2.   When it should be done.
3.   How it should be done.
4.   Why it should be done.✗
5.   How the maneuver relates to overall pilot proficiency.
6.   Acceptable performance limits.
7.   Common problems, errors, shortcomings, and how to avoid them.

You and your instructor should discuss each of the above seven points at the start of each lesson <u>before</u> getting into the plane. Your instructor may wish to use a model airplane, a chalkboard, slides, reference materials, etc. as training aids to facilitate your preflight discussion.

After each flight, you and your instructor should evaluate your performance based on:

1.   What you did well.
2.   Areas to work on.
3.   Reason(s) for inadequate performance.
4.   How to improve performance.
5.   Maneuvers to study for the next flight.

BEECH, CESSNA, AND PIPER CHECKLISTS

Throughout this book, checklists are reproduced from the FAA-approved flight manuals for Beechcraft Skippers, Cessna 152s, and Piper Tomahawks **FOR ILLUSTRATIVE PURPOSES ONLY**. These airplanes were selected because they illustrate the most popular trainers currently available at FBOs. Please recognize that the checklists have, in many cases, been taken out of context and are intended ONLY as specific illustrations of the general procedures presented throughout this book.

You MUST rely on and use the FAA-approved flight manual issued for YOUR AIRPLANE. Remember that these FAA-approved flight manuals are continually being revised by the manufacturer, who issues the manual as a ringbook (the manufacturer sends out insertable revision pages as changes are made).

RECREATIONAL PILOT FAA PRACTICAL TEST STANDARDS

The FAA has issued "Practical Test Standards" (PTSs) for the recreational pilot FAA practical (flight) test. The purpose of these PTSs is to structure the procedures that designated examiners (and also FAA inspectors) use to administer the flight test, i.e., which maneuvers are tested and how. The following nine paragraphs have been taken from the FAA Recreational Pilot PTSs to provide you insight into this new approach to FAA flight tests.

1. **Practical Test Standard Concepts.** Federal Aviation Regulations (FARs) specify the areas in which knowledge and skill must be demonstrated by the applicant before the issuance of a pilot certificate or rating. The FARs provide the flexibility to permit the FAA to publish practical test standards containing specific TASKS (procedures and maneuvers) in which pilot competence must be demonstrated.

2. **Flight Instructor Responsibility.** An appropriately rated flight instructor is responsible for training the student to the acceptable standards as outlined in the objective of each TASK within the appropriate practical test standard. The flight instructor must certify that the applicant is able to perform safely as a private pilot and is competent to pass the required practical test for the certificate or rating sought.

3. **Examiner Responsibility.** The examiner (the FAA inspector or FAA-designated pilot examiner) who conducts the practical test is responsible for determining that the applicant meets the standards outlined in the objective of each TASK within the appropriate practical test standard. The examiner shall meet this responsibility by accomplishing an ACTION that is appropriate for each TASK. For each TASK that involves "knowledge only" elements, the examiner will orally quiz the applicant on those elements. For each TASK that involves both "knowledge and skill" elements, the examiner will orally quiz the applicant regarding knowledge elements and ask the applicant to perform the skill elements. The examiner will determine that the applicant's knowledge and skill meets the objective in all required TASKS. Oral questioning may be used at any time during the practical test.

4. **Use of the Practical Test Book.** The FAA requires that each practical test be conducted in strict compliance with the appropriate practical test standards for the issuance of a pilot certificate or rating. When using the practical test book, the examiner must evaluate the applicant's knowledge and skill in sufficient depth to determine that the standards of performance listed for all TASKS are met.

   a. When the demonstration of a TASK is not practicable, e.g., night flying, competence should be evaluated by oral testing.

   b. The examiner is not required to follow the precise order in which the AREAS OF OPERATION and TASKS appear in each section. The examiner may change the sequence or combine TASKS with similar objectives to conserve time. Examiners will develop a plan of action that includes the order and combination of TASKS to be demonstrated by the applicant in a manner that will result in an efficient and valid test.

   c. Suggested Examples of Combining TASKS:

      1) Descending turns may be combined with high-altitude emergencies,

      2) Rectangular course may be combined with airport traffic pattern, and

      3) Navigation during flight by reference to instruments may be combined with visual navigation.

   d. Other TASKS with similar OBJECTIVES may be combined to conserve time. However, the OBJECTIVES of all TASKS must be demonstrated and evaluated at some time during the practical test.

   e. Examiners will place special emphasis upon areas of aircraft operation that are most critical to flight safety. Among these areas are correct aircraft control and sound judgment in decision making. If these areas are shown in the OBJECTIVE, additional emphasis will be placed on them. The examiner will also emphasize stall/spin awareness, spatial disorientation, collision avoidance, wake turbulence avoidance, low-level wind shear, use of the checklist, and other areas as directed by future revisions of this standard.

5. **Use of Distractions During Practical Tests.** Numerous studies indicate that many accidents have occurred when the pilot's attention has been distracted during various phases of flight.

   a. Many accidents have resulted from engine failure during takeoffs and landings, but under conditions in which safe flight was possible had the pilot used correct control technique and divided attention properly. Distractions found to cause problems are

      1) Preoccupation with situations inside or outside the cockpit,

      2) Maneuvering to avoid other traffic, or

      3) Maneuvering to clear obstacles during takeoffs, climbs, approaches, or landings.

   b. To strengthen this area of pilot training and evaluation, the examiner will provide realistic distractions throughout the flight portion of the practical test. Some examples of distractions are

      1) Simulating engine failure;

      2) Simulating radio tuning and communications;

      3) Identifying a field suitable for emergency landings;

      4) Identifying features or objects on the ground;

      5) Reading the outside air temperature gauge;

      6) Removing objects from the glove compartment or map case; and

      7) Questioning by the examiner.

6. **Practical Test Prerequisites.** An applicant for a practical test is required by FARs to

   a. Pass the appropriate pilot written test since the beginning of the 24th month before the month in which the flight test is taken;

   b. Obtain the applicable instruction and aeronautical experience prescribed for the pilot certificate or rating sought;

   c. Possess a current medical certificate appropriate to the certificate or rating sought;

   d. Meet the age requirement for the issuance of the certificate or rating sought; and

   e. Obtain a written statement from an appropriately certificated flight instructor certifying that the applicant has been given flight instruction in preparation for the practical test within 60 days preceding the date of application. The statement shall also state that the instructor finds the applicant competent to pass the practical test, and that the applicant has satisfactory knowledge of the subject area(s) in which a deficiency was indicated by the airman written test report.

7. **Satisfactory Performance.** The ability of an applicant to perform the required TASKS is based on

   a. Executing TASKS within the aircraft's performance capabilities and limitations, including use of the aircraft's systems;

   b. Executing emergency procedures and maneuvers appropriate to the aircraft;

   c. Piloting the aircraft with smoothness and accuracy;

   d. Exercising good judgment;

   e. Applying aeronautical knowledge; and

   f. Showing mastery of the aircraft within the standards outlined in this book, with the successful outcome of a TASK never seriously in doubt.

8. **Unsatisfactory Performance.** If, in the judgment of the examiner, the applicant does not meet the standards of performance of any TASK performed, the associated PILOT OPERATION is failed and, therefore, the practical test is failed. The examiner or applicant may discontinue the test at any time after the failure. If the test is discontinued, the applicant is entitled to credit for only those TASKS satisfactorily performed. However, during the retest and at the discretion of the examiner, any TASK may be re-evaluated including those previously passed.

   a. The tolerances stated in the OBJECTIVE represent the minimum performance expected in good flying conditions.

   b. Consistently exceeding (i.e., violating) tolerances or failure to take prompt corrective action when tolerances are exceeded is unsatisfactory performance.

   c. Any action, or lack thereof, by the applicant that requires corrective intervention by the examiner to maintain safe flight will be disqualifying. The applicant must use proper and effective scanning techniques to clear the area before performing maneuvers. Ineffective performance in these areas will be disqualifying.

9. **Recording Unsatisfactory Performance.** The term *PILOT OPERATION* is used in regulations to denote areas (procedures and maneuvers) in which the applicant must demonstrate competence prior to being issued a pilot certificate. When a disapproval notice is issued, the examiner will record the applicant's unsatisfactory performance in terms of PILOT OPERATIONS appropriate to the practical test conducted.

TASKS TESTED ON YOUR FAA FLIGHT TEST

Also see Chapter 14, "FAA Practical Test," which begins on page 235. Appendix A, page 249, lists the titles of each of the 34 Tasks and provides cross-references to the chapter and page number in this book where they are discussed and reprinted.

The FAA has identified 34 Tasks to be tested and organized them into 8 Areas of Operation:

      I. Preflight Preparation
     II. Airport and Traffic Pattern Operation
    III. Normal Takeoff and Landing
    IV. Maximum Performance Takeoff and Landing
     V. Flight at Critically Slow Airspeed
    VI. Flight Maneuvering by Reference to Ground Objects
   VII. Navigation
  VIII. Emergency Operation

For each of the 34 Tasks, the FAA standards specify in "OBJECTIVES" what you are to do. For example, "normal and crosswind takeoff" is one Task. A reprint from the FAA PTSs as used by FAA examiners is presented on page 12. It is printed in italics and presented in a shaded box, as all reprints of standards will be. The FAA standards for each of the 34 Tasks are reproduced in the appropriate chapters of this book.

III. Area of Operation: Normal Takeoff and Landing

A. TASK: **NORMAL AND CROSSWIND TAKEOFF** *(ASEL)*
   PILOT OPERATION - 8
   REFERENCE: AC 61-21. (Report the Flight Publication)

Objective. To determine that the applicant:

1. Exhibits knowledge by explaining the elements of normal and crosswind takeoffs, including airspeeds, configurations, and emergency procedures.

2. Verifies the wind direction.

3. Aligns the airplane on the runway centerline.

4. Applies full aileron deflection in the proper direction, where crosswind exists.

5. Advances the throttle smoothly to maximum allowable power.

6. Checks the engine instruments.

7. Maintains directional control on the runway centerline.

8. Adjusts aileron deflection during acceleration (crosswind conditions).

9. Rotates at the recommended* airspeed, accelerates to V_y and establishes wind-drift correction (crosswind conditions).

10. Establishes the pitch attitude for V_y and maintains V_y, ±10 kts.

11. Retracts the wing flaps as recommended or at a safe altitude.

12. Maintains takeoff power to a safe maneuvering altitude.

13. Maintains a straight track over the extended runway centerline until a turn is required.

14. Completes after-takeoff checklist.

* The term "recommended" refers to the manufacturer's recommendation. If the manufacturer's recommendation is not available, the description contained in AC 61-21 will be used.

"Pilot Operation - 8" refers to FAR 61.98, "Flight Proficiency," which specifies eight categories of flight operations that CFIs are to use for instructing recreational pilot applicants. Thus, this is only an FAA cross-reference with little or no significance to student pilots and CFIs. For your information, the eight items in 61.98 are:

1. Preflight operations, including weight and balance determination, line inspection, airplane servicing, powerplant operations, and aircraft systems;

2. Airport and traffic pattern operations, collision and wake turbulence avoidance;

3. Flight maneuvering by reference to ground objects;

4. Pilotage with the aid of magnetic compass;

5. Flight at critically slow airspeeds, and the recognition of and recovery from imminent and full stalls entered from straight flight and from turns;

6. Emergency operations, including simulated aircraft and equipment malfunctions;

7. Maximum performance takeoffs and landings; and

8. Normal and crosswind takeoffs and landings.

Each of the 34 Tasks provides a "reference," a number that refers to an FAA publication. The references used are

Number	Title
AIM	Airman's Information Manual
FAR 61	Federal Aviation Regulations Part 61, "Certification: Pilots and Flight Instructors"
FAR 91	Federal Aviation Regulations Part 91, "General Operating and Flight Rules"
AC 00-6	Aviation Weather
AC 00-45	Aviation Weather Services
AC 61-21	Flight Training Handbook
AC 61-23	Pilot's Handbook of Aeronautical Knowledge
AC 61-84	Role of Preflight Preparation
AC 67-2	Medical Handbook for Pilots
AC 91-13	Cold Weather Operation of Aircraft
AC 91-55	Reduction of Electrical System Failures Following Aircraft Engine Starting

The pertinent material from these FAA publications is outlined and integrated in the appropriate chapters in this book.

See Appendix C, which begins on page 255, for an outline of Federal Aviation Regulations which may pertain to recreational pilots. FAR 61.101, "Recreational Pilot Privileges and Limitations," is most pertinent to recreational pilots (see page 262).

CHAPTER TWO
AIRPLANES AND AERODYNAMICS

The purpose of this chapter is to introduce you to the parts of the airplane and to aerodynamics, i.e., the forces acting on the airplane in flight. As you study this and subsequent chapters, write all "new" terms, definitions, etc. on a separate sheet of paper. At the end of each study session, review these new concepts to make sure you understand them.

If you become bored or confused by the detail, skim the chapter to obtain an overview. Then later, as you study subsequent chapters, you can return to study (and learn) the material in this chapter as needed. Also, this chapter will make more sense after you have experienced several flights.

THE AIRPLANE

The diagram on the next page is a high-wing aircraft (the Cessna 152). On low-wing aircraft, e.g., the Beech Skipper and the Piper Tomahawk, the wings are affixed to the bottom rather than the top of the fuselage. See page 17 for more discussion on high-wing vs. low-wing airplanes.

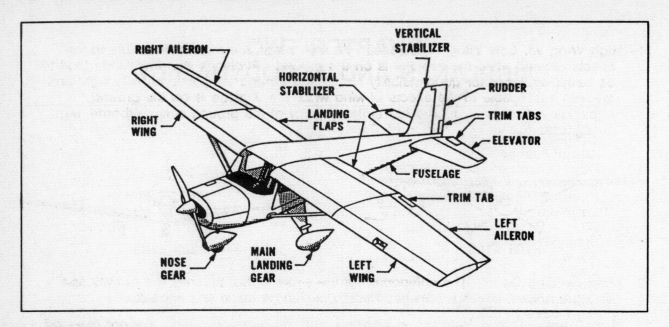

1. **Right and Left Wing** -- The wing of the airplane provides lift by creating a low pressure area on the top of the wing and a high pressure area on the bottom. The wing tends to move from high pressure to low pressure, thus creating lift. Lift is explained under a separate sideheading on page 27.

2. **Fuselage** -- the main component of the airplane. Its function is to act as a carrier for the wings and tail section. It also is designed to produce a limited amount of lift.

3. **Horizontal Stabilizer** -- This structure, located in the rear of the airplane, is designed to provide continuous longitudinal ("pitch") stability. It produces negative lift, which offsets the heaviness of the nose of the airplane.

4. **Elevator** -- a movable part on the rear of the horizontal stabilizer. It is used to move the airplane about the lateral axis. See the diagram on page 18. It provides the input of pitch and helps control altitude.

5. **Vertical Stabilizer** -- This surface provides directional ("yaw") stability. It acts like a weathervane.

6. **Rudder** -- This surface, which is connected to the vertical stabilizer, moves the airplane around its vertical axis and is used to yaw the airplane. See the "Axes of Rotation" sideheading and the accompanying diagram on page 18.

7. **Rudder and Elevator Trim Tabs** -- These provide a means to decrease or increase control pressures and help to establish hands-off flight (i.e., when the plane will almost fly by itself).

8. **Right and Left Ailerons** -- These surfaces, located on the outside trailing edges of the wings, control the airplane around its longitudinal axis (See the diagram on page 18) and provide the input of roll control.

9. **Aileron Trim Tabs** -- These are small movable section(s) of one or both ailerons that permit adjustment so the wings remain level; i.e., you can compensate for more weight on either side of the airplane.

10. **Landing Flaps** -- These are located on the inside trailing edges of the wings. They can be extended to provide greater wing area at slower speeds. This provides more lift and drag and allows an airplane to land, take off, or fly at slower speeds.

11. **High Wing vs. Low Wing** -- Airplanes with high wings are more susceptible to the effects of wind while the airplane is on the ground. Airplanes with low wings tend to be better airplanes for good visibility above and around the plane while in flight and are less susceptible to the effects of wind while the airplane is on the ground. Airplanes with high wings provide better visibility of the ground when airborne, e.g., for sightseeing.

HIGH WING   LOW WING

12. **Main Landing Gear** -- The component of the airplane that touches the runway first during a normal landing. It is stressed to take large loads and impacts.

13. **Nose Gear** -- This is designed to steer the airplane on the ground. It is not stressed for excessive impacts or loads. It <u>is</u> designed to carry the weight of the forward portion of the airplane.

14. **Nosewheel (tricycle) vs. Tailwheel (conventional)** -- Nosewheel airplanes have the "third" wheel in front of the main landing gear (i.e., under the nose). Tailwheel airplanes have the "third" wheel under the tail. Tailwheel airplanes can land on much rougher terrain and, consequently, are used by bush pilots. In a tailwheel airplane, this gear supports the weight of the rear portion of the airplane. Nosewheel airplanes have much better handling and visibility characteristics while taxiing. Almost all new airplanes are nosewheel design.

15. **Retractable Landing Gear** -- Retracting the gear reduces the drag, and increases the airspeed without additional power. The landing gear normally retracts into the wing or fuselage through an opening that is covered by doors after the gear is retracted. The smooth door thus provides for the unrestricted flow of air across the opening which houses the gear. The retraction or extension of the landing gear is accomplished either electrically or hydraulically by landing gear controls from within the cockpit. Warning indicators are usually provided in the cockpit to indicate whether the wheels are extended and locked, or retracted. In nearly all airplanes equipped with retractable landing gear, a system is provided for emergency gear extension in the event landing gear mechanisms fail to lower the gear.

CATEGORIES OF AIRCRAFT

A. The discussion in this book pertains only to airplanes. There are 3 other categories of aircraft: gliders, rotorcraft, and lighter than air. Each category, except gliders, has *classes*, e.g., single-engine land.

    1. Airplanes

        a. Single-engine land
        b. Multiengine land
        c. Single-engine sea
        d. Multiengine sea

2. Gliders

3. Rotorcraft

    a. Gyroplanes -- thrust from a pusher propeller and lift from an unpowered rotorblade.

    b. Helicopter -- rotorblade is powered to obtain lift.

4. Lighter than air

    a. Hot air (e.g., balloons)
    b. Gas (e.g., blimps)

AXES OF ROTATION

A. The airplane has three axes of rotation around which it moves.

    1. **Lateral (pitch) axis** -- an imaginary line from wingtip to wingtip.

        a. Rotation about the lateral axis is called pitch and is controlled by the elevators. This rotation is referred to as longitudinal control or longitudinal stability. This may seem confusing, but consider that as the airplane rotates about the lateral axis, the longitudinal axis (the front to rear axis) moves up and down.

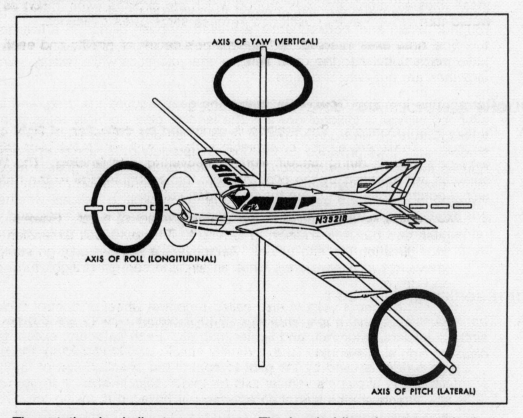

        b. The rotation is similar to a seesaw. The bar holding the seesaw is the lateral axis but the rotation is longitudinal.

        c. This is known as the airplane's "pitch."

   2. **Longitudinal (roll) axis** -- an imaginary line from the nose to the tail.

      a. Rotation about the longitudinal axis is called roll and is controlled by the ailerons. This rotation is referred to as lateral control or lateral stability. This may seem confusing, but consider that as the airplane rotates about the longitudinal axis (i.e., rolls), the lateral axis (the line through the wingtips) moves up and down.

      b. The rotation is similar to a barbecue spit, where the spit is the longitudinal axis but the rotation is lateral.

      c. This is known as the airplane's "bank."

   3. **Vertical (yaw) axis** -- an imaginary line extending vertically through the intersection of the lateral and longitudinal axes.

      a. Rotation about the vertical axis is called yaw and is controlled by the rudder. This rotation is referred to as directional control or directional stability.

      b. The rotation is similar to a weathervane, where the post holding the vane is the vertical axis but the rotation is directional.

      c. This is known as the airplane's "heading."

B. The airplane can rotate around one, two, or all three axes simultaneously. Think of these axes as imaginary axles around which the airplane turns, much as a wheel would turn around axles positioned in these same three directions.

   1. The three axes intersect at the airplane's center of gravity and each one is perpendicular to the other two.

FLIGHT CONTROLS AND CONTROL SURFACES

A. Primary Flight Controls. The airplane is controlled by deflection of flight control surfaces. These are hinged or movable surfaces with which the pilot adjusts the airplane's attitude during takeoff, flight maneuvering, and landing. The flight control surfaces are operated by the pilot through connecting linkage to the rudder pedals and a control yoke. See also the next sideheading.

   1. The control yoke is similar to the steering wheel of a car. However, you can push and pull it in addition to turning it. The push/pull dimension controls the third direction (up and down). Remember, a car can only go straight or turn (move in two dimensions), while an airplane can go straight, turn, or move up and down.

      a. The control yoke is also called a control wheel or control stick. In some airplanes, it is a stick that can be moved right or left and forward or back.

   2. The rudder is attached to the vertical stabilizer. Controlled by the rudder pedals, the rudder is used by the pilot to control the direction (left or right) of yaw about the airplane's vertical axis for minor adjustments. It is not used to make the airplane turn, as is often erroneously believed (banking the airplane makes it turn).

   3. The elevators are attached to the horizontal stabilizer. The elevators provide the pilot with control of the pitch attitude about the airplane's lateral axis. The elevators are controlled by pushing or pulling the control yoke.

4.   The movable portions of each wing are the ailerons. The term "aileron" is the French word for "little wing." The ailerons are located on the trailing (rear) edge of each wing near the outer tips. When deflected up or down they in effect change the wing's camber (curvature) and its angle of attack. This changes the wing's lift and drag characteristics.

    a.   Their primary use is to bank (roll) the airplane around its longitudinal axis. The banking of the wings results in the airplane turning in the direction of the bank, i.e., toward the direction of the low wing.

    b.   The ailerons are interconnected in the control system to operate simultaneously in opposite directions of each other. As the aileron on one wing is deflected downward, the aileron on the opposite wing is deflected upward.

    c.   The ailerons are controlled by turning the control yoke.

B.   Secondary Flight Controls. In addition to the primary flight controls, most modern airplanes also have another group called "secondary controls." These include trim devices of various types, spoilers, and wing flaps.

    1.   Trim tabs are commonly used to relieve the pilot of maintaining continuous pressure on the primary controls. Thus, you can "retrim" at each power setting and/or flight attitude to neutralize control pressure.

    2.   Spoilers, found only on certain airplane designs and most gliders, are mounted on the upper surface of each wing. Their purpose is to "spoil" or disrupt the smooth flow of air over the wing to reduce the wing's lifting force. It is a means of increasing the rate of descent without increasing the airplane's speed.

    3.   Wing flaps are installed on the wings of most modern airplanes. Flaps increase both lift and drag and have three important functions:

        a.   First, they permit a slower landing speed which decreases the required landing distance.

        b.   Second, they permit a comparatively steep angle of descent without an increase in speed. This makes it possible to safely clear obstacles when making a landing approach to a small field.

        c.   Third, they may also be used to shorten the takeoff distance and provide a steeper climb path.

CONTROLLING YAW, PITCH, AND ROLL

A.   Control of Yaw means Directional Control About the Vertical Axis. Directional control of the airplane is maintained with the rudder. The rudder is a movable surface hinged to the trailing edge of the vertical stabilizer (fin) and attached by mechanical linkage to the two rudder pedals located in the cockpit.

    1.   When you press the right rudder pedal, the rudder is deflected to the right, which causes the relative wind to deflect the tail to the left and the nose to the right.

    2.   If left rudder pressure is applied, the reverse occurs and the nose is deflected to the left.

3. It is important to understand that the purpose of the rudder during flight is only to control yaw and not to turn the airplane. The airplane is turned by banking the airplane (see C. below for a discussion of "Lateral Control").

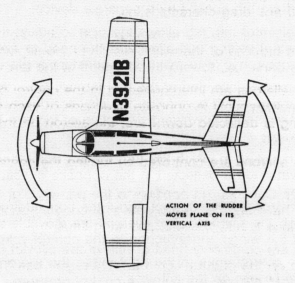

ACTION OF THE RUDDER
MOVES PLANE ON ITS
VERTICAL AXIS

4. Some airplanes are equipped with a rudder trim tab, which can hold the rudder slightly to either side when constant rudder pressure is needed over a period of time so the pilot does not have to apply constant pressure on the pedal(s).

B. **Control of Pitch means Longitudinal Control About the Lateral Axis.** To maintain longitudinal control around the lateral axis, you use the elevators and the elevator trim tab.

1. The elevator control provides a way to change the wings' angle of attack. The importance of the wings' angle of attack is discussed on pages 25 and 31.

2. On most airplanes the elevators are movable control surfaces hinged to the horizontal stabilizer. They are attached to the control yoke in the cockpit by mechanical linkage.

    a. This allows the pilot to change the angle of attack of the entire horizontal stabilizer. The horizontal stabilizer normally has a negative angle of attack to provide a downward force (rather than a lifting force) in the rear of the plane to offset the heaviness of the airplane's nose.

    b. Applying back pressure on the control yoke (i.e., pulling the yoke toward the pilot) raises the elevators. The raised elevators increase the horizontal stabilizer's negative angle of attack and consequently increase the downward tail force. This forces the tail down, increasing the angle of attack of the wings.

    c. Applying forward pressure to the control yoke (i.e., pushing it away) lowers the elevators. The lowered elevators decrease the horizontal stabilizer's negative angle of attack and consequently decrease the downward force on the tail. The tail rises, decreasing the angle of attack of the wings.

3.   The elevator trim tab is a small auxiliary control surface hinged at the trailing edge of the elevators. This trim tab is a part of the elevators but may be moved upward or downward independently of the elevator. The elevator trim tab acts on the elevators, which in turn act upon the entire airplane. It is operated from the cockpit by a separate device.

   a.   The elevator trim tab allows the pilot to adjust the angle of attack for a constant setting and eliminates the need to exert continuous pressure on the control yoke to maintain a constant angle of attack.

   b.   An upward deflection of the trim tab will force the elevators downward with the same result as moving the elevator downward with the control yoke. Conversely, a downward deflection of the trim tab will force the elevator upward.

   c.   The direction in which the trim tab is deflected will always cause the entire elevator to be deflected in the opposite direction.

C.   Control of Roll means Lateral Control About the Longitudinal Axis. Lateral control is obtained through the ailerons. The ailerons are movable surfaces hinged to the outer trailing edge of the wings and attached to the control yoke by mechanical linkage.

   1.   Moving the control yoke to the right raises the aileron on the right wing and lowers the aileron on the left wing.

   2.   Moving the control yoke to the left raises the aileron on the left wing and lowers the aileron on the right wing.

   3.   When an aileron is lowered, the angle of attack on that wing will increase, which increases the lift. When an aileron is raised, the angle of attack will decrease, which decreases the lift. This permits rolling (banking) the airplane laterally around the longitudinal axis.

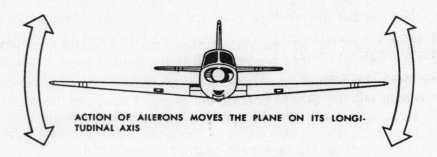

ACTION OF AILERONS MOVES THE PLANE ON ITS LONGI-TUDINAL AXIS

   4.   An aircraft turns primarily due to banking of the wings. With wings level, all lift is perpendicular to the earth. With wings banked, the lift has a horizontal component as well as a vertical component.

   a.   The horizontal component (i.e., when the wings are lifting sideways as well as up) counteracts the centrifugal force, which is pulling the airplane straight ahead.

   b.   Rudder is required to "coordinate" the turn.

5. Many airplanes are equipped with an aileron trim tab. This is a small movable part of the aileron hinged to the trailing edge of the main aileron. It can be moved independently of the ailerons. Aileron trim tabs function similarly to elevator trim tabs:

   a. Moving the trim tab produces an effect on the aileron which in turn affects the entire airplane.

   b. If the trim tab is deflected upward, the aileron is deflected downward. This increases the angle of attack on that wing and results in greater lift on that wing.

   c. The reverse happens if the trim tab is deflected downward.

D. The amount of control that the pilot has over the airplane depends on the speed of the airflow striking all of these control surfaces. The greater the airspeed the greater the effect of stability as a restoring force. "Airplane Stability" is a separate sideheading on page 36.

FORCES ACTING ON THE AIRPLANE IN FLIGHT

A. Among the aerodynamic forces acting on an airplane during flight, four are considered to be basic because they act upon the airplane during all maneuvers. These basic forces are

   1. Lift, the upward acting force.
   2. Weight (or gravity), the downward acting force.
   3. Thrust, the forward acting force.
   4. Drag, the rearward acting force.

B. While in steady flight the attitude, direction, and speed of the airplane will remain constant until one or more of the basic forces changes in magnitude.

   1. In steady flight, the opposing forces are in equilibrium.

   2. Lift and thrust are considered positive forces (+), while weight and drag are considered negative forces (-).

   3. In steady flight, the sum of the opposing forces is zero. In other words, lift equals weight and thrust equals drag.

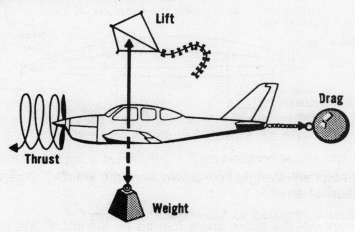

C.   When pressure is applied to one or more of the airplane controls, one or more of the basic forces change(s) in magnitude and become(s) greater than the opposing force, causing the airplane to move in the direction of the applied force(s).

   1.   EXAMPLE. If power is applied (increasing thrust) and altitude is maintained, the airplane will accelerate. As speed increases, drag increases until a point is reached at which drag again equals thrust. Then the airplane will continue in steady flight at a higher speed.

D.   Airplane designers make an effort to increase the performance of the airplane by increasing the efficiency of the desirable forces of lift and thrust while reducing, as much as possible, the undesirable forces of weight and drag.

DEFINITIONS

   Defining some of the terms used extensively in this section will be helpful in continuing the discussion of the four forces.

A.   Acceleration -- the force involved in overcoming inertia. It is defined as a change of velocity per unit of time, and means changing speed and/or changing direction, including starting from rest (positive acceleration) and stopping (deceleration or negative acceleration).

B.   Airfoil -- any surface, such as an airplane wing, designed to obtain reaction such as lift from the air through which it moves. Note that the diagram is a cross-section of a wing. That is, this is the profile of the part of the wing flush against the fuselage.

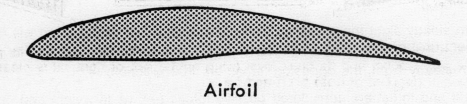

Airfoil

C.   Camber -- the curvature of the airfoil (e.g., the wing) from the leading edge to the trailing edge.

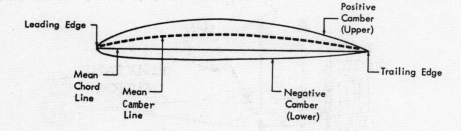

D.   Chord -- an imaginary straight line drawn from the leading edge to the trailing edge of a cross section of an airfoil.

E.   Angle of Incidence -- the acute angle formed by the chord line of the wing and the longitudinal axis of the airplane. It is the angle at which the wing is attached to the fuselage. Since it was determined by airplane design, it is a fixed angle and cannot be changed by the pilot. Angle of incidence should not be confused with angle of attack.

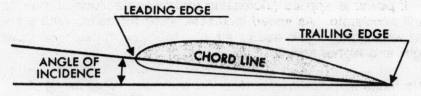

F. Angle of Attack -- the acute angle between the chord line of the wing and the direction of the relative wind. It can usually be changed by pitch and power.

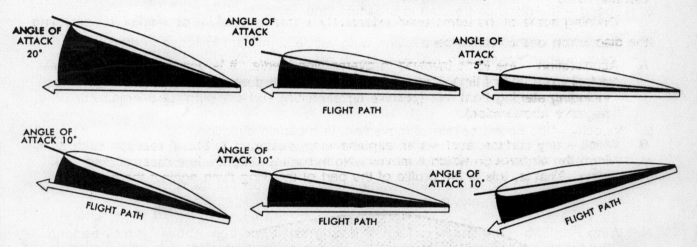

G. Attitude -- An airplane's attitude means relationship to the horizon, i.e., its pitch (nose angle) up or down and its bank level (wing angle), left or right. It is measured in number of degrees of both pitch and bank.

H. Vector -- the graphic representation of a force. It is drawn as a straight line with direction indicated by an arrow and magnitude indicated by its length. When an object is being acted upon by two or more forces, the combined effect of these forces may be represented by a resultant vector. The resultant vector may then be measured to determine the direction and magnitude of the combined forces.

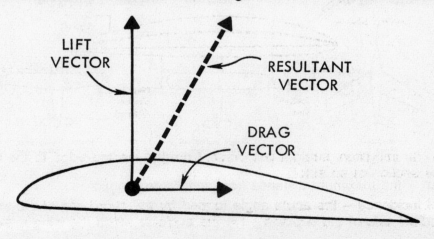

I.   Relative Wind -- the direction of the airflow produced by an object moving through the air. The relative wind for an airplane in flight flows parallel with and opposite to the direction of flight. Therefore, the actual flightpath of the airplane determines (is the opposite of) the direction of the relative wind.

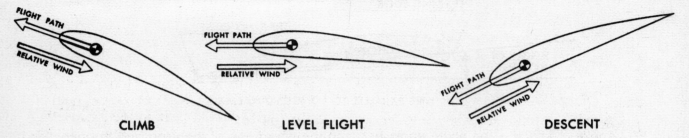

J.   Speed -- the distance traveled in a certain time.

K.   Stall -- the loss of lift by the airplane wing with a significant increase in drag. This occurs when the smooth airflow over the wing is disrupted.

    1.   Remember, a stall is an aerodynamic effect. It does NOT mean the engine has stopped.

L.   Velocity -- the speed or rate of movement in a certain direction.

M.   Wing Area -- the entire surface of the wing including control surfaces.

    1.   Control surfaces are the movable surfaces that control the attitude of the airplane, e.g., elevators and ailerons.

N.   Wing Planform -- the shape or form of a wing as viewed from above. It may be long and tapered, short and rectangular, or various other shapes. See the illustration below.

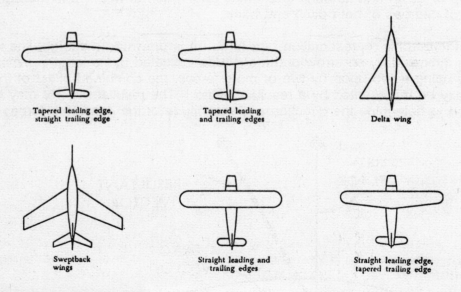

O.   Wingspan -- the maximum distance from wingtip to wingtip.

LIFT

A. Lift is the upward force created by an airfoil when it is moved through the air. Although lift may be exerted to some extent by many external parts of the airplane, the three principal airfoils on an airplane are:

1. The wing
2. The propeller
3. The horizontal tail surfaces

B. Bernoulli's Principle states in part that "the internal pressure of a fluid (liquid or gas) decreases at points where the speed of the fluid increases." In other words, high speed flow is associated with low pressure, and low speed flow is associated with high pressure.

1. This principle is applicable to an airplane wing since it is designed and constructed with a curve or camber. When air flows along the upper wing surface it travels a greater distance in the same period of time (i.e., faster) than the airflow along the lower wing surface.

2. Therefore, the pressure above the wing is less than it is below the wing. This generates a lift force over the upper curved surface of the wing.

C. At the same time, the lower surface of the wing, by its shape, deflects the air downward. Since for every action there is an equal and opposite reaction (Newton's third law of motion), additional upward force is generated.

1. Thus, both the development of low pressure above the wing and reaction to the force and direction of air being deflected from the wing's lower surface contribute to the total lift. See the illustration below.

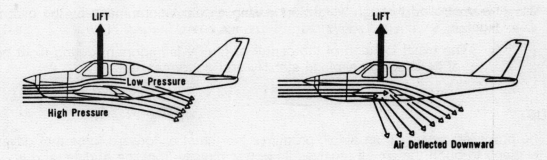

D. The amount of lift generated by the wing depends upon several factors:

1. Speed of the wing through the air
2. Angle of attack
3. Planform of the wing
4. Wing area
5. Air density

E. Lift acts upward and perpendicular to the relative wind and to the wing span. Although lift is generated over the entire wing, an imaginary point is established which represents the resultant of all lift forces. This single point is the center of lift, sometimes referred to as the center of pressure (CP).

1. The location of the center of pressure relative to the center of gravity (weight) is very important from the standpoint of airplane stability. Stability is covered in more detail beginning on page 36.

GRAVITY (WEIGHT)

A.   Gravity is the downward force that tends to draw all bodies vertically toward the center of the earth.

   1.   The airplane's center of gravity (CG) is the imaginary but determinable point on the airplane at which all weight is considered to be concentrated. It is the point of balance.

   2.   For example, if it were possible to suspend an airplane from a rope attached to its center of gravity, the airplane would balance.

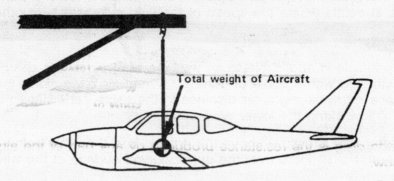

Total weight of Aircraft

B.   The center of gravity is located along the longitudinal centerline of the airplane (imaginary line from the nose to the tail) and somewhere near the center of lift of the wing.

   1.   The location of the center of gravity depends upon the location and weight of the load (including cargo, fuel, passengers, etc.) placed in the airplane.

   2.   It is controlled through weight and balance calculations made by the pilot prior to flight.

      a.   The exact location of the center of gravity is important during flight because of its effect on airplane stability and performance.

THRUST

A.   The propeller, acting as an airfoil, produces the thrust or forward force that drives the airplane through the air. It receives its power directly from the engine, and is designed to displace a large mass of air to the rear.

   1.   This thrust must be strong enough to counteract the force of drag and to give the airplane the desired forward motion.

DRAG

A.   Drag is the rearward acting force resulting from the forward movement of the airplane through the air. Drag acts parallel to and in the same direction as the relative wind. Every part of the airplane exposed to the air while the airplane is in motion produces some resistance and contributes to the total drag. Total drag may be classified into two main types: induced drag and parasite drag.

   1.   Induced drag is the undesirable but unavoidable byproduct of lift. It increases as the angle of attack increases. The greater the angle of attack (up to the critical angle), the greater the amount of lift developed, and the greater the induced drag.

a.   When the airflow around the wing is deflected downward (see the diagram under paragraph C. of the "Lift" sideheading on page 27), there is a rearward component to the lift vector which is induced drag.

b.   The amount of air deflected downward increases greatly at higher angles of attack. Therefore, the higher the angle of attack or the slower the airplane is flown, the greater the induced drag.

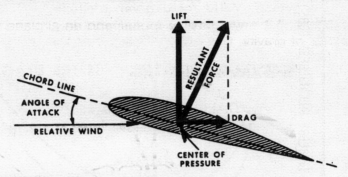

2.   Parasite drag is the resistance produced by any part of the airplane that disrupts airflow.

a.   Several factors affect parasite drag:

1)   The more streamlined an object, the less the parasite drag.

2)   The more dense the air moving past the airplane, the greater the parasite drag.

3)   The larger the size of the object in the airstream, the greater the parasite drag.

4)   As speed increases, the amount of parasite drag increases as the square of the velocity. If the speed is doubled, four times as much drag is produced.

b.   Parasite drag can be further classified into form drag, skin friction, and interference drag.

Example of skin friction drag.

Example of form drag.

1)   Form drag is caused by the frontal area of the airplane components being exposed to the airstream.

2)   Skin friction drag is caused by air passing over the airplane's surfaces. It increases considerably if the airplane surfaces are rough and dirty.

3)   Interference drag is caused by interference of the airflow between adjacent parts of the airplane such as the intersection of wings and tail sections with the fuselage. Fairings are used to streamline these intersections and decrease interference drag.

3. The airplane's total drag determines the amount of thrust required **at a given airspeed**. The graph below illustrates the variation in parasite, induced, **and total drag** with speed for a typical airplane in steady level flight.

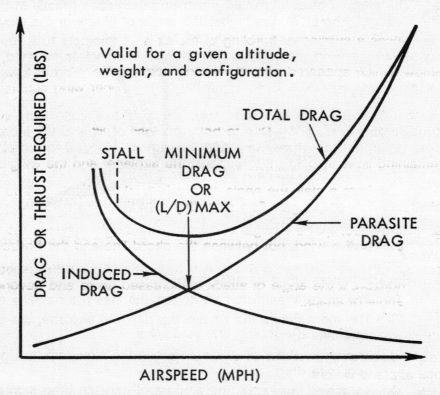

B. Thrust must equal drag in level flight. Therefore, the curve for the total drag also represents the thrust required for constant altitude. Also note on the above chart that the airspeed at which minimum drag occurs is the same airspeed at which the maximum lift/drag ratio (L/D) takes place. At this point, least thrust is required for level flight. This is important for determining the range for the airplane.

C. The force of drag can be controlled to a certain extent by the pilot. Loading the airplane properly, retracting the landing gear and flaps when not used, and keeping the surface of the airplane clean all help to reduce total drag.

STALLS

A. When the angle of attack is increased to approximately 18° to 20° on most airfoils, the airstream can no longer follow the upper curvature of the wing because of the excessive change in direction. This is the critical angle of attack.

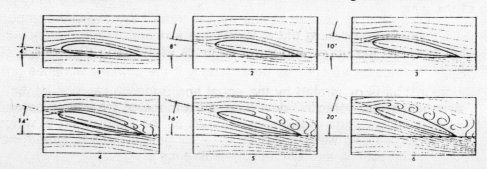

1. As the critical angle of attack is approached, the airstream begins separating from the rear of the upper wing surface. As the angle of attack is further increased, the airstream is forced to flow straight back, away from the top surface of the wing and from the area of highest camber. See the diagrams at the bottom of page 30.

2. This causes a swirling or burbling of the air as it attempts to follow the upper surface of the wing. When the critical angle of attack is reached, the turbulent airflow, which appeared near the trailing edge of the wing at lower angles of attack, quickly spreads forward over the entire upper wing surface.

3. This results in a sudden increase in pressure on the upper wing surface and a considerable loss of lift. Due to both this loss of lift and the increase in form drag (a larger area of the wing and fuselage is exposed to the airstream), the remaining lift is insufficient to support the airplane, and the wing stalls.

4. To recover from a stall, the angle of attack must be decreased so that the airstream can once again flow smoothly over the wing surface.

   a. Remember that the angle of attack is the angle between the chord line and the relative wind, not between the chord line and the horizon.

   b. An airplane can be stalled in any attitude of flight with respect to the horizon, if the angle of attack is increased up to and beyond the critical angle of attack.

B. Factors affecting an airplane's stalling characteristics:
   1. Weight distribution -- center of gravity.
   2. Total airplane weight.
   3. Bank -- wing loading.
   4. Pitch attitude -- critical angle of attack.
   5. Control coordination -- ailerons and elevator.
   6. Drag -- landing gear and/or flap position.
   7. Power setting.

C. See Chapter 9, "Slowflight, Stalls, and Spins."

RELATIONSHIPS BETWEEN LIFT, WEIGHT, THRUST, DRAG, AND ANGLE OF ATTACK

The following discussion recapitulates some of the above definitions and emphasizes the interrelatedness of the aerodynamic forces.

A. Relationship between Angle of Attack and Lift.

   1. The angle of attack is the acute angle between the relative wind and the chord line of the wing.

   2. At small angles of attack most of the wing lift is a result of the difference in pressure between the upper and lower surfaces of the wing (Bernoulli's Principle).

      a. Additional lift is generated by the equal and opposite reaction of the airstream being deflected downward from the wing (Newton's Law).

3.   As the angle of attack is increased, the airstream is forced to travel faster over the top of the wing (because of the greater distance over the upper surface of the wing), creating a greater pressure differential between the upper and lower surfaces. At the same time, the airstream is deflected downward at a greater angle causing an increased opposite reaction.

   a.   Both the increased pressure differential and increased opposite reaction increase lift and also drag.

   b.   Therefore, as angle of attack is increased (up to the critical angle of attack), lift is increased.

B.   Relationship of Thrust and Drag in Straight-and-Level Flight.

1.   During straight-and-level flight, thrust and drag are equal in magnitude if a constant airspeed is maintained.

   a.   When the thrust of the propeller is increased, thrust momentarily exceeds drag and the airspeed will increase provided straight-and-level flight is maintained.

      1)   Drag increases very rapidly with an increase in airspeed.

      2)   At some new and higher airspeed, thrust and drag forces again become equalized and speed again becomes constant.

2.   If all the available power is used, thrust will reach its maximum, airspeed will increase until drag equals thrust, and once again the airspeed will become constant. This will be the top speed for that airplane in that attitude and atmospheric condition.

3.   When thrust becomes less than drag, the airplane will decelerate to a slower airspeed provided straight-and-level flight is maintained. At some point, thrust and drag again will become equal. If the airspeed becomes too slow, or more precisely if the angle of attack is too great, the airplane will stall.

   a.   The stall occurs because as the airplane slows, the angle of attack must be increased to maintain level flight and prevent a descent. The relative wind forms a progressively larger angle with the chordline of the wing until the critical angle is reached and the stall occurs.

C.   Relationship of Lift and Weight in Straight-and-Level Flight.

1.   Lift, the upward force on the wing, always acts perpendicular to the direction of the relative wind.

2.   In steady state straight-and-level flight (constant altitude), lift counterbalances the airplane weight. Thrust and drag are also equal.

3.   When entering a climb or a descent, by raising or lowering the nose, the angle of attack, and therefore lift, changes momentarily.

4.   Once a climb or descent is established, upward and downward, and forward and rearward forces are again balanced. The airspeed stabilizes at a value different than in straight-and-level flight if there is no power change.

   a.   In steady state descents and climbs, lift and weight are not vertical nor are thrust and drag, but upward-downward and forward-rearward forces are equal. (?)

GROUND EFFECT

A. It is possible to fly an airplane just clear of the surface (ground or water) at a slightly slower airspeed than that required to sustain level flight at higher altitudes.

    1. Near the surface the vertical component of the airflow around the wing is restricted.

    2. This alters the wing's upwash, downwash, and wingtip vortices.

B. The principal aerodynamic effects due to promixity of the ground are the changes in the aerodynamic characteristics of the wing.

    1. The reduction of the wingtip vortices due to ground effect alters the spanwise lift distribution and reduces the induced angle of attack and induced drag.

C. An airplane leaving ground effect (i.e., taking off) will

    1. Require an increase in angle of attack to maintain the same lift coefficient.

    2. Experience an increase in induced drag and thrust required.

    3. Experience a decrease in stability and a slight nose-up pitch.

    4. Produce a reduction in static source pressure and an increase in indicated airspeed.

D. An airplane entering ground effect (landing) will encounter the opposite phenomena.

E. Ground effect permits airplanes to lift off the ground at airspeeds lower than adequate to continue a safe climb.

    1. You must make sure you have reached a safe airspeed before rotating off the runway.

    2. On landings, you must be aware of the airplane's tendency to "float" down the runway when ground effect is encountered.

        a. Further power reductions are required and/or

        b. Additional airspeed reduction through continued and increased control yoke back pressure is appropriate.

HOW AIRPLANES TURN

A. The lift produced by an airplane's wings is used to turn the airplane. When banked, the horizontal component of lift turns the airplane. See the diagram on the next page.

    1. Until a force acts on the airplane, it tends to fly straight ahead due to inertia.

        a. Inertia describes the phenomenon that moving items continue to move in the same direction, i.e., not turn.

    2. When the airplane begins to turn, centrifugal force pulls the airplane away from the turn, i.e., tends to make it fly straight ahead.

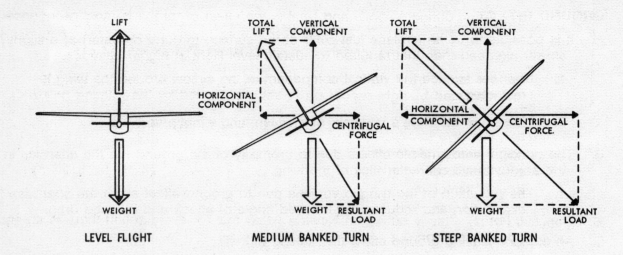

LEVEL FLIGHT   MEDIUM BANKED TURN   STEEP BANKED TURN

3. The horizontal component of lift (in a bank) counteracts the centrifugal force.

   a. Therefore, the greater the bank, the sharper the turn or the greater the rate of turn because more of the total lift goes into the horizontal component.

4. The rudder does not turn the airplane. It controls the yaw about the vertical axis.

   a. This permits the "coordination" of the rudder and ailerons.

   b. Coordinated flight is when the airplane goes "straight ahead" through the relative wind, i.e., not sideways (about its vertical axis).

B. In a bank, the total lift consists of both horizontal lift (counteracting centrifugal force) and vertical lift (counteracting weight and gravity).

   1. Therefore, given the same amount of total lift, there is less vertical lift in a bank than in straight-and-level flight.

   2. Thus, to maintain altitude in a turn, you must

   a. Increase back pressure on the control yoke (for a higher angle of attack to produce more lift), and/or

   b. Increase power.

C. The turn of an airplane is stopped by decreasing the bank of the airplane to zero.

TURNING TENDENCY (TORQUE EFFECT)

A. By definition, "torque" is a force or combination of forces (described in B through E below) that produces or tends to produce a twisting or rotating motion of an airplane.

   1. Airplanes are designed in such a manner that the torque effect is not noticeable to the pilot when the airplane is in straight-and-level flight at a cruise power setting.

   2. The effect of torque increases in direct proportion to engine power and airplane attitude, and inversely with airspeed.

   a. If the power setting is high, the airspeed slow, and the angle of attack high, the effect of torque is greater.

b. Thus, during takeoffs and climbs, the effect of torque is most pronounced.

1) The pilot must apply sufficient right rudder pressure to counteract the left-turning tendency and maintain a straight takeoff path.

3. The four forces involved in the tendency of an airplane to turn to the left (counteracted by right rudder pressure) are created by the rotating propeller. The four forces are

a. Reactive force
b. Spiraling slipstream
c. Gyroscopic precession (on tailwheel airplanes, when the tail is lifted)
d. "P" factor

B. **Reactive Force.** This is based on Newton's Law that for every action there is an equal and opposite reaction.

1. An airplane's propeller rotates in a clockwise direction (as seen from the rear). This produces a force that tends to roll the entire airplane counterclockwise about its longitudinal axis.

2. Just as downward deflection of air by the lower surface of a wing causes lift, the clockwise turning of the propeller causes the airplane to roll counterclockwise.

C. **Spiraling Slipstream.** This is based on the reaction of the air to a rotating propeller blade.

1. As the airplane propeller rotates through the air in a clockwise direction (as viewed from the rear), the propeller blade forces air rearward in a spiraling clockwise direction of flow around the fuselage.

2. A portion of this spiraling slipstream strikes the left side of the vertical stabilizer. The airplane's tail is forced to the right and the nose is forced to the left, causing the airplane to rotate around the vertical axis.

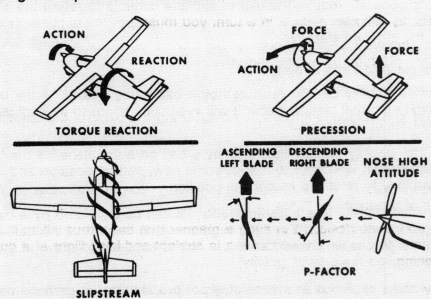

ACTION
REACTION
TORQUE REACTION

FORCE
ACTION
FORCE
PRECESSION

SLIPSTREAM

ASCENDING LEFT BLADE
DESCENDING RIGHT BLADE
NOSE HIGH ATTITUDE
P-FACTOR

D. **Gyroscopic Precession.** This is based on one of the gyroscopic properties which apply to any object spinning in space, even a rotating airplane propeller.

1. As the nose of the airplane is raised or lowered, or moved left or right, a deflective force is applied to the spinning propeller which results in a reactive force known as precession.

2. Precession is the resultant action or deflection of a spinning wheel (propeller in this case) when a force is applied to its rim. The preceding diagram shows a left turning force (true for a tailwheel plane as the tail is raised as pictured), but tricycle gear airplanes experience a right turn force when rotated on takeoff.

E. **"P" Factor or Asymmetric Propeller Loading.** The effects of "P" factor or asymmetric propeller loading usually occur when the airplane is flown at a high angle of attack.

1. The downward moving blade, which is on the right side of the propeller arc (as seen from the rear), has a higher angle of attack, greater action and reaction, and therefore higher thrust than the upward-moving blade on the left. (?)

2. This results in a tendency for the airplane to yaw around the vertical axis to the left. Again this is most pronounced when the engine is operating at a high power setting and the airplane is flown at a high angle of attack. (?)

AIRPLANE STABILITY

A. Stability is the inherent ability of a body, after its equilibrium is disturbed, to return to its original position. In other words, a stable airplane will tend to return to the original condition of flight if disturbed by a force such as turbulent air.

1. This means that a stable airplane is easy to fly.

2. It does not mean that a pilot can depend entirely on stability to return the airplane to the original condition. Even in the most stable airplanes, some conditions will require the use of airplane controls to return the airplane to the desired attitude. Less effort is needed to control the airplane, however, because of the inherent stability.

B. Stability is classified into three types

1. Positive stability can be illustrated by a ball inside a bowl. If the ball is displaced from its normal resting place, it will eventually return to its original position at the bottom of the bowl.

2. Neutral stability can be illustrated by a ball on a flat plane. If the ball is displaced, it will come to rest at some new, neutral position and show no tendency to return to its original position.

3. Negative stability is actually instability. It can be illustrated by a ball on the top of an inverted bowl. Even the slightest displacement of the ball will activate greater forces which will cause the ball to continue to move in the direction of the applied force (e.g., gravity).

4. Obviously, airplanes should display positive stability, or perhaps neutral stability, but never negative stability.

C.   Stability may be further classified as static and/or dynamic.

1.   Static stability means that if the airplane's equilibrium is disturbed, forces will be activated which will initially tend to return the airplane to its original position. However, these restoring forces may be so great that they will force the airplane beyond the original position and continue in that direction.

2.   Dynamic stability is a property that dampens the oscillations set up by a statically stable airplane, enabling the oscillations to become smaller and smaller in magnitude until the airplane eventually settles down to its original condition of flight.

3.   Therefore an airplane should possess positive stability that is both static and dynamic in nature. (?)

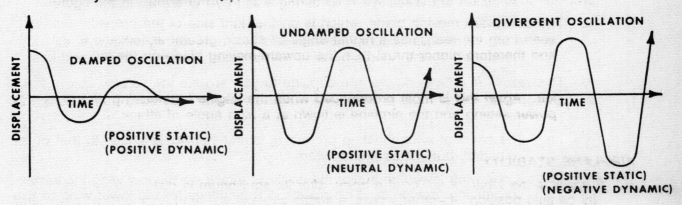

D.   Longitudinal Stability About the Lateral Axis.   Longitudinal stability is important to the pilot because it determines to a great extent the pitch characteristics of the airplane, particularly as this relates to the stall characteristics.

1.   It would be unsafe and uncomfortable for the pilot if an airplane continually displayed a tendency to either stall or dive when the pilot's attention was diverted for some reason.

2.   The location of the center of gravity with respect to the center of lift determines to a great extent the longitudinal stability of the airplane.

a.   Negative - if center of lift is in front of the center of gravity.
b.   Neutral - if center of lift is at the center of gravity.
c.   Positive - if center of lift is behind the center of gravity.

E.   Lateral Stability About the Longitudinal Axis. Lateral stability is the stability displayed around the longitudinal axis of the airplane. An airplane that tends to return to a wings-level attitude after being displaced from a level attitude by some force, such as turbulent air, is considered to be laterally stable. Three factors affect lateral stability:

1.   The dihedral is the angle at which the wings are slanted upward from the root to the tip. The stabilizing effect of the dihedral occurs when the airplane sideslips slightly as one wing is forced down in turbulent air.

   a.   This sideslip results in a difference in the angle of attack between the higher and lower wing with the greatest angle of attack on the lower wing.

   b.   The increased angle of attack produces increased lift on the lower wing with a tendency to return the airplane to wings-level flight. Note the direction of the relative wind during a slip by the arrows in the figure below.

   c.   A slip or sideslip occurs when the airplane turns slightly sideways, as illustrated by the figures below which indicate wing sweepback and keel effect.

2.   Sweepback is the angle at which the wings are slanted rearward from the root to the tip.

   a.   The effect of sweepback in producing lateral stability is similar to that of the dihedral, but not as pronounced.

   b.   If one wing lowers in a slip, the angle of attack on the low wing increases, producing greater lift. This results in a tendency for the lower wing to rise and return the airplane to level flight.

   c.   Sweepback augments dihedral to achieve lateral stability. (?)

   d.   Another reason for sweepback is to place the center of lift farther rearward, which affects longitudinal stability more than it does lateral stability.

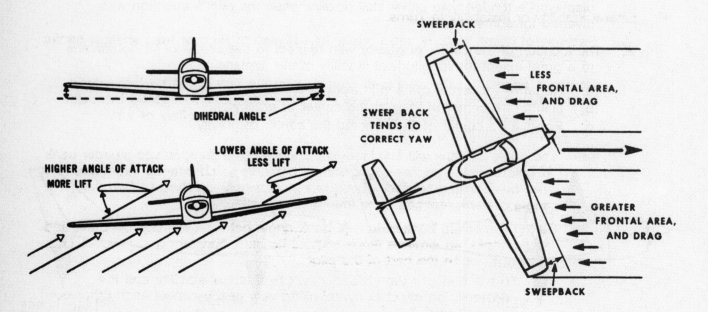

3.   Keel effect depends on the action of the relative wind on the side area of the airplane fuselage. In a slight slip the fuselage provides a broad area on which the relative wind will strike, forcing the fuselage to parallel the relative wind. This aids in producing lateral stability.

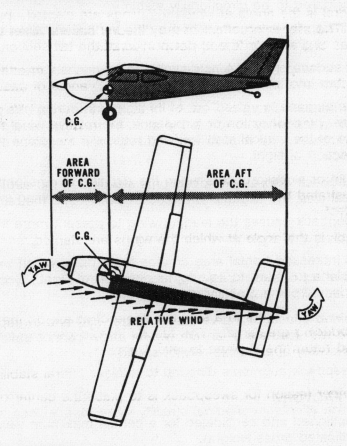

F.   Lateral Stability or Instability in Turns.

1.   Because of lateral stability, most airplanes will tend to recover from shallow banks automatically.

2.   However, as the bank is increased, the wing on the outside of the turn travels faster than the wing on the inside of the turn. The increased speed increases the lift on the outside wing, causing a destabilizing rolling effect or an overbanking tendency.

   a.   The angle of bank will continue to increase into a steeper and steeper bank unless the pilot applies slight control pressure to counteract this tendency. The overbanking tendency becomes increasingly significant when the angle of bank reaches more than 30°.

   b.   During a medium banked turn (a bank angle between the shallow bank and steep bank), an airplane tends to hold its bank constant and requires less control input on the part of the pilot.

      1)   This is because the stabilizing effect of lateral stability and the destabilizing effect of overbanking very nearly cancel each other out.

      2)   A pilot can discover these various areas of bank through experimentation.

G.   Directional Stability About the Vertical Axis (Yaw). Directional stability is displayed around the vertical axis and depends to a great extent on the quality of lateral stability. If the longitudinal axis of an airplane tends to follow and parallel the flightpath of the airplane through the air, whether in straight flight or curved flight, that airplane is considered to be directionally stable.

1.   Directional stability is accomplished by the vertical stabilizer or fin to the rear of the center of gravity on the upper portion of the tail section.

a.   The surface of this fin acts similar to a weathervane. It causes the airplane to turn into the relative wind.

b.   If the airplane is yawed out of its flightpath during straight flight or turn, either by pilot action or turbulence, the relative wind exerts a force on one side of the vertical stabilizer and returns the airplane to its original direction of flight.

2.   Wing sweepback also aids in directional stability. If the airplane is rotated about the vertical axis, the airplane is forced sideways into the relative wind.

a.   Sweepback causes the leading wing to present more frontal area to the relative wind than the trailing wing.

b.   This increased frontal area creates more drag, which tends to force the airplane to return to its original direction of flight. See E.3., keel effect, under "Airplane Stability" on page 39.

3.   The combined effects of the vertical stabilizer (fin) and sweepback can be compared with feathers of an arrow. An arrow cannot travel through the air sideways at any appreciable rate of speed.

LOADS AND LOAD FACTORS

A.   An airplane is designed and certificated for a certain maximum weight during flight (maximum certificated gross weight).

1.   It is important that the airplane be loaded within the specified weight limits before flight. If the airplane is overloaded, certain flight maneuvers that impose an extra load on the airplane structure may also impose stresses exceeding the design capabilities of the airplane.

2.   Overstressing the airplane can also occur if the pilot engages in maneuvers creating high loads, regardless of how much weight is in the airplane.

a.   These maneuvers increase both the load that the airplane structure must support and the airplane's stalling speed.

3.   The loads imposed on the wings in flight are stated in terms of load factor. Load factor is the ratio of the total load supported by the airplane's wings to the actual weight of the airplane and its contents:

$$\text{Load Factor} = \frac{\text{actual load supported by the wings}}{\text{total weight of the airplane}}$$

a.   EXAMPLE. An airplane has a gross weight of 2,000 lb. During flight it is subjected to aerodynamic forces which increase the total load that the wing must support to 4,000 lb. The load factor is thus 2.0 (4,000 ÷ 2,000 = 2). The airplane wing is producing "lift" equal to twice the gross weight of the airplane.

4. Another way of expressing load factor is the ratio of a given load to the pull of gravity or "G." If the weight of the airplane is equal to "1 G," and if a load of three times the actual weight of the airplane were imposed upon the wing due to curved flight, the load factor would be equal to "3 G's."

B. Load Factors and Airplane Design. To be certificated by the FAA, the structural strength (load factor) of airplanes must conform with prescribed standards set forth by FARs. Airplanes are classified as to strength and operational use by means of the category system.

1. The normal category has a maximum load factor of 3.8 Gs.

    a. Permissible maneuvers include:

        1) Any maneuver incident to normal flying.
        2) Stalls.
        3) Lazy eights, chandelles, and steep turns in which the angle of bank does not exceed 60°.

2. The utility category has a maximum load factor of 4.4 Gs.

    a. Permissible maneuvers include:

        1) All operations in the normal category.
        2) Spins (if approved for that airplane).
        3) Lazy eights, chandelles, and steep turns in which the angle of bank is more than 60°.

3. The acrobatic category has a maximum load factor of 6.0 Gs.

    a. There are no restrictions except those shown to be necessary as a result of required flight tests.

4. Note the increase in maximum load factor with an increasing severity of maneuvers permitted. Small airplanes may be certificated in more than one category if the requirements for each category are met, e.g., an airplane heavily loaded may deserve Normal Category restrictions whereas when lightly loaded may deserve Utility Category restrictions.

5. This system indicates what operations can be performed in a given airplane without exceeding the load limit. Pilots are cautioned to operate the airplane within the load limit for which the airplane is designed so as to enhance safety and still benefit from the intended use of the airplane.

C. Effect of Turns on Load Factor. A turn is made by banking the airplane so that horizontal lift from the wings pulls the airplane from its straight flightpath. In a constant altitude coordinated turn, the load factor (resultant load) is the result of two forces: (1) pull of gravity and (2) centrifugal force.

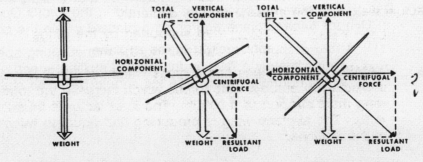

LEVEL FLIGHT   MEDIUM BANKED TURN   STEEP BANKED TURN

1.   The load factor increases at a rapid rate after the angle of bank reaches 50°. The wing must produce lift equal to this load factor if altitude is to be maintained.

    a.   The 90° banked, constant altitude turn is not mathematically possible.

    b.   At an angle of bank of slightly more than 80° the load factor exceeds 6, which is the limit load factor for an acrobatic airplane.

    c.   The approximate maximum bank for conventional light airplanes is 60° which produces a load factor of 2.

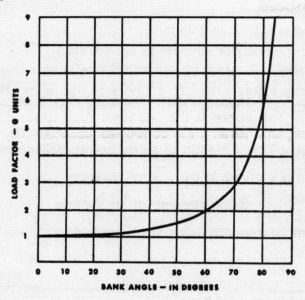

D.   **Effect of Load Factor on Stalling Speed.** As bank angle increases, load factor goes up. When load factor goes up, the wing requires a higher angle of attack to support the increased load. When the wing reaches the critical angle of attack, a stall occurs.

1.   The maximum speed at which an airplane can be safely stalled is the design maneuvering speed.

    a.   The design maneuvering speed is a valuable reference point for the pilot.

    b.   When operating below this speed a damaging positive flight load should not be produced. The airplane should stall before the load becomes excessive. Any combination of flight control usage, including full deflection of the controls or gust loads created by turbulence, should not create an excessive air load if the airplane is operated below maneuvering speed.

        1)   CAUTION: Certain adverse wind shear or gusts may cause excessive loads even at speeds below maneuvering speed.

    c.   Design maneuvering speed can be found in the *Pilot's Operating Handbook* (POH) for each airplane and/or on a placard within the cockpit.

        1)   A rule of thumb for determining the maneuvering speed is approximately 1.7 times the normal stalling speed. Thus, an airplane which normally stalls at 35 kts should never be stalled when the airspeed is above 60 kts (35 kts x 1.7 = 59.5 kts).

E. **Effect of Turbulence on Load Factor.** Turbulence in the form of vertical air currents can, under certain conditions, cause severe load stress on an airplane wing.

   1. When an airplane flying at a high speed with a low angle of attack suddenly encounters a vertical current of air moving upward, the relative wind changes to an upward direction as it meets the airfoil. This increases the angle of attack of the wing.

   2. All certificated airplanes are designed to withstand loads imposed by turbulence of considerable intensity. Nevertheless, gust load factors increase with increasing airspeed.

      a. Therefore, it is wise in extremely rough air, as in thunderstorm or frontal conditions, to reduce the speed to the design maneuvering speed.

      b. As a general rule when severe turbulence is encountered, the airplane should be flown at the maneuvering speed shown in the *FAA-Approved Airplane Flight Manual, Pilot's Operating Handbook*, or placard in the airplane. This speed is the one least likely to result in structural damage to the airplane (even if the control surfaces are fully deflected), yet it allows a sufficient margin of safety above stalling speed in turbulent air.

F. V_g diagram (velocity versus "G" loads).

   1. It shows the flight operating strength of an airplane.

   2. On the diagram below, load factor is on the vertical axis with airspeed on the horizontal axis. (?)

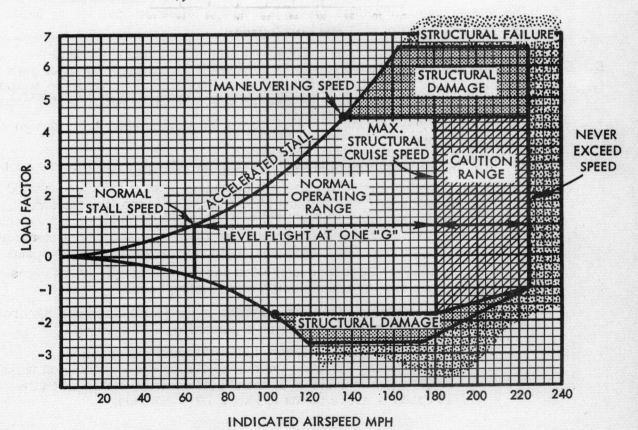

3. The lines of maximum lift capability (curved lines) are the first items of importance on the Vg diagram.

    a. The subject airplane in the preceding diagram is capable of developing no more than one positive G at 62 mph, the wing level stall speed of the airplane.

    b. The maximum load factor increases dramatically with airspeed. The maximum positive lift capability of this airplane is 2 G at 92 mph, 3 G at 112 mph, 4.4 G at 137 mph, etc.

        1) These are the "coordinates" of points on the curved line up to A.

    c. Any load factor above this line is unavailable aerodynamically. That is, the subject airplane cannot fly above the line of maximum lift capability (it will stall).

4. Point A is the intersection of the positive limit load factor (curved line up to A) and the line of maximum positive lift capability (line AB).

    a. The airspeed at this point is the minimum airspeed at which the limit load can be developed aerodynamically.

    b. Any airspeed greater than point A provides a positive lift capability sufficient to damage the airplane.

        1) Any airspeed less than point A does NOT provide positive lift capability sufficient to cause damage from excessive flight loads.

    c. The usual term given to the speed at point A is the "maneuvering speed."

5. The limit airspeed (or redline speed) is a design reference point for the airplane. The subject airplane is limited to 225 mph.

    a. If flight is attempted beyond the limit airspeed, structural damage or structural failure may result.

6. Thus, the airplane in flight is limited to a regime of airspeeds and Gs which do not exceed

    a. The limit (or redline) speed (line BC).
    b. The limit load factor (lines AB and ED).
    c. The maximum lift capability (curved lines up to A, down to E).

7. The airplane must be operated within this "envelope" to prevent structural damage and ensure the anticipated service life of the airplane.

FLIGHT INSTRUMENTS

A. <u>Altimeter</u>. The *altimeter* measures the height of the airplane above a given level. Since it is the only instrument that gives altitude information, the altimeter is one of the most important instruments in the airplane.

B. <u>Vertical Speed Indicator</u>. The *vertical speed or vertical velocity indicator* indicates whether the airplane is climbing, descending, or in level flight. The rate of climb or descent is indicated in feet per minute. If properly calibrated, the indicator will register zero in level flight.

C. <u>Airspeed Indicator</u>. The *airspeed indicator* is a sensitive differential-pressure gauge which measures the difference between pitot or impact pressure and static pressure (the atmospheric pressure at the airplane's flight level).

    1.   Single-engine light airplanes use a standard color code on airspeed indicators. Although the colors are standard, the beginning and end of each arc will vary according to individual make and model of airplane.

        a.   Flap operating range (the white arc).

        b.   Power-off stalling speed with the wing flaps and landing gear in the landing position (the lower limit of the white arc).

        c.   Maximum flaps extended speed (the upper limit of the white arc). This is the highest airspeed at which the pilot should extend full flaps. Flaps at higher airspeeds could result in severe strain or structural failure.

        d.   Normal operating range (the green arc).

        e.   Power-off stalling speed with the wing flaps and landing gear retracted (the lower limit of the green arc).

        f.   Maximum structural cruising speed (the upper limit of the green arc). This is the maximum speed for normal operation.

        g.   Caution range (the yellow arc). The pilot should avoid this area unless in smooth air.

        h.   Never-exceed speed (the red line). This is the maximum speed at which the airplane can be operated in smooth air. This speed should never be exceeded intentionally.

    2.   Other Airspeed Limitations. Some other important airspeed limitations are not marked on the face of the airspeed indicator. These speeds are generally found on placards in view of the pilot and in the *FAA-Approved Airplane Flight Manual* or Owner's Handbook.

        a.   Maneuvering speed is the "rough air" speed and the maximum speed for abrupt maneuvers. If heavy turbulence is encountered during flight, the airspeed should be reduced to maneuvering speed or lower to minimize stress on the airplane structure.

   b. Landing gear operating speed is the maximum speed for extending or retracting the landing gear if using an airplane so equipped.

   c. Best angle-of-climb speed is important when a short-field takeoff is required to clear an obstacle.

   d. Best rate-of-climb speed is the airspeed that will give the pilot the most altitude in a given period of time.

3. The following are abbreviations for performance speeds. The letter V stands for velocity.

   V_A - design maneuvering speed.

   V_C - design cruising speed.

   V_F - design flap speed.

   V_{FE} - maximum flap extended speed.

   V_{LE} - maximum landing gear extended speed.

   V_{LO} - maximum landing gear operating speed.

   V_{LOF} - lift-off speed.

   V_{NE} - never-exceed speed.

   V_R - rotation speed.

   V_s - the stalling speed or the minimum steady flight speed at which the airplane is controllable.

   V_{SO} - the stalling speed or the minimum steady flight speed in the landing configuration. *(FlAps DowN = DIRTY)*

   V_{S1} - the stalling speed or the minimum steady flight speed obtained in a specified configuration. *(FlAps uP - cleaN)*

   V_X - speed for best angle of climb.

   V_Y - speed for best rate of climb.

D. Turn-and-Slip Indicator. The *turn-and-slip indicator* was one of the first instruments used for controlling an airplane without visual reference to the ground or horizon. Its principal uses in airplanes are to indicate rate of turn and to serve as an emergency source of bank information if the attitude indicator fails.

1. The turn-and-slip indicator is actually a combination of two instruments: the turn needle and the ball or inclinometer (like a carpenter's level).

   a. The turn needle is gyro-operated to show rate of turn.

   b. The ball reacts to gravity and/or centrifugal force to indicate the need for directional trim.

2. The turn needle indicates the rate (in number of degrees per second) at which the airplane is turning about its vertical axis. Unlike the attitude indicator, the turn indicator does not give a direct indication of the banked attitude of the airplane.

3. The ball part of the turn and slip indicator is a simple inclinometer consisting of a sealed, curved glass tube containing kerosene and a black agate or steel ball bearing which is free to move inside the tube. The fluid provides a dampening action which ensures smooth and easy movement of the ball.

    a. The tube is curved so that when the airplane is horizontal (i.e., during coordinated straight-and-level flight), the ball tends to seek the lowest point (gravity). Two reference markers aid in determining when the ball is in the center of the tube.

    b. During a coordinated turn, turning forces are balanced, causing the ball to remain centered in the tube. See the turn-and-slip indicator on the left of the following diagram.

    c. If turning forces are unbalanced, i.e., a slip or skid, the ball moves away from the center of the tube in the direction of the excessive force.

        1) In a skid, the rate of turn is too great for the angle of bank, and excessive centrifugal force moves the ball to the outside of the turn. To achieve coordinated flight from a skid requires the pilot to increase the bank or use less rudder in the direction of the turn, or a combination of both. See the turn-and-slip indicator in the middle of the following diagram.

        2) In a slip, the rate of turn is too slow for the angle of bank, and the lack of centrifugal force moves the ball to the inside of the turn. To achieve coordinated flight from a slip requires the pilot to decrease the bank or use more rudder in the direction of the turn, or a combination of both. See the turn-and-slip indicator on the right of the diagram above.

        3) Remember: In slips you have used too little rudder (or opposite rudder). In skids you have used too much rudder.

    d. The ball then is actually a balance indicator. It is a visual aid to determine coordinated use of the aileron and rudder control. During a turn it indicates the relationship between the angle of bank and rate of turn. It indicates the "quality" of the turn or whether the airplane has the correct angle of bank for the rate of turn.

E. <u>Turn Coordinator</u>. Another type of turn indicator is used quite extensively. This *turn coordinator* is illustrated below.

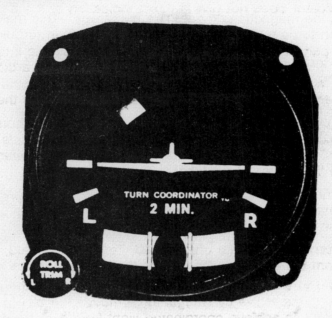

1. In place of the turn needle indication of the turn and slip indicator, this instrument displays a miniature airplane to show the movement of the airplane about the longitudinal axis.

    a. Your view of the miniature airplane is from the tail so when you bank to the right, the miniature airplane also banks to the right. It will also tilt in a wings level skid or when taxiing.

    b. The movement of the miniature airplane on the instrument is proportional to the roll rate of the airplane. The turn and slip indicator does not give roll rate.

    c. When the roll rate is reduced to zero (i.e., when the bank is held constant), the instrument indicates the rate of turn.

    d. This new design realigns the gyro so that it senses airplane movement about the yaw and roll axis and pictorially displays the resultant motion.

2. The conventional inclinometer (ball) is also incorporated in this instrument.

F. <u>Heading Indicator</u>. The *heading indicator* (or directional gyro) is fundamentally a mechanical instrument designed to facilitate use of the magnetic compass.

1. Errors in the magnetic compass are numerous. This makes straight flight and precision turns to headings difficult, particularly in turbulent air.

2. Heading indicators, however, are not affected by the forces that make the magnetic compass difficult to interpret.

G. <u>Attitude Indicator</u>. The *attitude indicator* (artificial horizon), with its miniature aircraft and horizon bar, depicts the attitude of the airplane.

1. The relationship of the miniature airplane to the horizon bar is the same as the relationship of the real airplane to the actual horizon.

2. The instrument gives an instantaneous indication of even the smallest changes in attitude.

H. Magnetic Compass. The *magnetic compass* (the only direction-seeking instrument in the airplane) contains steel magnetized needles fastened to a float around the edge of which is mounted a compass card.

1. The compass card has letters for cardinal headings.

a. Each 30° interval is represented by a number, the last zero of which is omitted. For example, 30° would appear as a 3 and 300° would appear as 30.

b. Between these numbers, the card is graduated for each 5°.

2. Compass errors: Compasses do not point to true north for the following reasons:

a. Magnetic variation -- The Earth is not magnetized uniformly and the magnetic north pole is not at the true north pole.

b. Compass deviation -- Electrical and magnetic fields within each airplane cause needle deviation.

c. Compass deflection -- Turns and acceleration/deceleration at certain headings cause needle deviation.

I. Use of Carburetor Heat. When conditions are conducive to carburetor icing during flight, periodic checks should be made to detect its presence. If detected, FULL carburetor heat should be applied immediately, and remain in the "on" position until the pilot is certain that all the ice has been removed. If ice is present, applying partial heat or leaving heat on for an insufficient time might aggravate the condition.

1. When carburetor heat is first applied there will be a drop in RPM in airplanes equipped with fixed-pitch propellers. There will be a drop in manifold pressure in airplanes equipped with controllable-pitch propellers.

2. If there is no carburetor ice present, there will be no further change in RPM or manifold pressure until the carburetor heat is turned off. Then the RPM or manifold pressure will return to the original reading before heat was applied.

3. If carburetor ice is present, there will be engine roughness after carb heat is applied, resulting from water from melted ice as it goes through the engine, accompanied by a gradual increase in RPM/MP as the ice melts. When the carburetor heat is turned off, the RPM or manifold pressure will rise to a setting greater than that before application of the heat. The engine should also run more smoothly after the ice melts.

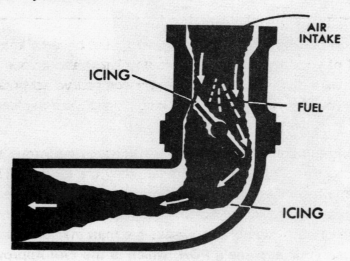

J. **Propellers.** A *propeller* is a rotating airfoil. Thus, it is subject to induced drag, stalls, and other aerodynamic principles that apply to any airfoil. The propeller provides the necessary thrust to pull, or in some cases push, the airplane through the air.

1. Fixed-pitch propeller. The pitch of this propeller is fixed by the manufacturer. It cannot be changed by the pilot. There are two broad categories of fixed-pitch propellers: the climb propeller and the cruise propeller.

2. Controllable-pitch propellers. The pilot sets the desired RPM for the propeller. The pitch or angle of the propeller then changes automatically to maintain the same RPM when the power is changed by the throttle. This is analagous to the shifting of an automatic transmission in a car.

K. **Emergency Locator Transmitters.** *Emergency locator transmitters* (ELTs) of various types are independently powered and of incalculable value in an emergency. They have been developed as a means of locating downed aircraft and their occupants. These electronic, battery-operated transmitters are not a fire hazard.

CHAPTER THREE
LEARNING YOUR AIRPLANE

Before and as you begin your flight training, you must become knowledgeable about the make and model of your airplane. The more you know about your airplane, the easier and more productive will be your flight time. A very competitive advantage over other student pilots will be your knowledge and understanding of your airplane's *Pilot's Operating Handbook* (POH).

In this chapter and throughout this book, we reproduce numerous excerpts from Beech Skipper, Cessna 152, and Piper Tomahawk *POH*s. They are for ILLUSTRATION PURPOSES ONLY. These are three recently manufactured and widely used representative single-engine trainer airplanes. By providing you with differing checklists, you are better able to understand the nature of each type of checklist rather than memorize a single checklist. **FOR FLIGHT, only use your airplane's *POH*, which is the *FAA-Approved Airplane Flight Manual*.**

The FAA requires an FAA-Approved *POH* (also called an *FAA-Approved Airplane Flight Manual*). These are usually 6" x 8" ring notebooks, so pages can be updated, deleted, added, etc. They typically have nine sections:

1. General . . . . Description of the airplane
2. Limitations . . . . Description of operating limits
3. Emergency Procedures . . . . What to do in each situation
4. Normal Procedures . . . . Checklists
5. Performance . . . . Graphs and tables of airplane capabilities
6. Weight and Balance . . . . Equipment list, airplane empty weight
7. Description of Operating Systems . . . . How they operate
8. Servicing and Maintenance . . . . Explanation of what and when
9. Supplements . . . . Usually describes available optional equipment

Most "late-model" popular airplanes have *POH*s reprinted as perfect-bound books (called Information Manuals) available at FBOs and aviation bookstores. IF POSSIBLE, purchase a *POH* for your training airplane before you begin your flight lessons. Read it cover-to-cover and study the normal operating checklists, and memorize the standard airspeeds and emergency procedures.

If a *POH* (information manual) is not available for purchase, borrow one overnight and photocopy the entire *POH* at a local copy center (estimated cost: 200 pages @ $.05 = $10.00). Even if you are told this is unnecessary, do it anyway. It will be very helpful.

This chapter covers 2 of the 34 "Tasks" in the FAA Practical Test Standards (PTSs). They are

1. Airplane Systems
2. Determining Performance and Limitations

COCKPIT FAMILIARITY

When you are purchasing a *POH* (or borrowing one to photocopy), take several pictures of the airplane's control panel you will be training in. Get in the back seat or hold your camera as far back in the cabin as you can. Take pictures of the flight controls, control panel, instruments, etc. through the windows and doors also.

If you are going to train in more than one airplane, take additional pictures of the control panels so you can understand the differences and adjust to different airplanes easier.

The objective is to learn the location and purpose of each switch, control, instrument, and gauge before you have to use them. In addition to your pictures, your *POH* should have diagrams similar to that of the Piper Tomahawk illustrated below. (Note: most trainers are not as fully equipped as in this illustration).

<u>Piper Tomahawk Instrument Panel</u>

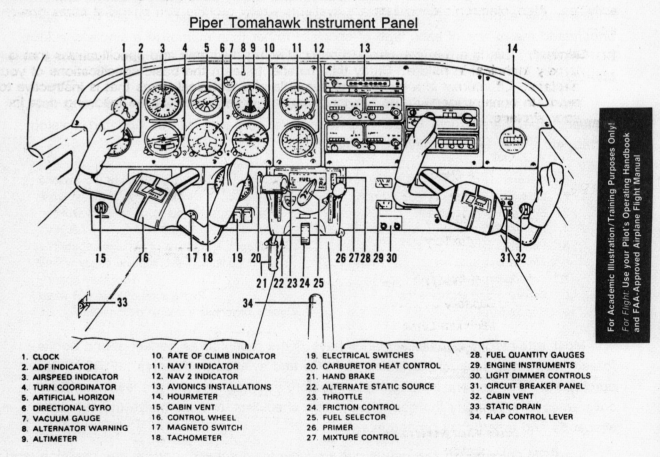

For Academic Illustration/Training Purposes Only!
For Flight: Use your Pilot's Operating Handbook and FAA-Approved Airplane Flight Manual

1. CLOCK	10. RATE OF CLIMB INDICATOR	19. ELECTRICAL SWITCHES	28. FUEL QUANTITY GAUGES
2. ADF INDICATOR	11. NAV 1 INDICATOR	20. CARBURETOR HEAT CONTROL	29. ENGINE INSTRUMENTS
3. AIRSPEED INDICATOR	12. NAV 2 INDICATOR	21. HAND BRAKE	30. LIGHT DIMMER CONTROLS
4. TURN COORDINATOR	13. AVIONICS INSTALLATIONS	22. ALTERNATE STATIC SOURCE	31. CIRCUIT BREAKER PANEL
5. ARTIFICIAL HORIZON	14. HOURMETER	23. THROTTLE	32. CABIN VENT
6. DIRECTIONAL GYRO	15. CABIN VENT	24. FRICTION CONTROL	33. STATIC DRAIN
7. VACUUM GAUGE	16. CONTROL WHEEL	25. FUEL SELECTOR	34. FLAP CONTROL LEVER
8. ALTERNATOR WARNING	17. MAGNETO SWITCH	26. PRIMER	
9. ALTIMETER	18. TACHOMETER	27. MIXTURE CONTROL	

After studying both your pictures and the *POH* diagram, sketch your control panel on a blank sheet of paper. Learn the position of each switch, control, instrument, and gauge.

As you study your *POH* and gain experience in the airplane, you will learn "normal" indications on each gauge and instrument and how to react to abnormal readings.

This "advance preparation" is very important. It will allow you to concentrate on the flight controls and the flight path of the airplane rather than searching the control panel for an instrument. "Advance preparation" also gives you confidence, i.e., lessens confusion.

PILOT'S OPERATING HANDBOOK (POH)

In conjunction with cockpit familiarity, you must pursue *POH* knowledge (not familiarity). Each of the nine sections listed on page 53 are commented on in the next few pages.

ALSO be aware that some *POH*s have two parts to each section: abbreviated procedures (which are checklists) and amplified procedures (which consist of discussion of the checklists). In this book, we generally reproduce only the checklists. In your airplane's *POH*, learn BOTH the abbreviated and the amplified procedures!

As a practical matter, after you study your *POH* and gain some experience in your airplane, you may wish to retype some of the standard checklists on heavy manila paper. This is more convenient than finding checklists in your *POH* while engaged in other cockpit activities. Also, electronic checklists are available which provide you checklist items one-at-a-time.

1. **General.** This is a general introduction containing diagrams and specifications that is largely technical in nature. Study this material to learn the basic specifications of your airplane. Of interest is a glossary of symbols and technical terms that is instructive to read. In conjunction with the "General" section of the *POH*, list the following data for your airplane.

Fuel

Type Used . . . . _____

Capacity of Each Tank: Left   Right

    Main . . . . _____   _____

    Auxiliary . . . . _____   _____

Oil

Type/Weight . . . . _____

Capacity . . . . _____

Minimum Level . . . . _____

Suggested Level . . . . _____

Tire Pressure

Mains . . . . _____

Nose . . . . _____

Brake Fluid Reservoirs

Location . . . . _____

Type of Fluid . . . . _____

Capacity . . . . _____

2. **Limitations.** This important section tells you the safe "limits" to which your airplane can be flown. Based on data in Section 2, complete and memorize the following "airspeed limits" and "weight limits" tables.

Airspeed Limits — Speed in (STATUTE) (KTS) or (MPH)

(STAlling or min. steady Flight
LAnding configuration)

V_{SO} ... Flaps Down .... (45.18) 52
(bottom of white arc)

V_{S1} ... Flaps UP .... (50.40) 58
(bottom of green arc)

V_{LOF} Lift off Speed .... (52.13) 60
(liftoff)

V_X Speed for best angle of climb .... (48.66) 56
(best angle-of-climb)

V_Y Speed for best Rate of Climb .... (65.12) 75
(best rate-of-climb)

V_{FE} - Setting 1 .... (86.89) 100
(flap extension - approach flaps)

V_{FE} - Setting 2 .... _____
(flap extension - full flaps)

V_A .... _____
(maneuvering speed/turbulence)

V_{NO} .... _____
(top of green, bottom of yellow)

V_{NE} .... (139.3) 160
(red line, never exceed)

$V_{MaxGlide}$ .... " 160
(Obtain from Section 3, POH)

Weight Limits

Max. Ramp 1389+222+15 1624		Basic Empty Weight 1388 + 222 =
Max. T/O 2200		Max. Payload _____
Max. Landing "		Max. Fuel Weight _____
Max. Zero Fuel 2200+222 1978		Max. Baggage _____

The following weight definitions are taken from the Beech Skipper's *POH*. Learn them and the relationship between the weights.

Maximum Ramp Weight .... Maximum weight approved for ground maneuvers (includes weight of start, taxi, and runway fuel).

Maximum Takeoff Weight .... Maximum weight approved for the start of the takeoff run.

Maximum Landing Weight ...... Maximum weight approved for the landing touchdown.

Maximum Zero Fuel Weight ...... Maximum weight exclusive of usable fuel.

Basic Empty Weight .... Weight of an empty basic airplane including unusable fuel, full operating fluids, and full oil, plus optional equipment.

Payload .... Weight of occupants and baggage.

Useful Load occ-bag-fuel+oil. Difference between ramp weight and basic empty weight.

1. *Max Ramp minus Max T/O* is the fuel used on engine start, warm-up, and taxi.

2. *Max T/O minus Max landing* is the fuel used en route.

3. *Max Ramp minus (Basic empty + Payload)* is the maximum fuel weight possible for that flight.

4. *Max zero fuel* is basic empty plus maximum payload.

5. *Max fuel weight* is total usable fuel x 6 lb/gal.

Note that the maximum can be hypothetical or the weight applicable to each flight. For each flight: your basic empty weight, plus fuel weight, plus payload, must NOT EXCEED maximum ramp weight.

3. **Emergency Procedures**. Read and study Section 3 very carefully. Emergencies occur very infrequently, if ever, but you want to be totally prepared for the possibility! For illustration, the Skipper, 152, and Tomahawk Section 3 Tables of Contents are reproduced below.

Beechcraft Skipper
Emergency Procedures

Emergency Airspeeds
Engine Failure
  During Take-off Ground Roll
  After Liftoff and in Flight
Rough Running Engine
Airstart
Electrical Smoke or Fire
Engine Fire (Ground)
Engine Fire in Flight
Emergency Descent
Glide

Landing Emergencies
  Landing Without Power
Systems Emergencies
  Alternator-Out Procedure
  Starter Engaged Warning Light Illuminated
  Alternate Static Air Source
  Unlatched Door in Flight
  Complete Loss of Electrical Power
  Emergency Exit
Spins

Cessna 152
Emergency Procedures

Engine Failures
  Engine Failure During Takeoff Run
  Engine Failure Immediately After Takeoff
  Engine Failure During Flight
Forced Landings
  Emergency Landing Without Engine
    Power
  Precautionary Landing With Engine
    Power
  Ditching

Fires
  During Start on Ground
  Engine Fire in Flight
  Electrical Fire in Flight
  Cabin Fire
  Wing Fire
Icing
  Inadvertent Icing Encounter
Landing With a Flat Main Tire
Electrical Power Supply System Malfunctions

Piper Tomahawk
Emergency Procedures

General
Emergency Procedures Checklist
Amplified Emergency Procedures (General)
Engine Inoperative Procedures
  Engine Power Loss During Takeoff (Not
    Airborne)
  Engine Power Loss During Takeoff (If
    Airborne)
  Engine Power Loss in Flight
  Power Off Landing

Fire
  Engine Fire During Start
  Fire in Flight
Loss of Oil Pressure
Loss of Fuel Pressure
High Oil Temperature
Alternator Failure
Spin Recovery (Unintentional Spin)
Open Door
Engine Roughness
Loss of Pitot-Static Pressure

4. **Normal Procedures**. Section 4 contains your daily checklists. These are what you rely on to avoid skipping an important procedure or step.

Beechcraft Skipper
Normal Procedures

Airspeeds for Safe Operation
Preflight Inspection
Before Engine Starting
External Power
  Starting Engine Using Auxiliary
    Power Unit
Engine Starting
Before Taxi
Before Takeoff
Takeoff
Climb
Cruise
Descent
Before Landing

Balked Landing
After Landing
Shutdown
Environmental Systems
Heating and Ventilation
Cold Weather Operation
Preflight Inspection
Engine
Taxiing
Noise Characteristics
Spins
Entry
Recovery

Cessna 152
Normal Procedures

Speeds for Normal Operation
Preflight Inspection
  Cabin
  Empennage
  Right Wing, Trailing Edge
  Right Wing
  Nose
  Left Wing
  Left Wing, Leading Edge
  Left Wing, Trailing Edge
Before Starting Engine
Starting Engine (Temperatures
  Above Freezing)
Before Takeoff

Takeoff
Normal Takeoff
Short Field Takeoff
Enroute Climb
Cruise
Descent
Before Landing
Landing
Normal Landing
Short Field Landing
Balked Landing
After Landing
Securing Airplane

Piper Tomahawk
Normal Procedures

General
Airspeeds for Safe Operations
Normal Procedures Checklist
Amplified Normal Procedures (General)
Preflight Check
Before Starting Engine
Starting Engine
Warm-Up
Taxiing
Ground Check
Before Takeoff

Takeoff
Climb
Cruising
Approach and Landing
Stopping Engine
Parking
Stalls
Turbulent Air Operation
Weight and Balance
Maneuvers
Spins

5. **Performance**. This section specifies how your airplane is capable of performing under various conditions. While this data (usually presented in graph form) may appear only technical and perhaps even distant, you **must** learn your airplane's performance capability. For each data set, graph, or chart, work a hypothetical example given various conditions, e.g., weight, temperature, etc. See the "Performance and Limitations PTS" on page 64.

Beechcraft Skipper
Performance

Introduction to Performance and Flight
  Planning
    Conditions
Comments Pertinent to the Use of
  Performance Graphs
Airspeed Calibration-Normal System
Altimeter Correction-Normal System
Airspeed Calibration-Alternate System
Altimeter Correction-Alternate System
Fahrenheit to Celsius Temperature
  Conversion
ISA Conversion

Stall Speeds
Wind Components
Take-Off Distance-Hard Surface
Take-Off Distance-Grass Surface
Climb
Time, Fuel, and Distance to Climb
Cruise Speeds
Cruise Performance
Range Profile-29 Gallons
Endurance Profile-29 Gallons
Landing Distance-Hard Surface-Flaps Down (30°)
Landing Distance-Grass Surface-Flaps Down (30°)

Cessna 152
Performance

Introduction
Use of Performance Charts
Sample Problem
  Takeoff
  Cruise
  Fuel Required
  Landing
Demonstrated Operating Temperature
Figure 5-1, Airspeed Calibration
Figure 5-2, Temperature Conversion Chart

Figure 5-3, Stall Speeds
Figure 5-4, Takeoff Distance
Figure 5-5, Maximum Rate of Climb
Figure 5-6, Time, Fuel, and Distance to Climb
Figure 5-7, Cruise Performance
Figure 5-8, Range Profile - 24.5 Gallons Fuel
           Range Profile - 37.5 Gallons Fuel
Figure 5-9, Endurance Profile - 24.5 Gallons Fuel
           Endurance Profile - 37.5 Gallons Fuel
Figure 5-10, Landing Distance

Piper Tomahawk
Performance

Introduction - Performance and Flight
  Planning
Flight Planning Example
Temperature Conversion
Airspeed Calibration
Stall Speed vs. Angle of Bank
Takeoff Performance - Zero Degrees
  Wing Flaps
Takeoff Performance Over 50 Ft. Barrier -
  Zero Degrees Wing Flaps
Takeoff Performance - One Notch Wing
  Flaps
Takeoff Performance Over 50 Ft. Barrier -
  One Notch Wing Flaps

Climb Performance
Fuel, Time, and Distance to Climb
Engine Performance
Speed Power - Best Power Mixture Below 75%
Speed Power - Best Economy Mixture
Best Power Range
Best Economy Range
Best Power Endurance
Best Economy Endurance
Fuel, Time, and Distance to Descend
Glide Performance
Landing Ground Roll

6. **Weight and Balance.** Weight and balance calculations and/or review should be done before each flight. Operation of **your** airplane in excess of maximum weight or outside of CG limits is extremely dangerous, i.e., life threatening. After studying the next 3 pages of definitions and basic principles, refer to Section 6 of your airplane's *POH* and work through several CG examples. Also refer to the example in Chapter 6 of this book. See the Performance and Limitations PTS on page 64. Remember, your weight and balance check is as important as checking to see if there is oil in the engine and fuel in the gas tank.

a.   Overview.

   1)   Maximum gross weight is the maximum weight of an airplane and its contents at takeoff.

   2)   In addition to having a maximum gross weight, the airplane must be loaded so that the center of gravity (CG) is in front of the center of lift. This provides aircraft stability about the lateral axis (for pitch) and means the nose will drop if the wings stall.

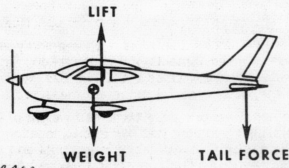

LIFT

WEIGHT   **TAIL FORCE**

Max gross wt. of my plane = 2200

b.   Maximum gross weight.

   1)   You need to know

6 lb per gal × 37 = 222 Lb.

   a)   Fuel weighs 6 pounds per gallon. *Holds 42 gal. Total - only 37 usable*

   b)   Oil weighs 7.5 pounds per gallon and a gallon equals 4 quarts.

Empty wt. =
1,381 Lb
222 " gas
15 " oil
───
1624
1610.

   2)   When calculating maximum gross weight, begin with the airplane's empty weight from the FAA-approved operating manual. Then add the weight of

   a)   Usable fuel

   •   Unusable fuel is included in the empty weight in airplane operating manuals. *(unusable in ours is 5 gal. (or 30 Lb)*

   b)   Oil (if not included in empty weight) *(our plane holds 8 qts = 2 gal. = 15 Lb.)*
   c)   Baggage   *(7.5 per gal = 15 Lb.)*
   d)   Passengers

   3)   Frequently, you will be trying to figure how much baggage, fuel, and/or passengers you can carry.

   a)   First, compute the total weight without the items to be carried. Then subtract the weight of the items to be carried from the maximum gross weight. *1624 Lbs*

   b)   The difference is the amount of weight available for carrying the last items. *576 avail. Lbs = payload*
   590

   4)   If the last items bring the total weight over maximum, you cannot bring all the items or you must determine how much fuel to drain in order to bring the airplane back within maximum gross weight. Divide the amount of excess weight by 6 pounds to convert to gallons of fuel to be drained. Remember to recompute your endurance and range.

c.   Weight and balance definitions (CG).

   1)   Arm (moment arm) -- the horizontal distance in inches from the reference datum line to the center of gravity of any item. The algebraic sign is plus (+) if measured aft of the datum and minus (-) if measured forward of the datum.

CG oF our Plane is 53.2 IN behind DATum Line.

2) Center of gravity (CG) -- the point about which an airplane would balance if it were possible to suspend it at that point. It is the mass center of the airplane, or the theoretical point at which the entire weight of the airplane is assumed to be concentrated.

3) Center of gravity limits -- the specified forward and aft points within which the CG must be located during flight for safe control and maneuverability. These limits are indicated on pertinent airplane specifications.

4) Center of gravity range -- the distance between the forward and aft CG limits indicated on pertinent airplane specifications.

5) Datum (reference datum) line -- an imaginary vertical plane or line from which all measurements of arm are taken. The datum is established by the manufacturer. Once the datum has been selected, all moment arms and the location of CG range are measured from this point.

6) Basic empty weight -- the combined weight of the airframe, engines, and all operating equipment that has a fixed location and is permanently installed in the airplane. It also includes optional and special equipment, fixed ballast, hydraulic fluid, unusable (residual) fuel, and undrainable (residual) oil.

7) Fuel load -- the expendable part of the load of the airplane. It includes only usable fuel, not fuel required to fill the lines or that which remains trapped in the tank sumps.

8) Moment -- the product of the weight of an item times its arm. Remember, an item's arm is its ± distance from the datum line. Moments are expressed in pound-inches (lb.-in.). Total moment is the weight of the airplane times the distance between the datum and the CG.

9) Standard weights -- established for numerous items involved in weight and balance computations.
    a) Gasoline is 6 pounds/U.S. gallon.
    b) Oil is 7.5 pounds/U.S. gallon.

(812 Lb) 10) Useful load -- the weight of the pilot, copilot, passengers, baggage, usable fuel, and drainable oil. It is the basic empty weight subtracted from the maximum allowable gross weight. This term applies to general aviation airplanes only.

d. Basic principles of weight and balance (CG).

1) Total weight is the airplane's basic empty weight plus the weight of everything loaded on it. This is quite simple.
    a) The difficulty comes when you must distribute this weight in such a manner that the entire mass of the loaded airplane is balanced around a point (CG) which must be located within specified limits.
    b) It becomes easier when the basic principles of weight and balance are understood.

2) The point where the airplane will balance can be determined by locating the center of gravity. Remember, it is the imaginary point at which all the weight is concentrated.
    a) To provide the necessary balance between longitudinal stability and elevator control, the center of gravity is usually located slightly forward of the center of lift.

b)   This loading condition causes a nose-down tendency, which is desirable during flight at a high angle of attack and slow speed.

3)   The safe zone within which the balance point (CG) must fall is called the CG range.

a)   The extremities of the range are called the forward and aft CG limits.

b)   These limits are usually specified in inches, along the longitudinal axis of the airplane, measured from a datum reference.

c)   The datum is an arbitrary point, established by airplane designers. It will probably vary in location between different airplanes.

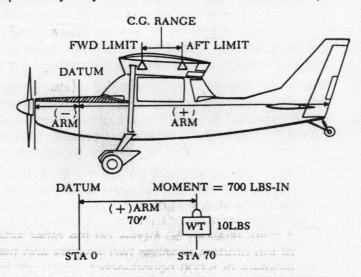

4)   The distance from the datum line (often just called "datum") to any component part of the airplane, or any object loaded on the airplane, is called an arm.

a)   When the object or component is located aft of the datum it is measured in positive inches. If located forward of the datum it is measured in negative inches.

•   The location of an object or part is often referred to as the station.

b)   Recall that the moment is the weight of an object times its arm (distance from the datum). The moment is a measurement of the gravitational force which causes a tendency of the weight to rotate about a point or axis. It is expressed in pound-inches.

5)   EXAMPLE. In the diagram at the top of the opposite page, assume that a weight of 50 pounds is placed on the board at a station or point 100 inches from the datum (fulcrum). The downward force of the weight at that spot can be determined by multiplying 50 pounds by 100 inches, which produces a moment of 5,000 pound-inches.

a)   To establish a balance, a total of 5,000 pound-inches must be applied to the other end of the board. Any combination of weight and distance which, when multiplied, produces 5,000 pound-inches moment forward (to the left) of the datum will balance the board.

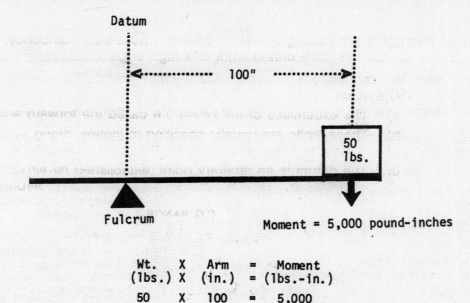

```
Wt.    X   Arm   =   Moment
(lbs.) X   (in.) =   (lbs.-in.)
50     X   100   =   5,000
```

NOTE: The datum is assumed to be located
       at the fulcrum.

b) If a 100-pound weight is placed at a point (station) 25 inches on the
    other side of the datum, and a second 50-pound weight is placed at
    a point (station) 50 inches on the other side of the datum, the sum
    of the product of these two weights and their distances will total a
    moment of 5,000 pound-inches which will balance the board.

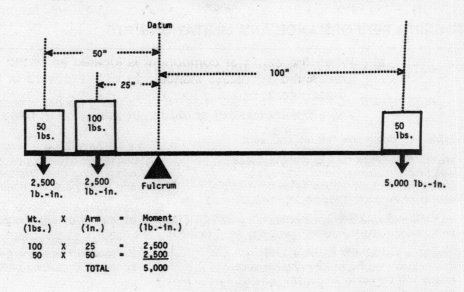

```
Wt.    X   Arm   =   Moment
(lbs.)     (in.)     (lb.-in.)
100    X   25    =   2,500
50     X   50    =   2,500
           TOTAL     5,000
```

7. **Description of Operating Systems.**

8. **Service and Maintenance.**

9. **Supplements.**

> These last 3 *POH* sections are self-
> explanatory and require a careful
> reading. They are extensions of
> Section 1. Some *POH*s have a
> Section 10, "Safety Tips," which is
> obviously important.

AIRPLANE SYSTEMS PTS

TASK: AIRPLANE SYSTEMS (ASEL)
   PILOT OPERATION -- 1
   REFERENCES: AC 61-21; Pilot's Operating Handbook and FAA-Approved Airplane Flight Manual.

Objective. To determine that the applicant exhibits knowledge by explaining the airplane systems as appropriate:

1. Primary flight controls and trim.

2. Wing flaps, leading edge devices, and spoilers.

3. Flight instruments.

4. Landing gear -
   a. brakes and tires.
   b. nosewheel or tailwheel steering.

5. Engine -
   a. controls and indicators.
   b. induction, carburetion, and injection.
   c. exhaust.

6. Propeller.

7. Fuel system -
   a. tanks, pumps, controls, and indicators.
   b. fueling procedures.
   c. normal operation.

8. Hydraulic system -
   a. controls and indicators.
   b. pumps and regulators.
   c. normal operation.

9. Electrical system -
   a. controls and indicators.
   b. alternators or generators.
   c. battery, ground power.
   d. normal operation.

10. Environmental system -
   a. heating.
   b. ventilation.
   c. controls and indicators.

11. Ice prevention and elimination.

12. Vacuum system.

DETERMINING PERFORMANCE AND LIMITATIONS PTS

TASK: DETERMINING PERFORMANCE AND LIMITATIONS (ASEL)
   PILOT OPERATION -- 1
   REFERENCES: AC 61-21, AC 61-23, AC 61-84; Pilot's Operating Handbook and
        FAA-Approved Airplane Flight Manual.

Objective. To determine that the applicant:

1. Exhibits knowledge by explaining airplane weight and balance, performance, and limitations, including adverse aerodynamic effects of exceeding the limits.

2. Uses the available and appropriate performance charts, tables, and data.

3. Computes weight and balance, and determines that the weight and center of gravity will be within limits during all phases of the flight.

4. Calculates airplane performance, considering density altitude, wind, terrain, and other pertinent conditions.

5. Describes the effect of atmospheric conditions on airplane performance.

6. Makes a competent decision on whether the required performance is within the operating limitations of the airplane.

NORMAL POWER SETTINGS AND AIRSPEEDS

These are for normal operations and especially for IFR flight. Obtain them from your CFI and confirm them in reading your *POH* and flying the airplane.

	Airspeed	Power MP*	RPM
Liftoff			
Climbout			
Cruise climb			
Cruise level			
Cruise descent			
Slow cruise level			
Traffic pattern			
Approach			
Landing (flare)			

*Not relevant to airplane with fixed pitch propeller.

These are the "numbers" you will use to fly by. Learn them and be comfortable with them. Assume two people are on board: you and your CFI, safety pilot, or examiner. Note the effects that varying weights have on these numbers.

TAKEOFF DATA

Prior to <u>each</u> flight, you should work through each of the following. Consult your *POH* and confirm with flight experience.

1. Weight and balance. (Your *POH* should have a worksheet to help you do your computations. Photocopy it and complete it both for takeoff and landing, i.e., after fuel burn.)

2. Runway length . . . . _____

3. Headwind component . . . . _____

4. Temperature . . . . _____

5. Field altitude MSL . . . . _____

6. Pressure altitude . . . . _____

7. Airplane weight, takeoff . . . . _____

8. Airplane weight, landing . . . . _____

9. End-of-runway conditions, obstructions, etc. _____

   _____

10. Normal takeoff distance
    Ground . . . . _____
    50 ft . . . . _____

11. Maximum performance takeoff
    Ground . . . . _____
    50 ft . . . . _____

12. Liftoff airspeed . . . . _____

13. Normal landing distance . . . . _____

14. Groundroll over 50-ft obstacle . . . . _____

CHAPTER FOUR
PREFLIGHT PROCEDURES

Before flying, you are required to perform a preflight inspection of your airplane. The purpose of the preflight inspection (often called "preflight" or "walkaround") is to ensure the airplane has no obvious problems prior to taking off. Each airplane has a specific list of preflight procedures recommended by the airplane manufacturer that are found in the airplane operating manual. You should always follow this checklist item by item.

This chapter covers 3 of the 34 "Tasks" in the FAA Practical Test Standards (PTSs). They are:

1. Visual Inspection
2. Cockpit Management
3. Engine Start

GENERAL OBJECTIVES OF THE PREFLIGHT

Normally, the preflight is carried out in a systematic walk around the plane. The preflight generally consists of the following:

1. Check to see that all leading edges and surfaces (wings, elevators, rudder, propeller, fuselage) are smooth and undamaged.

    a. Be sure that the airplane is in an airworthy condition.
    b. No external damage should be apparent.

2. All of the moving control surfaces (ailerons, elevators, rudder) should move smoothly and freely for their entire movement span. They must also be securely attached, with no missing, loose, or broken nuts, bolts, or rivets.

    a. First, remove all control locks. Control locks keep the control surfaces fixed so they do not bang back and forth in the wind. They are either external (e.g., clamps holding the ailerons from moving) or on the control yoke (e.g., a pin to prevent the control yoke from turning or moving in or out).

b.   You may have to place flaps in the full down position so the internal components can be examined.

c.   Any ice, snow, and frost must be removed from the airplane.

3.   Check to see that there are no oil puddles or other leakages under the plane, inside the engine cowling, or on the wheel struts (parts attaching the wheels to the plane).

4.   Check to see that the tires are properly inflated and not cut, unduly worn, etc. Also, the struts (shock absorbers) should be properly inflated.

a.   Check that windshield and cabin windows are clean.

5.   Check to see that the gas tanks are full (or at desired levels). A visual inspection of each tank should be made to roughly verify fuel gauge indications. For example, if gauges indicate "full," the tank should not appear half full or empty. A fuel sample should be taken from each sump drainage valve at lowest points of each tank and from other parts of the fuel system. Look for three items:

a.   Presence of water.
b.   Contamination -- foreign matter.

6.   In the engine compartment, check to see that

a.   Oil is at desired level.
b.   Brake fluid is okay (this check is not possible on some airplanes).
c.   No fuel or oil leakages apparent.
d.   All wires appear connected and snug.
e.   Cowling is secure upon completion.

7.   Check to see that the pitot tube is uncovered and hole is clear, and that the static air source has clear openings.

a.   The stall warning vane and fuel vents should also be free of obstruction.

8.   Make sure all necessary documents, maps, safety equipment, etc. are aboard. The word ARROW will help you to remember the required documents:

a.   **A**irworthiness Certificate.

b.   **R**egistration Certificate.

c.   **R**adio station license.

d.   **O**perating limitations, or *FAA-Approved Airplane Flight Manual*.

e.   **W**eight and balance information (also in the flight manual).

f.   Flotation gear if the flight is to be conducted over water.

g.   Example illustrations of items a, b, and c are presented on pages 214 and 215 of Chapter 12, "Navigation."

h.   Engine and airframe logbooks (must be available, but not necessarily aboard the airplane).

9.   Operating limitations can be presented in an *FAA-Approved Airplane Flight Manual*, in the form of placards (small metal or plastic plaques), or a combination of both.

a.   Newer airplanes must have an *FAA-Approved Airplane Flight Manual* aboard (even though many placards also appear).

1)   Weight and balance information is also in the flight manual.

2)   All airplanes manufactured after March 1, 1979, must have an *FAA-Approved Airplane Flight Manual*.

b. In many older airplanes, manufacturers met the operating limitation requirements by mounting placards in the cockpit and putting a copy of the weight and balance information aboard.

c. In older airplanes without an *FAA-Approved Airplane Flight Manual*, be sure the weight and balance information is aboard, and the placards have not been removed or painted over.

　　1) If the placards are not visible, the airplane is considered not airworthy (and may be considered so by the FAA and the insurance company in the event of an accident).

d. The airplane as loaded must be within weight and balance operating limitations per the airplane operating manual. See weight and balance discussion in Chapter 11 "Solo Flight," and in *PRIVATE PILOT HANDBOOK* Chapter 6 "Weight and Balance.".

10. You should have on board your student pilot and medical certificate, and your pilot logbook with an endorsement by your instructor attesting that you have received the instruction required to operate within 50 NM of your home airport.

a. Prior to receiving your recreational pilot certificate, you will either be with your CFI or by yourself (which requires specific CFI logbook and student pilot certificate endorsements).

11. The airplane must be untied, unchocked, and clear of obstructions to the propellers, wings, etc. (i.e., it must be ready to taxi out of the ramp area).

12. Baggage must be secure, baggage door locked, and passenger door locked.

The preflight must be complete, i.e., no important step may be left out. Use of the written checklist or development of a systematic set of procedures (followed in the same order) as you gain familiarity with the airplane is of utmost importance.

Finally, if anything comes to your attention that may be a problem, ask someone more experienced and/or knowledgeable to look at it. For example, some oil found inside the cowling may be from an engine oil leak or a spill from the last time oil was added (check with a mechanic, the lineman, or the last person to fly the plane).

VISUAL INSPECTION PTS

TASK: *VISUAL INSPECTION (ASEL)*
　　　PILOT OPERATION - 1
　　　REFERENCES: AC 61-21; Pilot's Operating Handbook; and FAA-Approved Airplane Flight Manual.

Objective. *To determine that the applicant:*

1. *Exhibits knowledge of airplane visual inspection by explaining the reasons for checking all items.*

2. *Inspects the airplane by following a checklist.*

3. *Determines that the airplane is in condition for safe flight emphasizing -*

　　a. *fuel quantity, grade, and type.*
　　b. *fuel contamination safeguards.*

c. *fuel venting.*
d. *oil quantity, grade, and type.*
e. *fuel, oil, and hydraulic leaks.*
e. *flight controls.*
f. *structural damage.*
g. *exhaust.*
h. *tiedowns, control locks, and wheel chocks removal.*
i. *ice and frost removal.*
j. *security of baggage, cargo, and equipment.*

PREFLIGHT CHECKLIST FOR A BEECH SKIPPER

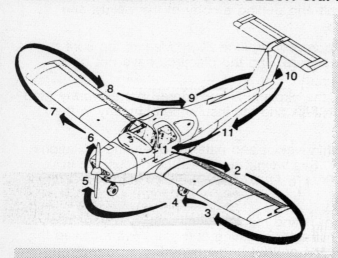

1. CABIN

    a. Pilot's Operating Handbook - AVAILABLE.

    b. Control Lock - REMOVE.

    c. Parking Brake - SET.

    d. Magneto/Start Switch - OFF.

    e. Battery Switch - ON.

    f. Fuel Quantity Indicators - CHECK QUANTITY.

    g. Battery Switch - OFF.

    h. Flush-type Fuel Drain Tool - OBTAIN.

2. LEFT WING TRAILING EDGE

    a. Flap - CHECK.

    b. Aileron - CHECK.

    c. Wing Tip - CHECK.

    d. Position and Strobe Light - CHECK.

3. LEFT WING LEADING EDGE

    a. Pitot Tube - CHECK (remove cover).

    b. Stall Warning - CHECK for movement of vane.

    c. Fuel Tank - CHECK QUANTITY; Cap - SECURE.

    d. Tie-down and Chocks - REMOVE.

4. LEFT LANDING GEAR

    a. Tire, Wheel and Brake - CHECK.

    b. Fuel Sump - DRAIN (use fuel-drain tool).

5. NOSE SECTION

    a. Propeller - CHECK.

    b. Induction Air Intake - CLEAR; Filter - CHECK condition and security of attachment.

    c. Landing Light - CHECK.

    d. Tire and Nose Gear - CHECK condition and inflation.

    e. Engine Oil - CHECK (operation with fewer than 4 quarts is not recommended); Cap - SECURE.

    f. Engine - CHECK GENERAL CONDITION.

    g. Access Door - SECURE.

    h. Fuel Strainer - DRAIN.

    i. Chocks - REMOVE.

6. RIGHT LANDING GEAR

    a. Tire, Wheel and Brake - CHECK.

    b. Fuel Sump - DRAIN (use fuel-drain tool).

7. RIGHT WING LEADING EDGE

    a. Fuel Tank - CHECK QUANTITY; Cap - SECURE.

    b. Tie-down and Chocks - REMOVE.

8. RIGHT WING TRAILING EDGE

    a. Position and Strobe Light - CHECK.

    b. Wing Tip - CHECK.

    c. Aileron - CHECK.

    d. Flap - CHECK.

9. RIGHT FUSELAGE

    a. Static Pressure Button - UNOBSTRUCTED.

    b. Emergency Locator Transmitter - ARMED.

10. EMPENNAGE

    a. Control Surfaces - CHECK.

    b. Tie-down - REMOVE.

    c. Position Light - CHECK.

11. LEFT FUSELAGE

    a. Static Pressure Button - UNOBSTRUCTED.

    b. All Antennas - CHECK.

NOTE: Check operation of lights if night flight is anticipated.

PREFLIGHT CHECKLIST FOR A PIPER TOMAHAWK

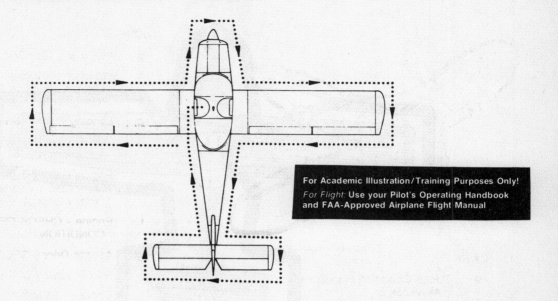

For Academic Illustration/Training Purposes Only!
For Flight: Use your Pilot's Operating Handbook
and FAA-Approved Airplane Flight Manual

1. **COCKPIT**
   a. Control wheel - RELEASE CONSTRAINTS.
   b. Ignition - OFF.
   c. Master switch - ON.
   d. Fuel Quantity Gauges - CHECK.
   e. Alternator Warning Light - CHECK.
   f. Master Switch - OFF.
   g. Primary Flight Controls - PROPER OPERATION.
   h. Flaps - PROPER OPERATION.
   i. Static Drain - DRAINED.
   j. Windows - CHECK CLEAN.
   k. Baggage - STOWED PROPERLY.
   l. Required Papers - ON BOARD.
   m. Parking Brake - SET ON.

2. **LEFT WING**
   a. Surface Condition - CHECK.
   b. Flap and Hinges - CHECK.
   c. Aileron and Hinges - CHECK.
   d. Wing Tip - CHECK.
   e. Lights - CHECK.
   f. Fuel Cap - OPEN.
   g. Fuel Quantity and Color - CHECK.
   h. Fuel Cap - CLOSE AND SECURE.
   i. Fuel Vent - OPEN.
   j. Fuel Tank Sump - DRAIN.
   k. Pitot Head - UNOBSTRUCTED.
   l. Stall Warning - CHECK.
   m. Landing Gear and Tire - CHECK.
   n. Brake Block and Disc - CHECK.
   o. Chock and Tie-Down - REMOVED.

3. **NOSE SECTION**
   a. Fuel Strainer - DRAIN.
   b. General Condition - CHECK.
   c. Propeller and Spinner - CHECK.
   d. Air Inlets - CLEAR.
   e. Engine Compartment - CHECK.
   f. Oil - CHECK QUANTITY.
   g. Dipstick - PROPERLY SEATED.
   h. Alternator Belt - CHECK TENSION.
   i. Cowling - CLOSED AND SECURE.
   j. Nose Wheel Tire - CHECK.
   k. Nose Gear Strut - PROPER INFLATION (3 inch exposure).
   l. Windshield - CLEAN.

4. **RIGHT WING** - Check as left wing.

5. **FUSELAGE (RIGHT SIDE)**
   a. General condition - CHECK.
   b. Antennas - CHECK.
   c. Side and Rear Window - CLEAN.
   d. Static Vents - UNOBSTRUCTED.

6. **EMPENNAGE**
   a. General Condition - CHECK.
   b. Hinges and Attachments - CHECK.

7. **FUSELAGE (LEFT SIDE)** - CHECK as right side.

PREFLIGHT CHECKLIST FOR A CESSNA 152

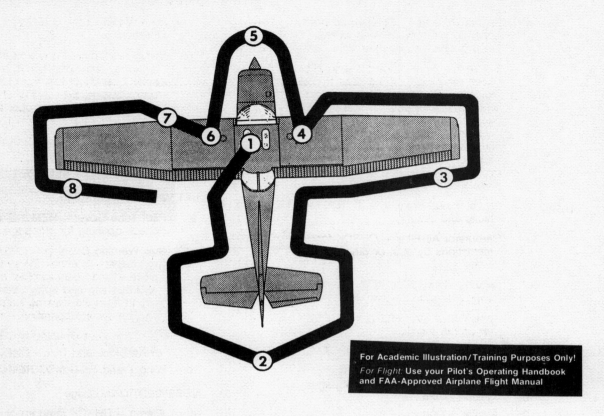

For Academic Illustration/Training Purposes Only!
For Flight: **Use your Pilot's Operating Handbook and FAA-Approved Airplane Flight Manual**

1. CABIN

    a.   Pilot's Operating Handbook -- AVAILABLE IN THE AIRPLANE.

    b.   Control Wheel Lock -- REMOVE.

    c.   Ignition Switch -- OFF.

    d.   Master Switch -- ON.

    ### WARNING

    When turning on the master switch, using an external power source, or pulling the propeller through by hand, treat the propeller as if the ignition switch were on. Do not stand, nor allow anyone else to stand, within the arc of the propeller, since a loose or broken wire, or a component malfunction, could cause the propeller to rotate.

    e.   Fuel Quantity Indicators -- CHECK QUANTITY.

    f.   Avionics Cooling Fan -- CHECK AUDIBLY FOR OPERATION.

    g.   Master Switch -- OFF.

    h.   Fuel Shutoff Valve -- ON.

2. EMPENNAGE

    a.   Rudder Gust Lock -- REMOVE.

    b.   Tail Tie-Down -- DISCONNECT.

    c.   Control Surfaces -- CHECK freedom of movement and security.

3. RIGHT WING Trailing Edge

    a.   Aileron -- CHECK freedom of movement and security.

4. RIGHT WING

    a.   Wing Tie-Down -- DISCONNECT.

    b.   Main Wheel Tire -- CHECK for proper inflation.

    c.   Before first flight of the day and after each refueling, use sampler cup and drain small quantity of fuel from fuel tank sump quick-drain valve to check for water, sediment, and proper fuel grade.

    d.   Fuel Quantity -- CHECK VISUALLY for desired level.

    e.   Fuel Filler Cap -- SECURE.

5. NOSE

    a. Engine Oil Level -- CHECK, do not operate with fewer than 4 quarts. Fill to 6 quarts for extended flight.

    b. Before first flight of the day and after each refueling, pull out strainer drain knob for about 4 seconds to clear fuel strainer of possible water and sediment. Check strainer drain closed. If water is observed, the fuel system may contain additional water, and further draining of the system at the strainer, fuel tank sumps, and fuel line drain plug will be necessary.

    c. Propeller and Spinner -- CHECK for nicks and security.

    d. Carburetor Air Filter -- CHECK for restrictions by dust or other foreign matter.

    e. Landing Light(s) -- CHECK for condition and cleanliness.

    f. Nose Wheel Strut and Tire -- CHECK for proper inflation.

    g. Nose Tie-Down -- DISCONNECT.

    h. Static Source Opening (left side of fuselage) -- CHECK for stoppage.

6. LEFT WING

    a. Main Wheel Tire -- CHECK for proper inflation.

    b. Before first flight of day and after each refueling, use sampler cup and drain small quantity of fuel from fuel tank sump quick-drain valve to check for water, sediment and proper fuel grade.

    c. Fuel Quantity -- CHECK VISUALLY for desired level.

    d. Fuel Filler Cap -- SECURE.

7. LEFT WING Leading Edge

    a. Pitot Tube Cover -- REMOVE and check opening for stoppage.

    b. Stall Warning Opening -- CHECK for stoppage. To check the system, place a clean handkerchief over the vent opening and apply suction; a sound from the warning horn will confirm system operation.

    c. Fuel Tank Vent Opening -- CHECK for stoppage.

    d. Wing Tie-Down -- DISCONNECT.

8. LEFT WING Trailing Edge

    a. Aileron -- CHECK freedom of movement and security.

9. BEFORE STARTING ENGINE make sure preflight inspection is complete.

FIRST FLIGHTS AND UNFAMILIAR AIRPLANES

Before getting ready to start the engine on your first flight and whenever you get ready to fly an unfamiliar airplane, take a few minutes to acquaint yourself with the cockpit, i.e., the flight controls, radios, and instruments. Almost all airplanes have a different configuration of instruments, radios, etc.

After your first flights and debriefing with your flight instructor, return to the airplane and sit in the pilot's seat and study the location of all instruments, radios, and control devices. Mentally review their location, operation, and use. Then mentally review your flight and how it could have been improved. After subsequent flight lessons you may find this procedure continues to be constructive if the airplane is available.

The next two pages contain diagrams of typical instrument panels and flight control arrangements of the Cessna 152 and the Beechcraft Skipper. The Piper Tomahawk's control panel appeared in Chapter 3 on page 54.

Cessna 152 Instrument Panel

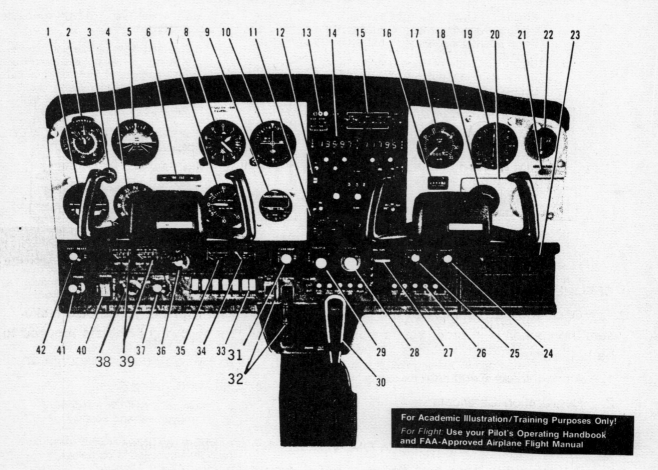

For Academic Illustration/Training Purposes Only!
For Flight: Use your Pilot's Operating Handbook
and FAA-Approved Airplane Flight Manual

1. Turn Coordinator
2. Airspeed Indicator
3. Suction Gage
4. Directional Indicator
5. Attitude Indicator
6. Airplane Registration Number
7. Vertical Speed Indicator
8. Altimeter
9. Digital Clock
10. Course Deviation and ILS Glide Slope Indicator
11. Transponder
12. ADF Radio
13. Marker Beacon Indicator Lights and Switches
14. Nav/Com Radio
15. Audio Control Panel
16. Flight Hour Recorder
17. Tachometer
18. Economy Mixture Indicator (EGT)
19. ADF Bearing Indicator
20. Additional Instrument Space
21. Low-Voltage Warning Light
22. Ammeter
23. Map Compartment
24. Cabin Heat Control
25. Cabin Air Control
26. Circuit Breakers
27. Wing Flap Switch and Position Indicator
28. Mixture Control
29. Throttle (With Friction Lock)
30. Microphone
31. Carburetor Heat Control
32. Elevator Trim Control Wheel and Position Indicator
33. Electrical Switches
34. Oil Pressure Gage
35. Oil Temperature Gage
36. Cigar Lighter
37. Instrument Panel and Radio Dial Lights Rheostat
38. Ignition Switch
39. Left and Right Fuel Quantity Indicators
40. Master Switch
41. Primer
42. Parking Brake Control

Beechcraft Skipper Instrument Panel

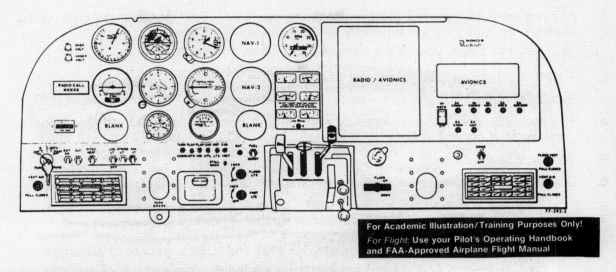

For Academic Illustration/Training Purposes Only!
For Flight: Use your Pilot's Operating Handbook and FAA-Approved Airplane Flight Manual

BEFORE STARTING THE ENGINE (COCKPIT MANAGEMENT)

Once you have completed the preflight and entered the airplane, you should make sure the cockpit is in order before starting the engine. The following items are required to be in the plane:

1. **A**irworthiness Certificate.

2. **R**egistration Certificate.

3. **R**adio station license.

4. **O**perating limitations (found in *FAA-Approved Airplane Flight Manual*).

5. **W**eight and balance data (found in *FAA-Approved Airplane Flight Manual*).

6. Recommended is flotation gear for each passenger if the flight is to be conducted over water (required when the flight is for hire).

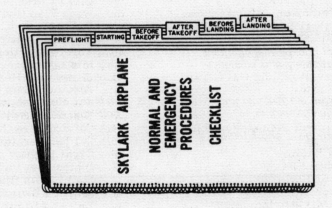

Flight Manual

You should have your pilot and medical certificates (your combined student pilot/ medical certificate is required prior to your solo). You should also have convenient

1. Any required navigational (sectional) charts available. Fold portions needed on the outside so that they will be ready for immediate reference.

    a. Do not forget your flight computer on cross-country flights.

2. A pad of paper and pencil or pen to make notes,

3. Expected radio frequencies noted for quick reference.

4. The seat adjusted for good visibility and full and convenient access to the rudders, brakes, and control yoke.

5. Your seatbelt fastened.

6. Checklists which are to be followed for starting, cruising, landing, shutting down, emergencies, etc.

7. An operating flashlight with extra batteries if night flight is a possibility.

Seat adjustments. You should adjust your seat and rudder pedals (if adjustable) so that you have complete and convenient control movement. Similarly, you should make sure each passenger's seat is firmly and appropriately adjusted. Relatedly, check that any carry-on luggage or other articles are securely fastened and cannot get in the way of the flight controls or control cables.

Seatbelts. Before starting your engine you should have your seat and shoulder belt fastened and secure. Also, each of your passengers should have seatbelts and shoulder harnesses securely fastened. Provide explanation and assistance to passengers as appropriate. You should also provide explanation of all appropriate emergency procedures.

COCKPIT MANAGEMENT PTS

TASK: COCKPIT MANAGEMENT (ASEL)
        PILOT OPERATION -- 1
        REFERENCE: AC 61-21.

Objective. To determine that the applicant:

1. Exhibits knowledge of cockpit management by explaining related safety and efficiency factors.

2. Organizes and arranges the material and equipment in an efficient manner.

3. Ensures that the safety belts and shoulder harnesses are fastened.

4. Adjusts and locks the foot pedals or pilot's seat to a safe position, and ensures full control movement.

5. Briefs the occupants on the use of safety belts and emergency procedures.

ENGINE START

A. Each airplane manufacturer (in cooperation with the engine manufacturer) has established a recommended set of procedures for starting the engine. You should always follow the specific checklist set forth in the operating manual for the airplane you are flying. The general procedures are to determine that

    1. The preflight check has been completed satisfactorily.

2. The cockpit is set to go (cockpit management!).

   a. Seatbelts and shoulder harnesses are fastened. Brief the occupants on the use of safety belts and emergency procedures.

   b. Seat is adjusted for best visibility and access to flight controls.

   c. Necessary maps, radio frequencies, etc. are conveniently available.

3. Fuel shut-off valve or selector is "on" fullest tank. Check operation, exercise valve; years of nonuse can lead to a frozen mechanism.

4. Radios and electrical equipment are off for starting.

5. Circuit breakers are all closed, i.e., not off.

6. The brakes are set (on).

7. Mixture is full rich.

8. Carburetor heat is off.

9. The throttle is "cracked," i.e., slightly open; 1/2 inch if engine is cold.

10. Prime as needed.

11. The airplane is positioned to avoid creating hazards.

12. Airplane movement after starting (avoid excessive RPM) must be avoided.

13. The propeller is clear and shout "CLEAR!" out the window to warn anyone nearby that you are about to start the engine.

14. The battery switch is on (master).

15. Rotating beacon is on (to warn others that you are in operation). Wait until you are in the air to turn on your strobe lights.

16. Engage starter (the same as starting an automobile). Release starter as soon as engine starts.

17. Adjust throttle to 800-1,000 RPM and check recommended oil pressure and other engine instruments.

18. Flaps are up.

19. Radios are on.

B. After the checklist has been completed, a general scan of the panel and surroundings should be made, including items such as

   1. Engine gauges, including oil pressure, are in green arcs.
   2. Ammeter is indicating a charge.
   3. Low voltage light is out.
   4. Radios are set to proper frequencies.
   5. Visually confirm flaps are up.
   6. Doors are closed and latched.

ENGINE START PTS

TASK: ENGINE START (ASEL)
PILOT OPERATION - 1
REFERENCES: AC 61-21, AC 61-23, AC 91-13, AC 91-55; Pilot's Operating Handbook and
FAA-Approved Airplane Flight Manual.

Objective. To determine that the applicant:

1. Exhibits knowledge by explaining engine starting procedures, including starting under various atmospheric conditions.

2. Performs all the items on the before-starting and starting checklists.

3. Accomplishes a safe starting procedure with emphasis on -

    a. positioning the airplane to avoid creating hazards.

    b. determining that the area is clear.

    c. adjusting the engine controls.

    d. setting the brakes.

    e. preventing undesirable airplane movement after engine start.

    f. avoiding excessive engine RPM and temperatures.

    g. checking the engine instruments after engine start.

STARTING CHECKLIST FOR A BEECH SKIPPER

A.   Engine Starting

1.   Mixture - FULL RICH

2.   Carburetor Heat - FULL COLD

3.   Throttle - PUMP 2 to 3 strokes for cold engine, then SET 1/4 TRAVEL

4.   Magneto/Start Switch - BOTH, and PUSH TO PRIME (for cold weather starts, prime 3 to 4 seconds before activating starter)

5.   Magneto/Start Switch - START and PRIME (release to BOTH position when engine fires and continue to prime as required)

6.   Engine Warm-up - 1000 to 1200 RPM

7.   Oil Pressure - INDICATION WITHIN 30 SECONDS

8.   External Power (if used) - OFF and DISCONNECT

9.   Alternator Switch - CHECK ON

10.   Alternator-out OVER VOLT/UNDER VOLT Lights - CHECK NOT ILLUMINATED

11.   Ammeter - CHECK (substantial charge rate decreases as battery is charged)

STARTING CHECKLIST FOR A CESSNA 152

A.   Starting Engine

1.   Mixture - RICH

2.   Carburetor Heat - COLD

3.   Prime - AS REQUIRED (up to 3 strokes - none if engine is warm)

4.   Throttle - OPEN 1/2 INCH (CLOSED if engine is warm)

5.   Propeller Area - CLEAR

6.   Master Switch - ON

7.   Ignition Switch - START (release when engine starts)

8.   Throttle - ADJUST for 1000 RPM or less

9.   Oil Pressure - CHECK

10.   Flashing Beacon and Navigation Lights - ON as required

11.   Radios - ON

STARTING CHECKLIST FOR A PIPER TOMAHAWK

A. Starting Engine When Cold
   1. Prime - AS REQUIRED.
   2. On last priming stroke leave primer in out position.
   3. Throttle - OPEN 1/2 INCH.
   4. Master Switch - ON.
   5. Electric Fuel Pump - ON.
   6. Mixture - FULL RICH.
   7. Starter - ENGAGE.
   8. Primer - PUSH IN SLOWLY AFTER ENGINE START.
   9. Throttle - ADVANCE SLIGHTLY.
   10. Oil Pressure - CHECK.
   11. Electric Fuel Pump - OFF.
   12. Fuel Pressure - CHECK.
   13. Primer - LOCKED.

COLD WEATHER STARTS

During cold weather the oil in an airplane engine becomes very thick. Before attempting a cold weather start, the propeller should be pulled through (turned) several times to loosen the oil (i.e., this is part of the preflight check). This saves battery energy, which is already low due to the low temperature. When pulling the propeller through by hand, treat it as if the ignition switch is turned on. Before starting this procedure, visually check that the throttle is closed, magnetos are off, and mixture is lean, and that no one else is standing in or near the propeller arc. Also, the parking brake should be on, the airplane chocked, tied down, etc. A loose or broken groundwire on either magneto could cause the engine to fire or backfire. In either case, the propeller turns very quickly one way or the other. Also, if you pull the propeller through backwards, the magnetos should not fire, lessening this risk.

Cold weather starting can be made easier by preheating the engine. Many fixed base operators (FBOs) at airports with cold winters offer preheating services. Additionally, there are several small, portable heaters available which can blow hot air into the engine to warm it. Preheating is generally required when outside temperatures are below zero, and is recommended by most engine manufacturers when the temperature is below 20°F.

To start a cold engine it should be primed first. The primer is a small manual or electric fuel pump which pumps a small charge of fuel directly into the cylinders. Most engines will require several priming strokes before starting the engine. Continuous priming may be required for several minutes after the engine has been started to keep it running. The procedure for starting an engine without preheat is the same, except that additional priming is needed, before pulling the propeller through by hand. Also, carburetor heat should be applied after the engine starts to help warm the engine more quickly.

After a cold engine has been started, it should be idled at low RPMs for 2 to 5 minutes to allow the oil to warm and begin circulating throughout the engine.

STARTING A HOT ENGINE

Hot engines tend to "load up," i.e., the cylinders may become overloaded with fuel. One procedure to clear the cylinders is to turn the engine over with the mixture control in the lean position or the throttle in the full open position (or, to do both works well in some airplanes). This helps clear the cylinders of the excess fuel and allows the engine to start. When turning the engine over with the throttle open (i.e., the same procedure as for starting an automobile engine that has flooded), BE VERY CAREFUL TO CLOSE THE THROTTLE AS THE ENGINE BEGINS TO START (and move mixture to rich). In an automobile, you do this procedure with the transmission in neutral, but this is not possible in an airplane.

The procedures for a hot engine versus a flooded engine in a Piper Tomahawk are contrasted below. Compare them with the "cold" start procedures discussed above.

Starting Engine When Hot	Starting Engine When Flooded
1. Throttle - CRACKED.	1. Throttle - OPEN FULL.
2. Master Switch - ON.	2. Master Switch - ON.
3. Electric Fuel Pump - ON.	3. Electric Fuel Pump - OFF.
4. Mixture - FULL RICH.	4. Mixture - IDLE CUT-OFF.
5. Starter - ENGAGE.	5. Starter - ENGAGE.
6. Throttle - ADJUST.	6. Mixture - ADVANCE.
7. Oil Pressure - CHECK.	7. Throttle - RETARD.
8. Electric Fuel Pump - OFF.	8. Oil Pressure - CHECK.
9. Fuel Pressure - CHECK.	9. Fuel Pressure - CHECK.

Fuel injected engines have unique starting problems in hot weather, and the manufacturer's recommended starting procedure for the particular engine in the airplane you are operating should be followed.

HAND PROPPING THE ENGINE

When hand propping an engine, it is mandatory to have two pilots familiar with the airplane: one to operate the controls (especially the brakes) and another to "pull through" (spin) the propeller. Please consider propping from behind the propeller even when another person is at the controls. The traditional approach with the person "pulling through" the propeller in front of the propeller follows.

1. To start the plane, the propeller is rotated in the clockwise direction (as seen from the cockpit).

2. Never lean into the propeller as you pull it. You must not be in a position where you would fall forward if your feet slip. You should have one foot forward and one foot back. As you pull down, you should shift your weight to your rear foot and back away.

3. You should not wrap your fingers around the propeller. You should have your fingers just over the trailing edge. This is to prevent injury if the engine backfires and turns backward.

a. Before pulling the propeller through slowly so the engine sucks gas into the cylinders, the person pulling the propeller should shout "brakes on, mag (magneto, i.e., ignition) off." The pilot inside the plane should confirm by repeating "brakes on, mag off." But always assume the mag switch is on. That is, always be in a safe position relative to the propeller and keep the area clear.

b. Before moving the propeller, the pilot outside should check the brakes by pushing on the propeller spinner (center of the propeller) to see that the airplane cannot be pushed backward.

c. After pulling the propeller through a few times, the propeller should be positioned with the left side (when facing the airplane from the front) at the 10 to 11 o'clock position. This will facilitate spinning the propeller by pulling down against the engine's compression.

d. When the person on the propeller is ready to attempt starting and the propeller (left blade when facing the nose of the plane) is at 10 to 11 o'clock, the person on the propeller should shout "brakes on, throttle cracked, mag on." The pilot in the plane should make the required adjustments and repeat "brakes on, throttle cracked, mag on."

e. After checking to see that the brakes are on (by pushing the spinner), the person on the propeller should then spin the propeller as hard as possible by pulling down on the left blade. Be sure to stand on firm ground. Stand close enough to the propeller to be able to step away easily. As the propeller is pulled through, the person should step back away from the propeller to avoid being hit as the engine starts.

4. Especially, if you are starting the engine yourself, you should stand behind the propeller on the right side when facing the direction the plane is facing. This will permit you to place one foot in front of the right main tire in addition to having the brakes set full on or having the airplane tied down (both if possible). Note, this is an extremely dangerous procedure. USE EXTREME CARE.

a. This approach should also be used when there is a pilot in the cockpit at the controls.

COMMON PREFLIGHT AND ENGINE STARTING ERRORS

1. Not recognizing the importance of the preflight inspection.

2. Not using a systematic approach (e.g., not using a checklist) during preflight.

3. Failing to unchock and/or untie the airplane.

4. Overpriming or priming when not necessary.

5. Operating the starter motor after you should have realized it was flooded or had some other problem, i.e., it would not start. This overheats the starter motor and drains the battery.

AIRCRAFT FUEL AND OIL

A. While you may choose almost any gasoline for your automobile, do not underestimate the importance of using the fuel specified by the manufacturer for your airplane engine. The substitution of any fuel other than the kind specified by the manufacturer of the airplane engine can be very dangerous. There are differences between automotive and aviation fuels, including the following:

1. The octane numbers shown for automotive fuels do not have the same meaning as those shown for aviation fuels. This could result in an appreciable difference in actual knock rating for two fuels which have the "same" number. If automotive fuel is used, this difference could lead to detonation, pre-ignition, and possible structural failure of the engine.

2. Most automotive fuels have higher vapor pressure which can lead to vapor lock. A condition of vapor lock in an airplane can be extremely dangerous because of power loss.

3. Tetraethyl lead in automotive fuels may contain an excess of chlorine and bromine, whereas aviation fuels contain only the minimum practical amount of bromine. The chlorine is very corrosive, and under certain conditions can lead to exhaust valve failures.

4. Automotive fuels may have a higher gum content. Gum deposits can result in valve sticking and poor fuel distribution.

5. Automotive fuels may have solvent characteristics not suitable for aircraft engines. Seals, gaskets, and flexible fuel lines are susceptible to attack.

B. Your airplane engine operates on a higher average power output than your automobile; 55% to 85% of maximum power as compared to 20% or 40% in your automobile. Your airplane engine is also operating under higher temperatures and pressures. It is subjected to a wider variation in climatic conditions and more rapid changes in atmospheric temperature and pressure. Every aircraft engine has been designed to use a specific grade of aviation fuel for satisfactory performance. Unless the manufacturer's recommendations are followed, damage to the engine or power failure may result.

C. Octane/Grade.

1. Anti-knock qualities of aviation fuels are designated by grades, such as 80/87, 100LL, 100/130, 108/135, and 115/145. The higher the grade, the more compression the fuel can stand without detonating. The more compression the fuel can stand without detonation, the more power can be developed from it. The first of the two numbers in a fuel designation indicates the lean-mixture rating (as during cruise), and the second the rich-mixture rating (as during takeoff and climb).

2. No engine manufacturer recommends that you use a fuel with a lower octane/grade rating than that specified for your engine. When you are faced with a shortage of the correct type of fuel, always use whatever alternate fuel grade is specified by the manufacturer or the next higher grade. Availability of different fuel grades at servicing facilities will be largely dependent on the classes of aircraft using the particular airport. The engine manufacturers have made information available concerning satisfactory alternate grade fuels for those which have been discontinued.

3. DO NOT USE AUTOMOTIVE FUEL unless an appropriate STC (supplemental type certificate) has been obtained for those engines approved for auto gas use.

CHAPTER FIVE
TAXIING

Taxiing is the controlled movement of the airplane on the ground under its own power. Taxiing occurs about the airport on ramps and taxiways, to move onto and off of the active runway. Ramps are the areas where airplanes are parked (tied down), fueled, etc. Taxiways are the "roadways" from the ramps to the end of the runways. Some small airports have virtually no taxiways, and taxiing is done on the runway itself.

This chapter covers 5 of the 34 "Tasks" in the FAA Practical Test Standards (PTSs). They are

1. Radio Communication . . . . Page 87
2. Taxi . . . . Page 91
3. Pre-Takeoff Check . . . . Page 91
4. Postflight Procedures . . . . Page 98
5. Airport and Runway Marking and Lighting . . . . Page 100

STARTING TO TAXI

A. After starting the engine, but before moving, set your directional gyro to your compass heading (if you have this flight instrument). This permits you to check its operation while taxiing, i.e., it should indicate the compass heading when you have reached the end of your takeoff runway. Other possible flight instruments:

    1. The altitude indicator should indicate a level bank after several minutes, even when taxiing.

    2. The turn coordinator should indicate the direction you turn while taxiing. The ball should move freely and roll to the opposite of the direction of the turn while taxiing.

B. Set your altimeter to the local field elevation.

C. Make sure the taxi area is clear.

D. Begin moving the airplane forward by gradually adding power (push the throttle in slowly) to increase the engine RPM. Reduce the power as soon as the plane begins moving because extra power was needed to overcome the plane's inertia, i.e., to get it moving.

    1. More power will be needed on a soft surface than on a hard surface.

    2. Failure to immediately reduce power will cause the plane to accelerate to an excessive and dangerous speed.

    3. Always taxi at slow speeds (equal to that of a brisk walk) so brakes are not needed to control taxi speed. Do not "ride" brakes.

E. Immediately tap the brakes to be sure they are operating properly (required by FAA PTSs). If there is any question about their operation, shut down the engine immediately.

F. You steer the airplane while taxiing by means of the rudder pedals.

    1. Ailerons and elevator should be placed in neutral position when there is no wind.

    2. Ailerons provide no control when there is no wind.

G. Check all wingtip clearances continuously. If there is any doubt about wingtip clearance, have someone walk along with the wingtip.

H. Taxi very slowly while on the ramp area near other planes and obstacles.

RADIO COMMUNICATIONS

A. Speak into the microphone (mike) at normal speech level and tone.

    1. When transmitting, hold your mike one to two finger widths from your lips.

B. Adjust any whistles, hums, scratches, etc. with the squelch adjustment.

C. Keep the mike convenient for use while flying.

D. Begin transmitting only after another pilot and controller have completed their exchange, i.e., do not block them out (you will be blocked out also).

E. When changing frequencies listen before transmitting so you do not "step on" another transmission.

F. An uncontrolled airport does not have a control tower, i.e., there is no traffic control over movements of aircraft on the ground or around the airport in the air. Often, fixed base operators (FBOs) operating at an uncontrolled airport will operate a radio on a UNICOM frequency (UNICOM is an acronym for Unified Communication).

   1. This frequency is most often 122.8 (122.7 and 123.0 are also used) and is indicated on the sectional aeronautical chart as the last item in the airport information block.

   2. All UNICOM frequencies including 122.8 will be indicated. The following identifier example is for a controlled airport. Uncontrolled airports have no control tower (CT) frequency (usually only airport name, altitude, longest runway length, and UNICOM frequency).

   Box indicates Special ⟶ [NAME] CT – 118.3*
   Traffic Area (See FAR 93)   ATIS 124.9
                         03 L 92 122.95 ⟵———— UNICOM
                         VFR Advsy 125.3
                         Airport of entry

G. UNICOMs at uncontrolled airports are used for providing advisory information for incoming aircraft and for air-to-air communication.

   1. To provide advisory information for incoming aircraft. This information includes the active runway, the wind direction and velocity, and any reported traffic in the area.

      a. When you approach the airport intended for landing, you call
         1) Destination (name of airport).
         2) Your type of plane and your call sign.
            a) Even though nothing is official by giving your call sign, other traffic will not confuse you with another airplane.
         3) Your approximate position from the airport (again to advise other traffic).
         4) Then request weather (generally only surface wind), active runway, and other traffic.

      b. EXAMPLE. "Jonesville UNICOM, Cessna 172, 5 north, inbound, request airport advisory."
         1) Note that the call sign may or may not be used.
         2) If ground personnel or other pilots may have an interest in your (personal) presence, use it.
         3) Normally for traffic advisories, pilots are just concerned with the type and location of other aircraft.

      c. Their response: "Cessna calling Jonesville, wind 340 at 10, runway 36 is active with 2 aircraft in the pattern, over."

      d. You can request information regarding available services, ask that local telephone calls be made, etc. on UNICOM (unlike on ATC frequencies which are strictly for aircraft traffic control).

      e. Finally, the same UNICOM frequencies are used at many airports and thus the frequency is usually cluttered with people calling many airports. Keep your transmission to a minimum.

2.   UNICOM is also for air-to-air communication, so that aircraft can advise each other about where they are in the traffic pattern.

   a.   As you enter the traffic pattern of an uncontrolled airport (with or without an assigned UNICOM frequency), you may wish to call your position and intent, e.g., "Jonesville traffic, Cessna 172 entering downwind, runway 36."

   b.   You may wish to call base leg and final leg of your airport traffic pattern, depending on weather, other traffic, availability of the frequency, etc., e.g., "Jonesville traffic, Cessna 172, base (or final), runway 36."

   c.   You may also wish to make similar radio calls when taxiing for long distances on the active runway or taking off, e.g., "Jonesville traffic, Cessna 172 taxiing onto active runway 36, for takeoff and departure to the north."

   d.   Note that you should use the airport's assigned UNICOM frequency for traffic advisories to other aircraft.

      1)   If the airport has no assigned UNICOM frequency, use MULTICOM 122.9.

3.   At controlled airports, other frequencies, e.g., 122.95, are assigned to FBOs as the UNICOM frequency. It is used to request services, fuel availability, call for taxis, etc. (weather advisories and traffic control are provided by ATC).

   a.   MULTICOM 122.9 has been assigned for air-to-air and air-to-ground vehicle communication.

   b.   The procedure for talking to another aircraft at a controlled airport is to ask tower, ground control, etc. to ask the aircraft you wish to contact to tune to 122.9 and then you do the same.

4.   Common Traffic Advisory Frequency (CTAF)

   a.   CTAF is usually

      1)   Tower frequency at airports with part-time control towers.

      2)   Flight Service Station (FSS) airport advisory frequency (usually 123.6) at airports without control towers where a FSS is located on the airport.

      3)   UNICOM at airports with no tower or FSS, and a UNICOM frequency is assigned.

      4)   MULTICOM (122.9) if no tower, FSS, or UNICOM.

   b.   The FAA recommends that you monitor the CTAF within 10 miles of an airport of departure and/or intended landing.

      1)   When inbound, announce your position and intentions 10 miles out and again in the traffic pattern.

      2)   When outbound, announce your intentions for taxi, takeoff, and departure.

RADIO COMMUNICATIONS PTS

TASK: RADIO COMMUNICATIONS (ASEL)
PILOT OPERATION - 2
REFERENCES: AC 61-21, AC 61-23; AIM.

Objective. To determine that the applicant:

1. *Exhibits knowledge by explaining two-way radio communication procedures recommended for use at uncontrolled airports.*

2. *Selects the frequencies appropriate for the facilities to be used (UNICOM, FSS, or flight watch facilities).*   122.8 123.6

3. *Transmits requests and reports using recommended standard phraseology.*

4. *Receives, acknowledges, and complies with radio communications.*

NOTE: For the applicant whose airplane IS NOT radio equipped, this task will be orally tested ONLY. For the applicant whose airplane IS radio equipped, this task may be simulated in flight by the examiner.

TAXI SPEED AND BRAKING

A. Taxi speed is controlled primarily with the throttle and, only secondarily, with the brakes. Recommended taxi speed is about the speed of a brisk walk. Develop your skill so as to taxi as if the brakes were inoperative. Use the brakes only when a reduction in engine speed is not sufficient.

B. The two prime considerations of taxi speed are (1) safe positive control and (2) the ability to stop or turn when and where desired. Additionally, you should always taxi slowly in ramp areas and near other aircraft. You should appear safe to fellow pilots as well as be safe.

C. Airplane brakes are generally toe brakes, i.e., on the top of the rudder pedals. Thus, when you apply pressure to the top of the rudder pedals, you are also applying the brakes. Rudder pedals are usually high enough that you have to consciously move your feet up on the rudder pedals to apply the brakes.

   1. Normally (i.e., when not using brakes) while taxiing, your heels are raised off the floor and placed on the base of the brake pedal for quick braking action with the ball of the foot, if required.

   2. NEVER APPLY BRAKES BEFORE LANDING OR BEFORE YOU HAVE THE PLANE FIRMLY ON THE RUNWAY UNDER COMPLETE CONTROL.

   3. The following diagram illustrates use of the rudder on the left and brakes on the right.

D. Some airplanes have heel brakes which are activated by separate small brakes just in front and to the inside of the rudder pedals. These, as the description implies, are activated by your heel.

E. Always use both brakes together with the same pressure. The ONLY time you use different pressure for directional purposes is for sharp turns at VERY LOW speeds, i.e., barely moving. At all other times, apply the brakes evenly and use the airplane's nosewheel or tailwheel (steerable with the rudder controls) for directional control.

TAXIING IN WIND

A. The wind is a very important consideration when operating an airplane on the ground. The objective is to keep the airplane firmly on the ground, i.e., not let the wind blow the airplane around.

   1. If a crosswind gets under the wing, it can lift the wing up and even blow the airplane over sideways. A wind from the rear can get under the tail of the airplane and blow the airplane over to the front.

   2. When taxiing in windy conditions, the objective is to use the control surfaces to keep the wing down that is pointing to the direction the wind is coming from. Also, the tail should be kept down if the wind is blowing from the rear.

   3. Caution is recommended. Avoid sudden bursts of power and sudden braking.

B. When taxiing in windy conditions, the control surfaces should be positioned as shown in the following diagram.(?)

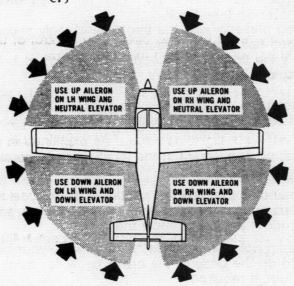

   1. When the wind is from any forward direction, the control yoke should be turned toward the wind.

      a. Wind from the front makes the plane act as it would in flight, i.e., turn the control yoke in the direction of the desired down wing.

      b. The aileron on the side the wind is coming from will be up and the wind flowing over the wing will hold the wing down (rather than lifting the wing which would permit the wind to get under the wing and possibly blow the airplane over on its back).

      c. The elevators should be in a neutral position, i.e., the control yoke neither held forward or back. This permits the nosewheel to carry its normal weight and to be used for directional control.

         1) NOTE: On tailwheel airplanes ONLY, the elevators should be up, i.e., control yoke or stick pulled back, to keep the tail firmly down so the tailwheel can provide directional control.

2. When the wind is from any rearward direction, the control yoke should be turned in the direction the wind is GOING.

    a. The aileron on the side the wind is coming from will be down, which will help keep the wind from getting under the wing and lifting it.

    b. By directing the control yoke in the direction the wind is GOING, it will be full forward, causing the elevator to be pointed down. This will deter the wind from getting under the tail, raising the tail, and possibly blowing the airplane over (tail over front).

        1) Note that on tailwheel airplanes the control yoke or stick is also held full forward to keep the tailwheel firmly on the ground for directional control.

3. It would be an extreme situation for an airplane to be blown (flipped) on its back.

    a. If the wind is blowing that hard, you should not even be in the airplane.

    b. However, watch out for jet blast, which has been known to blow small airplanes over on their backs.

    c. The more likely result is losing directional control of the airplane, running into something, or running off the runway due to

        1) Panic, or

        2) Incorrect response which aggravates the situation.

C. After each of your first few lessons, you should return to the airplane just after your post-flight debriefing with your flight instructor. As explained in the previous chapter, the purpose is to become conversant in the location and operation of the flight instruments, radios, and controls.

    1. To this end, you should practice the control surface positions for taxiing in the wind. Imagine there is a strong headwind and you are going to taxi in a circle.

    2. Adjust the controls for each 45° of the turn and observe the control surfaces and their effect in the wind.

TAXIING NOSEWHEEL AIRPLANES

A. Taxiing an airplane equipped with a nosewheel is relatively simple. Nosewheel airplanes generally have the best ground handling characteristics (relative to tailwheel airplanes). The nosewheel is usually connected to the rudder pedals by a mechanical linkage.

    1. Despite these advantages, it is poor technique to use excessively high power settings, to taxi at high speeds, or to attempt to control the direction and taxi speed with the brakes.

B. When starting to taxi, the airplane should always be allowed to roll forward slowly so the nosewheel turns straight ahead in order to avoid turning into an adjacent airplane or nearby obstruction.

    1. Aligning the nosewheel straight ahead during the preflight inspection also prevents side stress on the nose gear and excessive wear on the nosewheel.

C. All turns conducted with a nosewheel airplane are started using the rudder pedals.

    1. Power may be applied after entering the turn to counteract the increase in friction during the turn.

    2. If it is necessary to tighten the turn after full rudder pedal deflection has been reached, the inside brake may be used as needed to aid in turning the airplane.

D. When stopping the airplane, it is advisable to always stop with the nosewheel straight in order to relieve any strain on the nose gear and to make it easier to start moving again.

    1. This is particularly true when positioning yourself for the "pre-takeoff" checklist during which you "run up" (operate at relatively high RPM) the airplane to check the ignition system.

TAXIING TAILWHEEL AIRPLANES

A. Taxiing a tailwheel-type airplane is usually more difficult than taxiing nosewheel equipped airplanes, because the tailwheel provides less directional control than a nosewheel. Also, tailwheel airplanes tend to turn so the nose of the aircraft points itself into the wind (this is referred to as weathervaning).

    1. The tendency for tailwheel airplanes to weathervane is greatest in a crosswind situation.

    2. Generally, brakes play a much larger role in taxiing tailwheel equipped airplanes.

B. When taxiing into the wind, or in a crosswind, it is best to use full "up" elevator (hold the control yoke back) so that the maximum load will be placed on the tailwheel.

    1. When taxiing downwind, hold the elevator control in the full forward position. This will prevent the wind from picking up the tail and blowing the airplane over on its nose. (?)

C. Since a tailwheel-type airplane rests on its tailwheel, as well as the main landing wheels, it assumes a nose high attitude when on the ground. In most cases, this causes the engine to restrict the pilot's forward vision.

    1. It may be necessary to weave the airplane right and left while taxiing to see and avoid collision with any objects or hazardous surface conditions in front of the nose.

    2. The weave, zigzag, or short S turns must be done slowly, smoothly, and cautiously.

TAXIING ON OTHER THAN CLEAN PAVEMENT

A. Operation of nosewheel equipped airplanes on other than clean pavement requires that the elevator control be held in the full back position (so the elevator is up, tail down, and nose up).

B. High RPM settings should be avoided (except on a soft field) so that the propeller will not be damaged by sand, stones, and other debris "sucked" up from the ground by the propeller.

C. When taxiing on soft surfaces, e.g., a muddy field, sufficient additional power should be used to keep the airplane rolling. If it stops, it would take considerable (maybe full) throttle to get the airplane moving again. Remember, full throttle will shower the airplane with debris.

TAXI PTS

TASK: **TAXI** *(ASEL)*

    PILOT OPERATION - 1

    REFERENCE: AC 61-21.

Objective. *To determine that the applicant:*

1. *Exhibits knowledge by explaining safe taxi procedures.*

2. *Adheres to signals and clearances and follows the proper taxi route.*

3. *Performs a brake check immediately after the airplane begins moving.*

4. *Controls taxi speed without excessive use of brakes.*

5. *Recognizes and avoids hazards.*

6. *Positions the controls for the existing wind conditions.*

7. *Avoids creating hazards to persons or property.*

PRE-TAKEOFF CHECK

A. The "pre-takeoff check" is the systematic procedure for making a last-minute check of the engine, controls, systems, instruments, and radio prior to flight.

1. Normally, the pre-takeoff check is performed after taxiing to a position near the takeoff end of the runway.

2. Taxiing to that position usually allows sufficient time for the engine to have warmed up to at least minimum operating temperatures and ensures adequate lubrication of the internal moving parts of the engine before operating the engine at high power settings.

3. Some people differentiate between a "ground checklist" and "pre-takeoff list." We have combined both, as most do. Both are done on a taxiway near the end of the active runway. The objective is to ascertain that all systems, instruments, etc. are working properly and are ready for flight.

4. As you taxi to the active runway, turn your airplane somewhat diagonal to the runway so you will not blast any airplanes behind you with your propeller backwash.

   a. In older airplanes with radial engines, the rule was to turn into the wind to provide as much cooling as possible for the engine. Generally, cooling is not a problem for today's airplane engines.

   b. If you have problems with overheating, you may wish to point the airplane into the wind to obtain the maximum cooling effect.

   c. Straighten your nosewheel before stopping, as your magneto check requires an engine run up which puts considerable stress on your nosewheel (which is better absorbed with the nosewheel straight).

B.   General pre-takeoff checklist. Touch a control or switch or adjust it to the prescribed position after identifying a checklist item (if an instrument gauge, the instrument reading should be said aloud).

1.   Check flight controls for free and proper operation. This means you must move your controls their entire distance and observe that the flight surfaces move correspondingly.

2.   Set trim tabs for takeoff.

3.   Check wing flaps for operation and set for takeoff.

4.   Set fuel selector to fullest tank.

5.   Set carburetor heat control to COLD.

6.   Hold brake ON.

7.   Adjust throttle to runup RPM (usually 1,500 to 1,700 RPM).

8.   Check each magneto for operation.

   a.   All reciprocating airplane engines have dual magnetos as a safety measure. Thus, if one fails there is a backup. Each magneto system is checked by turning the other magneto system off to see if the engine continues running with not more than a 100 to 200 RPM reduction.

   b.   Do this by turning the ignition key from BOTH to RIGHT, then back to BOTH, then to LEFT, and then back to BOTH.

   c.   You turn the switch to BOTH in between RIGHT and LEFT to allow normal combustion (with both spark plugs firing) before going to the left mag system.

   d.   Return magneto switch to BOTH ON.

9.   Check carburetor heat by setting to HOT and notice a 50-100 RPM decline.

   a.   Return carburetor heat to off position.

10. Adjust throttle to idle RPM (usually 700-1,000).

11. Set heading indicator to correspond with compass heading.

12. Check engine instruments for normal indications.

13. Set flight instruments, including altimeter, heading indicator, turn coordinator, and attitude indicator, if you have them in your airplane.

14. Check seat locked and seatbelt and shoulder harness fastened.

15. Check cabin door locked and windows secured.

16. Recognize any discrepancy. Taxi back and inquire or have maintenance performed. DO NOT TAKE ANY CHANCES!!

17. Review the critical takeoff performance airspeeds and distances.

18. Review and be prepared to execute take-off emergency procedures (see Chapter 6, "Takeoffs").

19. Check clock for time.

20. Check runway and final approach for other aircraft.

21. Set mixture control to RICH.

    a. Although the engine is started with a full rich mixture, it is usually a good procedure to taxi the airplane with a somewhat leaner full setting to avoid fouling the spark plugs with the full rich mixture.

    b. If this is done, the mixture must again be set to full rich before takeoff. The full rich mixture is used for full power, i.e., generally during takeoffs only.

PRE-TAKEOFF CHECKLIST FOR A BEECH SKIPPER

1. Seat Belts and Shoulder Harnesses - CHECK
2. Parking Brake - SET
3. Avionics - CHECK
4. Engine Instruments - CHECK
5. Flight Instruments - CHECK and SET
6. Fuel Selector - CHECK ON
7. Throttle - 1800 RPM
8. Magnetos - CHECK (175 RPM maximum drop, within 50 RPM of each other)
9. Carburetor Heat - CHECK and set COLD for takeoff
10. Throttle - IDLE
11. Elevator Trim - SET TO TAKE-OFF RANGE
12. Rudder Trim - SET TO 0
13. Flaps - CHECK OPERATION, THEN UP
14. Controls - CHECK FREEDOM OF MOVEMENT AND PROPER DIRECTION
15. Mixture - FULL RICH (or as required by field elevation)
16. Doors - SECURE
17. Parking Brake - RELEASE
18. Engine Instruments - CHECK

For Academic Illustration/Training Purposes Only! *For Flight:* Use your Pilot's Operating Handbook and FAA-Approved Airplane Flight Manual

PRE-TAKEOFF CHECKLIST FOR A CESSNA 152

1. Parking Brake - SET
2. Cabin Doors - CLOSED and LATCHED
3. Flight Controls - FREE and CORRECT
4. Flight Instruments - SET
5. Fuel Shutoff Valve - ON
6. Mixture - RICH (below 3,000 feet)
7. Elevator Trim - TAKEOFF
8. Throttle - 1700 RPM
    a. Magnetos - CHECK (RPM drop should not exceed 125 RPM on either magneto or 50 RPM differential between magnetos)
    b. Carburetor Heat - CHECK (for RPM drop)
    c. Engine Instruments and Ammeter - CHECK
    d. Suction Gauge - CHECK
9. Throttle - 1,000 RPM or LESS
10. Radios - SET
11. Strobe Lights - AS DESIRED
12. Throttle Friction Lock - ADJUST
13. Brakes - RELEASE

For Academic Illustration/Training Purposes Only! *For Flight:* Use your Pilot's Operating Handbook and FAA-Approved Airplane Flight Manual

PRE-TAKEOFF CHECKLIST FOR A PIPER TOMAHAWK

1. Brakes - SET
2. Throttle - 1800 RPM
3. Magnetos - CHECK (max. drop 175 RPM, maximum differential of 50 RPM)
4. Vacuum - 5.0" Hg + .1
5. Oil Temp - CHECK
6. Oil Pressure - CHECK
7. Carburetor Heat - CHECK
8. Throttle - RETARD
9. Magnetos - CHECK grounding at low RPM, then set to BOTH
10. Master Switch - CHECK ON
11. Flight Instruments - CHECK
12. Fuel Selector - PROPER TANK
13. Mixture - SET
14. Electric Fuel Pump - ON
15. Carburetor Heat - OFF
16. Engine Gauges - CHECK
17. Static Source - NORMAL
18. Seats - securely LATCHED in track
19. Seat Backs - ERECT
20. Belts/Harness - FASTENED
21. Empty Seat - seat belt snugly FASTENED
22. Flaps - SET
23. Trim Tab - SET
24. Controls - FREE
25. Doors - CLOSED and LATCHED
26. Overhead Latch - ENGAGED

For Academic Illustration/Training Purposes Only! For Flight: Use your Pilot's Operating Handbook and FAA-Approved Airplane Flight Manual

PRE-TAKEOFF CHECK PTS

> **TASK: PRETAKEOFF CHECK (ASEL)**
>
> **PILOT OPERATION - 1**
>
> **REFERENCES:** AC 61-21; Pilot's Operating Handbook and FAA-Approved Airplane Flight Manual.
>
> **Objective.** To determine that the applicant:
>
> 1. Exhibits knowledge of the pretakeoff check by explaining the reasons for checking the items.
> 2. Positions the airplane to avoid creating hazards.
> 3. Divides attention inside and outside of the cockpit.
> 4. Ensures that the engine temperature is suitable for run-up and takeoff.
> 5. Follows the checklist.
> 6. Adjusts each control or switch as prescribed by the checklist.
> 7. Ensures that the airplane is in safe operating condition emphasizing -
>   a. flight controls and instruments.
>   b. engine and propeller operation.
>   c. seat adjustment and lock.
>   d. safety belts and shoulder harnesses fastened and adjusted.
>   e. doors and windows secured.
> 8. Reviews the critical takeoff performance airspeeds and distances.
> 9. Describes takeoff emergency procedures.

TAXIING ONTO THE ACTIVE RUNWAY

A. Make sure your pre-takeoff checklist is complete.

B. If radio equipped, state your intent on the appropriate UNICOM or MULTICOM frequency, e.g., "St. Augustine traffic, Beech Skipper taxiing out onto runway 4 for takeoff, north departure."

C. Check for traffic! No matter who authorizes what, you want to be sure that another plane is not going to land on you or collide with you.

D. Taxi onto the runway and align the airplane with the runway center line before applying power.

TAXIING OFF THE ACTIVE RUNWAY

A. After landing but before turning off the runway, be sure to slow the airplane down to a safe taxi speed, i.e., the speed of a fast walk.

B. Finally, you should refer to your "after-landing" checklist which is generally cowl flaps open, flaps up, carburetor heat off, and trim set for takeoff.

   1. We have combined the after-landing checklist and the stopping engine checklists for the Skipper, 152, and Tomahawk on page 96.

PARKING THE AIRPLANE

A. Position (park) the airplane on the ramp to facilitate taxiing and parking by other airplanes.

   1. Frequently, airport ramps are marked with painted lines which indicate where and how to park. At other airports, airplane "tie down" ropes (or chains) mark parking spots.

   2. Almost always, there are three ropes provided for each airplane: one rope positioned for the middle of each wing and one rope to tie the tail. If the ramp is not paved, each of the tiedown ropes (chains) is usually marked by a tire.

B. Park the plane to avoid being hit or prop washed by other aircraft. You should "chock" and/or tie down your airplane so it cannot roll or be blown into another plane or other object.

   1. Chocks are usually blocks of wood placed both in front of and behind a tire to keep the plane from rolling.

C. At most transient ramps, you should not use your parking brake, as the FBO personnel frequently move aircraft.

   1. Always check with a lineperson before leaving your plane both locked and with the parking brakes on.

   2. The normal procedure is plane locked and parking brakes off -- wheel chocks or tie-downs secure the airplane.

SHUTTING DOWN THE ENGINE

A. You should have a standard checklist for shutting down (turning off) your engine. This will assure that all steps are taken, e.g., flaps up and battery off.

B. General engine shutdown checklist.

   1. Make sure your after-landing checklist is complete, i.e., flaps up, carburetor heat off, cowl flaps open, etc.

2. Set the parking brakes ON if appropriate (see above).

3. Set throttle to IDLE or 1,000 RPM.

4. Turn electrical units and radios OFF.

5. Turn ignition switch OFF then ON (this indicates that the magneto ground wires are, in fact, grounded, i.e., the magnetos will not be operational when turned OFF).

6. Set mixture control to IDLE CUT-OFF.

7. Turn ignition switch to OFF after engine stops.

8. Turn master electrical switch to OFF.

9. Install control lock.

10. Place chocks at wheels.

11. Tie down airplane.

C. The combined after-landing and stopping engine checklists for the Skipper, 152, and Tomahawk are given below.

AFTER-LANDING AND STOPPING ENGINE CHECKLIST FOR A BEECH SKIPPER

1.	Carburetor Heat - COLD	8.	Electrical and Avionics Equipment - OFF
2.	Landing Light - AS REQUIRED	9.	Throttle - 1,000 RPM
3.	Flaps - UP	10.	Mixture - IDLE CUT-OFF
4.	Elevator Trim Tab - SET TO TAKE-OFF RANGE	11.	Magneto/Start Switch - OFF, after engine stops
5.	Rudder Trim - SET TO 0	12.	Battery and Alternator Switches - OFF
6.	Parking Brake - SET	13.	Control Lock - INSTALL
7.	Fuel Boost Pump - OFF	14.	Wheel Chocks - INSTALL; Parking Brake - Release

AFTER-LANDING AND STOPPING ENGINE CHECKLIST FOR A CESSNA 152

1.	Wing Flaps - UP	5.	Mixture - IDLE CUT-OFF (pull full out)
2.	Carburetor Heat - COLD	6.	Ignition Switch - OFF
3.	Parking Brake - SET	7.	Master Switch - OFF
4.	Radios, Electrical Equipment - OFF	8.	Control Lock - INSTALL

AFTER-LANDING AND STOPPING ENGINE CHECKLIST FOR A PIPER TOMAHAWK

1.	Flaps - RETRACT	5.	Mixture - IDLE CUT-OFF
2.	Electric Fuel Pump - OFF	6.	Magnetos - OFF
3.	Radios - OFF	7.	Master Switch - OFF
4.	Throttle - FULL AFT		

TYING DOWN THE AIRPLANE

A. Obviously, hangar storage is the best means of protecting aircraft from the elements, flying debris, vehicles, vandals, etc. Even in hangars, planes should be "chocked" to avoid scrapes and bumps from rolling.

B. Airplanes stored outside are normally "tied down."

    1. Chains or ropes are used to secure the airplane to the ground from three locations on the airplane: usually, the midpoint of each wing and the tail.

    2. Tie-down hooks or eyelets are provided at these locations on most airplanes.

C. Tie down knot for ropes.

    1. Pull the rope through the hook or eyelet, and then use two half-hitches as illustrated below.

        a. The first half-hitch should be tied one foot away from the hook or eyelet and the second half-hitch should be about a foot away from the first half-hitch.

        b. The second half-hitch holds the first.

        c. Note that an extra loop is used on the second half-hitch to secure the knot. In the diagram below, the rope should be pulled tight in the direction of the arrow. This "catches" the rope between the second half-hitch knot and the rope extending from the first half-hitch and the second half-hitch.

        d. It is relatively quick and easy to tie and untie.

    2. When convenient and appropriate, practice the knot five or six times.

    3. Make sure the ropes are properly secured to the ground at appropriate intervals.

D. When leaving the airplane tied down for an extended period of time or when expecting windy weather, you should install the control or "gust" locks which hold the control yoke stationary so the control surfaces cannot bang back and forth in the wind.

    1. On older planes this is sometimes accomplished by clamping the aileron, elevator, and rudder to adjacent stationary surfaces so they cannot move.

    2. Alternatively, the control yoke (or stick in older airplanes) can be secured tightly with a seatbelt.

POSTFLIGHT PROCEDURES PTS

TASK: POSTFLIGHT PROCEDURE (ASEL)
PILOT OPERATION - 2
REFERENCES: AC 61-21, AC 61-23, Pilot's Operating Handbook and FAA-Approved Airplane
Flight Manual.

Objective. To determine that the applicant:

1. Exhibits knowledge by explaining the elements of after-landing procedures, including parking, temperature stabilization, shutdown, securing, and postflight inspection.

2. Selects the designated or suitable parking area, considering wind conditions and obstructions.

3. Parks the airplane properly.

4. Follows the checklist for engine shutdown, cockpit securing, and deplaning passenger.

5. Secures the airplane properly.

6. Performs a satisfactory postflight inspection.

COMMON TAXIING ERRORS

1. Not being ready to go after telling ground control "ready to taxi." Be ready to copy clearance and go.

2. Too fast on the ramp.

3. Lack of wingtip awareness.

4. Not positioning controls for taxiing in wind.

5. Distractions - especially on ramp.

6. Riding the brakes - easiest bad habit to develop.

7. Nosewheel not straight for runup.

8. Not knowing meaning of "taxi into position and hold."

9. Too fast to make turns.

10. Back-taxiing on the runway without clearance or careful observation for landing traffic - VERY dangerous. Back-taxiing is taxiing on a runway in the direction opposite from the one you are going to take off from or have just landed on.

11. Not telling ground control from which runway and at which intersection you are clear, and where on the airport you wish to go (if you know).

12. Shutting down the engine with the radios on. This is very hard on radios due to the electrical surge at start-up and shut-down.

13. Forgetting to turn off master switch and/or mags.

14. Forgetting to install control locks.

15. Forgetting to tie down the airplane, or tying it down inadequately.

16. Parking on the ramp so as to inconvenience others.

17. Propeller blasting dust and debris into open hanger areas or onto parked airplanes.

AIRPORT MARKING AIDS

Taxiway and runway markings are used during taxi, takeoff, and landing. Thus, the following material is also relevant to Chapter 6, "Takeoffs," and Chapter 8, "Landings." Study the following runway and taxiway markings now:

A. Runway Numbers - Runway numbers and letters are determined from the approach direction. The runway number is the whole number nearest one-tenth the magnetic azimuth of the centerline of the runway, measured clockwise from magnetic north; e.g., a runway with a magnetic heading of 343° would be numbered "34." The letter, or letters, differentiate between left (L), right (R), or center (C) parallel runways:

   1. For two parallel runways "L" "R"
   2. For three parallel runways "L" "C" "R"

B. Basic Runway Marking - markings used for operations under Visual Flight Rules: centerline marking and runway direction numbers.

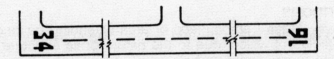

C. Non-Precision Instrument Runway Marking - markings on runways served by a non-visual navigation aid and intended for landings under instrument weather conditions: basic runway markings plus threshold ("hold line") marking. See below.

   1. An instrument runway is one that has been approved for instrument approaches.

   2. A non-precision runway is one without an ILS approach (this topic is beyond the scope of this book. See *INSTRUMENT PILOT FLIGHT MANEUVERS & HANDBOOK* for discussion of instrument approaches).

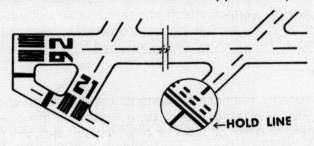

D. Precision Instrument Runway Marking - markings on runway served by nonvisual precision approach aids and on runways having special operational requirements, non-precision instrument runway marking, touchdown zone marking, fixed distance marking, plus side stripes. See below.

   1. Precision approaches generally refer to ILS approaches. See *INSTRUMENT PILOT FLIGHT MANEUVERS & HANDBOOK*.

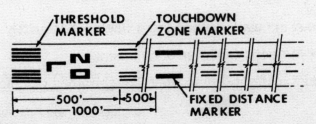

E.   Threshold - a heavy, solid line or set of solid lines perpendicular to the runway
     centerline designating the beginning of that portion of a runway usable for landing.

F.   Displaced Threshold - a threshold that is not at the beginning of the paved runway.
     The paved area behind the displaced runway threshold is available for taxiing, the
     takeoff of aircraft, and the landing rollout, but not for other landing purposes. See
     below.

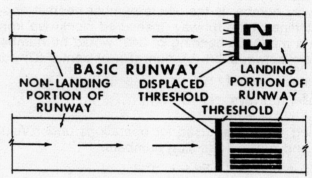

G.   Overrun and Stopway Areas - any surface or area extending beyond the usable runway
     which appears usable but which, due to the nature of its structure, is unusable. It is
     marked on the runway pavement as below.

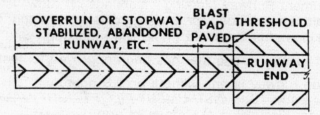

H.   Closed Runway - a runway surface which appears usable but which, due to the nature
     of its structure or other reasons, has become unusable. See below.

I.   Taxiway Marking - The taxiway centerline is marked with a continuous yellow line. The
     taxiway edge may be marked with two continuous yellow lines six inches apart.

     1.   Taxiway HOLDING LINES consist of two continuous and two dashed lines,
          spaced six inches between lines, perpendicular to the centerline.

AIRPORT AND RUNWAY MARKING AND LIGHTING PTS

TASK: AIRPORT AND RUNWAY MARKING AND LIGHTING (ASEL)
        PILOT OPERATION -- 2
        REFERENCES: AC 61-21; AIM.

Objective. To determine that the applicant:

1. Exhibits knowledge by explaining airport and   2. Identifies and interprets airport, runway, and
    runway markings and lighting aids.   taxiway marking aids.

                                                          3. Identifies and interprets airport lighting aids.

CHAPTER SIX
TAKEOFFS

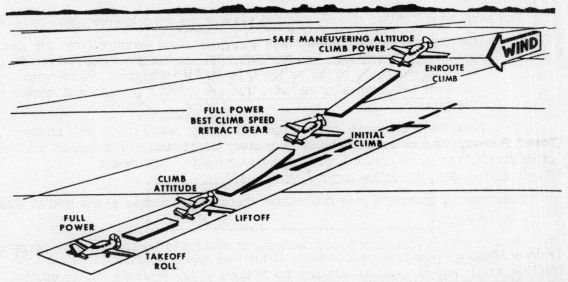

Takeoffs are made by accelerating the airplane to an airspeed at which the airplane can climb to a safe maneuvering altitude. Takeoffs consist of takeoff roll, lift-off, and initial climb.

1. The takeoff roll accelerates the airplane from a standstill to an airspeed that provides sufficient lift to become airborne.

2. The lift-off (also called rotation) is the act of becoming airborne as a result of the wings lifting the airplane off the ground or the pilot rotating the nose up, which increases the angle of attack to start a climb.

3. The initial climb begins when the airplane leaves the ground and a pitch attitude has been established to climb away from the takeoff area. Normally, it is considered complete when the airplane has reached a safe maneuvering altitude or an en route climb has been established.

This chapter begins with descriptions of normal takeoffs and concludes with other takeoff situations: crosswind, gusting wind, short-field, soft-field, and tailwheel airplanes. You also may wish to study Chapter 2, "Airplanes and Aerodynamics," before or after studying this chapter, but before your first flight. See the discussion of traffic patterns operation in Chapter 8, "Landings," for procedures to leave the pattern after takeoff.

This chapter covers 3 of the 34 "Tasks" in the FAA Practical Test Standards (PTSs). They are

    1.   Normal and Crosswind Takeoff
    2.   Short-Field Takeoff
    3.   Soft-Field Takeoff

NORMAL TAKEOFF ROLL
(The PTS for normal and crosswind takeoffs appear on page 108.)

A.   The takeoff is normal when

    1.   The takeoff surface is firm with no obstructions along the takeoff path and is of sufficient length to permit the airplane to gradually accelerate to normal climbing speed.

    2.   The airplane is headed directly into the wind or the wind is very light.

        a.   The airplane's groundspeed is much lower when taking off into the wind than if the takeoff were made downwind. Lower groundspeed results in reduced wear and stress on the tires and landing gear. Note, your airplane flies relative to the wind through which it passes, not relative to the ground.

        b.   Also, there is shorter ground roll and consequently much less space is required to develop the lift necessary for takeoff.

B.   Prior to taxiing onto the active runway, you must

    1.   Satisfactorily complete your pre-takeoff checklist (discussed at the end of Chapter 5, "Taxiing").

    2.   Be conversant with emergency procedures relating to takeoffs and be prepared to execute them.

    3.   Be very confident that you have plenty of runway to take off safely, and you have taken into account any obstacles you must clear.

        a.   If you have any questions, you should consult your airplane operating manual and compute your takeoff distance after computing density altitude.

    4.   Check for other traffic in the air and on the ground.

    5.   Notify traffic of your intentions if you are radio equiped.

C.   The takeoff roll is, essentially, taxiing the airplane fast enough to allow it to begin to fly.

    1.   Taxi the airplane to the middle of the runway and point it down the center line of the runway. Check the windsock to confirm no crosswind. See page 106 if a crosswind exists.

2. Before beginning (or as you begin) your takeoff roll, study the runway and related ground reference points, such as nearby buildings, trees, runway lights (at night), etc.

    a. This will give you a frame of reference for directional control during takeoff.

    b. You will also be more confident about having everything under control.

3. Engage full power smoothly.

    a. Use full power to decrease time and length of takeoff roll, which saves both tires and engines.

    b. Scan your engine instruments to assure full power and no other problems, e.g., too low or too high oil pressure.

4. Use the rudder for directional control. As you add power, the torque effect (P-factor) will require you to add right rudder to maintain your desired direction.

    a. Conduct your takeoff roll in the center of the runway.

5. Allow the elevators to assume a neutral position, i.e., no pilot pressure is required.

    a. This assumes the elevator trim is set according to the airplane operating manual recommendation.

    b. The elevator position should be held steady to avoid flutter.

6. Ailerons should also be held steady with adjustments to maintain level wings (see the effects of crosswinds beginning on page 106).

7. Throughout the roll you should scan the horizon (rather than stare straight ahead at the runway). Also scan the airspeed indicator and engine instruments, including the tachometer, oil pressure gauge, and fuel flow gauge (if so equipped).

    a. The primary concern is directional control and wing attitude relative to the runway and horizon.

    b. With experience, you will also find it comfortable to scan the control panel including engine instruments.

NORMAL LIFT-OFF

A. As the airplane reaches rotation speed (i.e., flying speed), slow but steady back pressure should be applied to the control yoke.

1. Rotation speed is sensed by glancing at the airspeed indicator and/or by the feel of the controls, depending on the pilot and type of airplane.

2. With the nose raised slightly above the horizon, the airplane will begin to lift off.

B. After lift-off, the pitch attitude should be adjusted to achieve the best rate of climb (V_Y) (see your *POH*).

1. The best <u>rate</u> of climb (V_Y) is the airspeed at which this particular airplane climbs the most in a given amount of <u>time</u>.

2. In contrast, the best <u>angle</u> of climb (V_X) is the airspeed at which this airplane will climb the most in a given <u>distance</u>. V_X is used on short-field takeoff (see the "Short-Field Takeoff" sideheading one page 109).

INITIAL CLIMB

A. Upon lift-off, the airplane should be flying at approximately the attitude that will allow it to accelerate to its best rate-of-climb airspeed (V_Y).

1. If the airplane has been properly trimmed, some back pressure will be required on the control yoke to hold this attitude until the proper climb speed is established.

    a. Lack of any back pressure on the elevator control may result in the airplane settling, even to the extent that it contacts the runway.

B. The airplane will pick up speed rapidly after it becomes airborne. However, only after it is certain that the airplane will remain airborne and a definite climb is established should the flaps and landing gear be retracted (if the airplane is so equipped). Many CFIs adhere to the rule of not retracting the landing gear until an emergency landing on the runway is no longer possible.

C. It is recommended by engine manufacturers, as well as the FAA, that takeoff (full) power be maintained until a safe maneuvering altitude of at least 500 feet above the surrounding terrain or obstacles is attained.

1. The combination of best rate-of-climb (V_Y) and maximum allowable power will give an additional margin of safety so that sufficient altitude is attained in minimum time from which the airplane can be safely maneuvered in case of engine failure or other emergency.

2. Also, in many airplanes the use of maximum allowable power automatically gives a richer mixture for additional cooling of the engine during the climb-out.

D. Since the power on the initial climb is fixed at the takeoff power setting, the airspeed must be controlled by making slight pitch adjustments using the elevators.

1. However, do not stare at the airspeed indicator when making these slight pitch changes. Instead, you should watch the attitude of the airplane in relation to the horizon.

2. It is better to first make the necessary pitch change and hold the new attitude momentarily, then glance at the airspeed indicator as a check to see if the new attitude is correct. Failure to do this is called "chasing the airspeed." Due to inertia, the airplane will not accelerate or decelerate immediately as the pitch is changed. It takes a little time for the airspeed to change.

3. If the pitch attitude has been under- or over-corrected, the airspeed indicator will show (belatedly) a speed that is more or less than that desired. When this occurs, the cross-checking and appropriate pitch-changing process must be repeated until the desired climbing attitude is established.

4. Be careful not to get the pitch attitude so high that you slow to stall speed.

5. When the correct pitch attitude has been attained, it should be held constant while cross-checking it against the horizon and other outside visual references. The airspeed indicator should be used only as a check to determine if the attitude is correct.

E. During initial climb, it is important that the takeoff path remain aligned with the runway centerline to avoid the hazards of drifting into obstructions or into the path of another aircraft which may be taking off from a parallel runway.

 1. Maintaining alignment with the runway centerline during a climbout involves maintaining right rudder pressure to counteract torque at climb speed, followed by a possible crab (realignment) of the nose to correct for wind drift.

F. During initial climb, you are on the upwind leg of the airport traffic pattern. See Chapter 8, "Landings," for a discussion of either remaining in the pattern or departing from it.

G. After the recommended climbing airspeed has been well established and a safe maneuvering altitude has been reached, power should be adjusted to the recommended climb setting and the airplane trimmed to relieve the control pressures. This will make it much easier to hold a constant attitude and airspeed.

H. Complete your after-takeoff checklist.

AFTER-TAKEOFF CHECKLIST

A. The FAA PTSs list "completes after-takeoff checklist" as a specific step for each of the following: normal, crosswind, soft-field, and short-field takeoffs. The operating manuals for most trainer airplanes (e.g., Beech Skipper, Cessna 152, and Piper Tomahawk) do not list specific after-takeoff checklists.

 1. On trainer airplanes, such steps include

 a. Reduce power at a safe maneuvering altitude.
 b. Make flap adjustments as recommended by airplane manufacturer.
 c. Adjust trim for climb.
 d. Establish climb airspeed.
 e. Adjust mixture as appropriate.
 f. Check for other aircraft traffic.

 2. On high performance airplanes, additional steps include

 a. Retract landing gear after a positive rate of climb has been established and a safe landing can no longer be made on remaining runway.

 b. Reduce manifold pressure (throttle) prior to reducing RPM.

 1) RPM is controlled by propeller pitch on constant speed propellers. Trainer airplanes have constant pitch, not constant speed, propellers.

 c. Adjust cowl flaps and monitor engine temperature.

 d. Adjust mixture and throttle (manifold pressure) for altitude change.

 3. Note that you should "think" and "say" the after-takeoff checklist by repeating:

 a. Adjust power back.
 b. Check traffic.
 c. Check instruments.

 4. Thus, you complete your after-takeoff checklist automatically and will be ready to do so on your FAA flight test.

CROSSWIND TAKEOFF

A. Crosswinds affect takeoffs the same way they affect taxiing. While taking off in a crosswind, the airplane will tend to weathervane into (i.e., point toward) the wind. The wind will also lift the wing pointing toward the wind, i.e., the wind gets under the wing.

   1. If the wind is coming from the right, it will have a tendency to lift the right wing up.

   2. The wind will then push on the tail, pivoting the airplane around the left wheel, pointing it into the wind.

   3. As the airplane gets lighter due to lift, the left wheel does not stay put and the whole airplane begins to skid to the left (even though it is pointed to the right).

B. The technique used during the initial takeoff roll in a crosswind is generally the same as that used in a normal takeoff, except that the aileron control must be held INTO the crosswind.

   1. This raises the aileron on the upwind wing to impose a downward force on the wing, counteracting the lifting force of the crosswind and preventing that wing from rising.

   2. FULL aileron should be held into the wind as the takeoff roll is started.

      a. Always verify wind direction as you taxi onto the runway by observing the windsock, grass, bushes, water surfaces, etc.

   3. During the ground roll, as the ailerons become effective for maneuvering the airplane about its longitudinal axis, relax the aileron pressure to keep the wings level. Full aileron deflection is usually not required during the entire ground roll.

   4. The takeoff path must be held straight with the rudder, which requires applying downwind rudder pressure.

      a. Remember, uncorrected, the airplane will tend to weathervane into the wind.

      b. When takeoff power is applied, torque or "P"factor, which yaws the airplane to the left, may be sufficient to counteract the weathervaning tendency caused by a light crosswind from the right.

         1) On the other hand, it may also aggravate the tendency to swerve left when the wind is from the left.

C. As the nosewheel or tailwheel raises off the runway, holding the aileron control into the wind may result in the downwind wing rising and the downwind main wheel lifting off the runway first, with the remainder of the takeoff roll being made on the other main wheel (i.e., on the side the wind is coming from).

   1. This is preferable to side skipping (which would occur if you did not turn the control yoke into the wind and use opposite rudder).

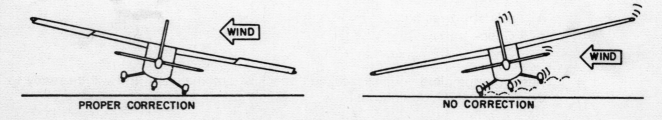

PROPER CORRECTION   NO CORRECTION

2. If a significant crosswind exists, the main wheels should be held on the ground slightly longer than in a normal takeoff so that a smooth but very definite lift-off can be made.

   a. Accomplish this by slightly less back pressure on the control yoke as you near lift-off speed.

   b. This procedure will allow the airplane to leave the ground under more positive control so that it will definitely remain airborne while the proper amount of drift correction is established.

   c. More importantly, it will avoid imposing excessive side loads on the landing gear and prevent possible damage that would result from the airplane settling back to the runway while drifting (due to the crosswind).

3. As both main wheels leave the runway and ground friction no longer resists drifting, the airplane would be slowly carried sideways with the wind unless you maintain adequate drift correction.

D. In the initial crosswind climb, the airplane will be slipping (upward wing down to prevent drift and opposite rudder to align your flightpath with the runway) into the wind sufficiently to counteract the drifting effect of the wind.

   1. When a definite climb is established, the airplane should be headed toward the wind to establish just enough "crab" to counteract the wind, and then the wings should be rolled level. The climb while in this "crab" should be continued so as to follow a ground track aligned with the runway direction.

   2. Complete your after-takeoff checklist.

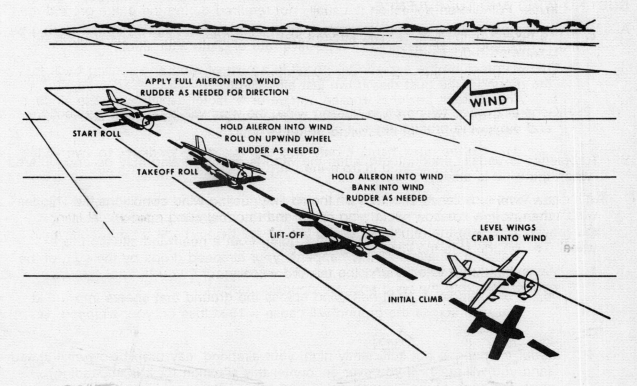

PRACTICAL TEST STANDARDS

NORMAL AND CROSSWIND TAKEOFF PTS

TASK: NORMAL AND CROSSWIND TAKEOFF (ASEL)
      PILOT OPERATION - 8
      REFERENCES: AC 61-21.

Objective. *To determine that the applicant:*

1. Exhibits knowledge by explaining the elements of normal and crosswind takeoffs, including airspeeds, configurations, and emergency procedures.

2. Verifies the wind direction.

3. Aligns the airplane on the runway centerline.

4. Applies full aileron deflection in the proper direction, where crosswind exists.

5. Advances the throttle smoothly to maximum allowable power.

6. Checks the engine instruments.

7. Maintains directional control on the runway centerline.

8. Adjusts aileron deflection during acceleration (crosswind conditions).

9. Rotates at the recommended (the term "recommended" refers to the manufacturer's recommendation) airspeed, accelerates to V_y, and establishes wind-drift correction (crosswind conditions).

10. Establishes the pitch attitude for V_y and maintains V_y, ± 10 kts.

11. Retracts the wing flaps as recommended or at a safe altitude.

12. Maintains takeoff power to a safe maneuvering altitude.

13. Maintains a straight track over the extended runway centerline until a turn is required.

14. Completes after-takeoff checklist.

GUSTING WIND AND TURBULENCE

A. When taking off in gusting wind, a slightly higher than normal rotation speed should be used. Thus, you will be assured of a positive rate of climb after lift-off.

   1. This will preclude the airplane taking off in a gust of wind and settling back to the ground if the gust dies down just after lift-off.

   2. Generally, when taking off in gusting wind, the wind will be changing directions and crosswind procedures will be required.

B. Turbulence is usually encountered when the wind is gusty. It also may be encountered when the wind is steady or calm.

   1. Low level turbulence should be handled like gusting wind conditions, i.e., higher than normal rotation speed and higher than normal climb speed.

      a. The purpose is to guard against going from a headwind situation to a tailwind situation. If this happens, your airspeed drops by the _sum_ of the headwind velocity and the tailwind velocity).

      b. For example, a 10-kt headwind across the ground that shears into a 5-kt tailwind across the ground will cause a 15-kt loss on your airspeed indicator.

   2. If your airspeed is not sufficiently high, your airspeed may drop below stall speed (and you will stall). If you ever encounter this situation (or it is impending), push the nose of the airplane down and apply full power, i.e., stall recovery technique.

C. Potholes in the sky. Before you make your first takeoff, recognize that the air is frequently choppy and the airplane will bounce around.

   1. Do not worry; the airplane will not come apart, nor will it fall out of the sky or turn upside down.

   2. Just as you get a rough ride on a bumpy road, you will get a rough ride when the air is choppy.

   3. Expect it, accept it, and note that the condition can be moderated by slower airspeed, just as it can in an automobile by slowing down on a bumpy road.

SHORT-FIELD TAKEOFF

A. The objective is takeoff and climb performance resulting in the shortest ground roll and the steepest angle of climb.

   1. This requires that the pilot operate the airplane at the limit of its takeoff performance capabilities. To take off safely, the pilot must exercise positive and precise control.

   2. The power setting, flap setting, airspeed, and procedures prescribed by the airplane's manufacturer should be observed. See your operating manual.

B. The speed for best angle-of-climb (V_x) is that which will result in the greatest gain in altitude for a given distance over the ground.

   1. It is usually slightly less than the speed for best rate-of-climb (V_y), which provides the greatest gain in altitude per unit of time.

   2. A deviation of 5 kts from the recommended speed will result in a significant reduction of climb performance.

   3. The FAA PTSs require V_x +5, -0 kts until over the obstacle or at least 50 ft AGL and then V_y ±5 kts.

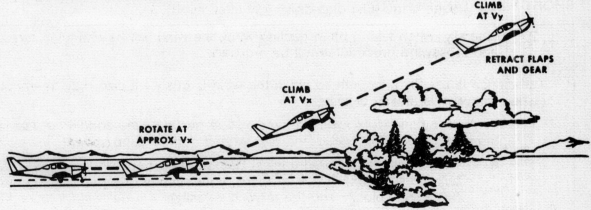

C. Taking off from short fields requires that the takeoff be started from the very beginning of the takeoff area and the airplane accelerated as rapidly as possible.

   1. Wing flaps may be lowered prior to starting the takeoff (if recommended by the manufacturer).

   2. At the field runway threshold, the airplane is aligned with the intended takeoff path and maximum allowable power applied smoothly and promptly with the brakes on. Make sure the engine is developing full takeoff power before you attempt the takeoff.

3. As the takeoff roll progresses, the airplane's pitch attitude and angle of attack should be adjusted to that which results in the minimum amount of drag and the quickest acceleration.

    a. In a nosewheel airplane, this is the normal attitude.

    b. In tailwheels, the tail should be allowed to rise off the ground slightly.

4. For the steepest climb-out and best obstacle clearance, the airplane should be allowed to roll with its full weight on the main wheels and accelerated to the lift-off speed, i.e., with the nosewheel barely on the ground.

5. Lift off smoothly and firmly (rotate) by applying back pressure on the elevator control as the best angle-of-climb speed (V_x) is attained.

6. After becoming airborne, a straight climb should be maintained at the best angle-of-climb speed (V_x) until the obstacles have been cleared, or if no obstacles are involved, until an altitude of at least 50 ft above the takeoff surface is attained.

    a. Since the airplane will accelerate more rapidly after lift-off, additional back pressure is necessary to hold a constant airspeed.

7. Upon reaching a safe altitude (50 ft AGL or above the obstacles), the pitch attitude is lowered slightly and the climb continued at the best rate-of-climb speed (V_Y) until reaching a safe maneuvering altitude.

8. On short-field takeoffs, the flaps and landing gear should remain in takeoff position until well clear of obstacles (or as recommended by the manufacturer) and the best rate-of-climb speed (V_Y) has been established.

9. Retract the wing flaps as recommended at a safe altitude.

    a. Complete your after-takeoff checklist.

SHORT-FIELD TAKEOFF PTS

TASK: SHORT-FIELD TAKEOFF *(ASEL)*
PILOT OPERATION - 7
REFERENCES: AC 61-21.

Objective. *To determine that the applicant:*

1. *Exhibits knowledge by explaining the elements of a short-field takeoff, including the significance of appropriate airspeeds and configurations, emergency procedures, and the expected performance for existing operating conditions.*

2. *Selects the recommended wing flap setting.*

3. *Positions the airplane at the beginning of the takeoff runway aligned on the runway centerline.*

4. *Advances the throttle smoothly to maximum allowable power.*

5. *Maintains directional control on the runway centerline.*

6. *Rotates at the recommended airspeed and accelerates to V_x (Best Angle)*

7. *Climbs at V_x or recommended airspeed, +5, -0 kts until obstacle is cleared, or until at least 50 ft above the surface, then accelerates to V_y and maintains V_y ±10 kts.*

8. *Retracts the wing flaps as recommended or at a safe altitude.*

9. *Maintains takeoff power to a safe maneuvering altitude.*

10. *Maintains a straight track over the extended runway centerline until a turn is required.*

11. *Completes after-takeoff checklist.*

SOFT-FIELD TAKEOFF

A. Takeoffs and climbs from soft fields require the use of operational techniques for getting the airplane airborne as quickly as possible to eliminate the drag caused by tall grass, soft sand, mud, snow, etc.

   1. It may or may not require climbing over an obstacle.

   2. These same techniques are also useful on a rough field where it is advisable to get the airplane off the ground as soon as possible to avoid damaging the landing gear.

   3. Soft surfaces or long wet grass retard the airplane's acceleration during the takeoff roll.

B. To minimize the hazards associated with takeoffs from soft or rough fields, support of the airplane's weight must be transferred as rapidly as possible from the wheels to the wings as the takeoff roll proceeds.

   1. This is done by establishing and maintaining a relatively high angle of attack or nose-high pitch attitude as early as possible by use of the elevator control.

   2. Wing flaps may be lowered prior to starting the takeoff (if recommended by the manufacturer) to provide additional lift and to transfer the airplane's weight from the wheels to the wings as early as possible.

C. The airplane should be taxied onto the takeoff surface as fast as possible, consistent with safety and surface conditions.

   1. Stopping on a soft surface, such as mud or snow, might bog the airplane down. Keep the airplane in continuous motion with sufficient power while lining up for the takeoff roll.

   2. As the airplane is aligned with the proposed takeoff path, takeoff power must be applied smoothly and as rapidly as the powerplant will accept without faltering.

     a. Use right rudder to maintain directional control as necessary.

   3. As the airplane accelerates, full back elevator pressure should be applied to establish a positive angle of attack and to reduce the weight on the nosewheel.

     a. In a tailwheel airplane, the tailwheel should be kept off the ground but the tail should still be kept as low as possible. This establishes the proper angle of attack and helps prevent nosing over in a very soft spot.

   4. Once the nosewheel lifts off, reduce the elevator control to the amount needed to keep the nosewheel just off the ground to increase airspeed to take off.

     a. As speed increases and lift develops throughout the takeoff run, the wings will progressively relieve the wheels of more and more of the airplane's weight,

       1) This minimizes the drag caused by surface irregularities or adhesion.

5. The airplane will virtually fly itself off the ground and may become airborne at an airspeed slower than a safe climb speed because of the action of "ground effect." See "Common Takeoff Errors" at the end of this chapter for an explanation of ground effect.

6. After the plane is airborne, the nose should be lowered very gently with the wheels just clear of the surface to allow the airplane to accelerate to the best rate-of-climb speed (V_y). The PTSs permit ±5 kts. (?)

    a. Use the best angle-of-climb speed (V_x) if obstacles must be cleared.

        1) The PTSs permit +5, -0 kts until obstacle is cleared. (?)

    b. Extreme care must be exercised immediately after the airplane becomes airborne and while it accelerates, to avoid settling back onto the surface.

    c. Maintain takeoff power to a safe maneuvering altitude.

7. After a definite climb is established and the airplane has accelerated to the best rate-of-climb speed (V_y), retract the landing gear and flaps if so equipped.

    a. In the event an obstacle must be cleared after a soft-field takeoff, the climb-out must be performed at the best angle-of-climb airspeed (V_x) until the obstacle has been cleared.

    b. Complete your after-takeoff checklist.

SOFT-FIELD TAKEOFF PTS

TASK: *SOFT-FIELD TAKEOFF (ASEL)*
PILOT OPERATION - 7
REFERENCE: AC 61-21.

Objective. To determine that the applicant:

1. Exhibits knowledge by explaining the elements of a soft-field takeoff, including the significance of appropriate airspeeds and configurations, emergency procedures, and hazards associated with climbing at an airspeed less than V_x.

2. Selects the recommended wing flap setting.

3. Taxies onto the takeoff surface at a speed consistent with safety.

4. Aligns the airplane on takeoff path without stopping and advances the throttle smoothly to maximum allowable power.

5. Adjusts and maintains a pitch attitude which transfers the weight from the wheels to the wings as rapidly as possible.

6. Maintains directional control on the center of the takeoff path.

7. Lifts off at the lowest possible airspeed and remains in ground effect while accelerating.

8. Accelerates to and maintains V_x, +5, -0 kts, if obstructions must be cleared, otherwise to V_y, ±10 kts.

9. Retracts the wing flaps, as recommended or at a safe altitude.

10. Maintains takeoff power to a safe maneuvering altitude.

11. Maintains a straight track over the center of the extended takeoff path until a turn is required.

12. Completes after-takeoff checklist.

CESSNA 152 TAKEOFF AND CLIMB CHECKLIST

A. Normal Takeoff
1. Wing Flap - 0°-10°
2. Carburetor Heat - COLD
3. Throttle - FULL OPEN
4. Elevator Control - LIFT NOSE WHEEL AT 50 KIAS
5. Climb Speed - 65-75 KIAS

B. Short Field Takeoff
1. Wing Flaps - 10°
2. Carburetor Heat - COLD
3. Brakes - APPLY
4. Throttle - FULL OPEN
5. Mixture - RICH (above 3,000 ft, LEAN to obtain maximum RPM)
6. Brakes - RELEASE

7. Elevator Control - SLIGHTLY TAIL LOW
8. Climb Speed - 54 KIAS (until all obstacles are cleared)
9. Wing Flaps - RETRACT slowly after reaching 60 KIAS

C. Climb
1. Airspeed - 70-80 KIAS
2. Throttle- FULL OPEN
3. Mixture - RICH below 3,000 ft, LEAN for maximum RPM above 3,000 ft

D. Airspeeds
1. Best rate-of-climb V_Y - 67 kts
2. Best angle-of-climb V_X - 55 kts
3. Takeoff rotation - 50 kts
4. Takeoff after 50 ft - 65-75 kts

PIPER TOMAHAWK TAKEOFF AND CLIMB CHECKLIST

A. Normal Takeoff
1. Flaps - SET
2. Tab - SET
3. Accelerate to 53 KIAS
4. Control Wheel - back pressure to rotate to climb attitude

B. Short Field, Obstacle Clearance
1. Flaps - 21° (first notch)
2. Accelerate to 53 KIAS
3. Control Wheel - back pressure to rotate to climb attitude
4. Accelerate to 61 KIAS until obstacle clearance
5. Accelerate to 70 KIAS after obstacle is cleared
6. Flaps - retract slowly

C. Soft Field, No obstacle
1. Flaps - 21° (first notch)
2. Accelerate and lift off nose gear as soon as possible
3. Lift off at lowest possible airspeed
4. Accelerate just above ground to best rate of climb speed, 70 KIAS
5. Flaps - slowly retract

D. Climb
1. Best rate (flaps up) - 70 KIAS
2. Best angle (flaps up) - 61 KIAS
3. Electrical fuel pump - OFF at desired altitude

E. Airspeeds
1. Best rate-of-climb V_Y - 70 kts
2. Best angle-of-climb V_X - 61 kts
3. Takeoff rotation - 53 kts
4. Takeoff after 50 feet - 60-70 kts

BEECHCRAFT SKIPPER TAKEOFF AND CLIMB CHECKLIST

A. Takeoff Power - Full Throttle
1. Power - SET takeoff power and mixture before brake release
2. Airspeed - ROTATE AT 56 KIAS, ACCELERATE TO 60 KIAS
3. ESTABLISH DESIRED CLIMB SPEED when clear of obstacles

For Academic Illustration/Training Purposes Only!
For Flight: **Use your Pilot's Operating Handbook and FAA-Approved Airplane Flight Manual**

B. Climb
1. Power - SET
2. Mixture - LEAN TO MAXIMUM RPM
3. Engine Temperature - MONITOR
4. Fuel Boost Pump - OFF

C. Airspeeds
1. Best rate-of-climb V_Y - 68 kts
2. Best angle-of-climb V_X - 61 kts
3. Takeoff rotation - 56 kts
4. Takeoff after 50 ft - 60 kts

TAKEOFFS IN TAILWHEEL AIRPLANES

A. Tailwheel airplanes are more susceptible to crosswinds and torque (P-factor) due to the limited directional control provided by the small tailwheel (relative to nosewheels which are larger and have more weight on them).

B. There are two main differences when taking off in a tailwheel airplane. Both have to do with the takeoff roll.

1. First, during the initial roll, the elevator should be held full back. This puts the maximum weight on the tailwheel, which will provide directional control (to counteract P-factor and crosswinds).

    a. As speed increases, the rudder will become more effective for directional control.

    b. Full back elevator must be maintained until sufficient speed is reached to permit reliance on the rudder for directional control.

2. Second, as the full back pressure is released, the tail will lift off and you will be "taxiing" (recall that a takeoff roll is taxiing to flying speed) on two wheels.

    a. If the airplane is trimmed properly, it will have the proper pitch. If not, you must correct the pitch angle with appropriate forward or backward pressure on the control yoke or stick.

    b. In contrast, tricycle gear airplanes are on three wheels until just prior to lift-off.

C. Other differences from nosewheel airplanes have already been noted regarding special takeoffs, e.g., crosswind, short field, and soft field.

WAKE TURBULENCE FROM OTHER AIRCRAFT

A. If it is necessary to take off behind another airplane, the possibility of wake turbulence must be anticipated, especially if the wind condition is calm or straight down the runway.

1. If turbulence is encountered, resulting in sudden deviations in flight attitudes, firm control pressure should be applied to make a shallow turn to fly out of the wake turbulence.

    a.   When in smoother air the airplane can then be realigned with the original flightpath.

2.   If a crosswind is present, the turn should be made into the wind since the wake turbulence will be blown downwind or away from your flightpath.

3.   If a heavy airplane is departing ahead of you, take off so as to lift-off before the heavier airplane's point of rotation. That way you will be above the wake turbulence. Recall that wake turbulence drifts downward at about 500 ft per minute.

    a.   If the heavier airplane has a steeper rate of climb than you, turn to the upwind side of the runway after lift off so you do not travel through the heavier airplane's wake.

    b.   Heavier airplanes are emphasized because they provide dangerous "wingtip vortices."

B. Vortex Generation.

1.   Lift is generated by the creation of a pressure differential between the top and bottom of the wing surface. The lowest pressure occurs over the upper wing surface and the highest pressure under the wing.

2.   This pressure differential triggers the rollup of the airflow behind the wing, resulting in swirling air masses trailing downstream of the wing tips. After the roll up is completed, the wake consists of two counter rotating cylindrical vortices, as shown to the right.

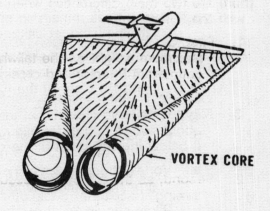

VORTEX CORE

C. Vortex Strength.

1.   The strength of the vortex is governed by the weight, speed, and shape of the wing of the generating airplane.

    a.   The vortex characteristics of any given airplane can be changed by extension of flaps or other wing configuring devices as well as by a change in speed.

    b.   The basic factor is weight, and the vortex strength increases proportionately with the weight of the airplane.

2.   During tests, peak vortex tangential velocities have been recorded at 224 ft per second, or about 133 kts.

3.   The greatest vortex strength occurs when the generating airplane is heavy, clean (flaps and gear up), and slow.

D. **Vortex Behavior.**

1. Vortices are generated from the moment the airplane leaves the ground since trailing vortices are a by-product of wing lift. Prior to takeoff or touchdown, pilots should note the rotation or touchdown point of the preceding airplane.

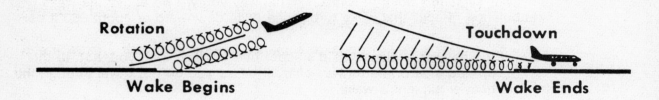

2. The vortex circulation is outward, upward, and around the wing tips when viewed from either ahead or behind the airplane.

    a. Tests with large airplanes have shown that the vortex flow field, in a plane cutting through the wake at any point downstream, covers an area about two wing spans in width and one wing span in depth.

    b. The vortices remain so spaced (about a wing span apart), even drifting with the wind, at altitudes greater than a wing span from the ground.

    c. In view of this, if persistent vortex turbulence is encountered, a slight change of altitude and lateral position (preferably upwind) will provide a flightpath clear of the turbulence.

3. Flight tests have shown that the vortices from large airplanes sink at a rate of about 400 to 500 ft per minute. They tend to level off at a distance about 900 ft below the flightpath of the generating airplane.

    a. Vortex strength diminishes with time and distance behind the generating airplane. Atmospheric turbulence hastens breakup.

    b. Pilots should fly at or above the large airplane's flightpath, altering course as necessary to avoid the area behind and below the generating airplane.

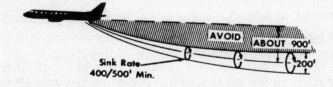

4. When the vortices of large airplanes sink close to the ground (within about 200 ft), they tend to move laterally over the ground at a speed of about 5 kts.

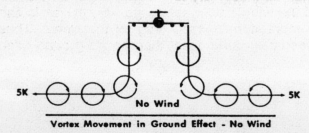

Vortex Movement in Ground Effect - No Wind

5. A crosswind will decrease the lateral movement of the upwind vortex and increase the movement of the downwind vortex.

    a. Thus, a light wind of 3 to 7 kts could result in the upwind vortex remaining in the touchdown zone for a period of time and hasten the drift of the downwind vortex toward another runway.

    b. Similarly, a tailwind condition can move the vortices of the preceding landing airplane forward into the touchdown zone. The light quartering tailwind requires maximum caution.

    c. Pilots should be alert to large airplanes upwind from their approach and takeoff flightpaths.

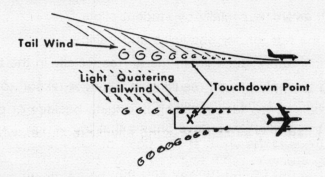

COMMON TAKEOFF ERRORS

A. The most common takeoff error is not correcting for crosswinds.

    1. As the airplane begins to accelerate and get light on the wheels, the plane will weathervane into the wind.

    2. As the airplane is turning into the wind, student pilots frequently try to turn it back to the center line of the runway with the aileron. This raises the wing on the side the wind is coming from, which allows the wind to get under the wing and blow the airplane sideways off the runway.

B. A second common takeoff error is not monitoring airspeed during the takeoff roll and not applying backward pressure on the control yoke when it is time to rotate.

    1. The result is to stay on the ground longer than you need to. This wears out tires.

    2. As soon as the airplane is ready to fly, you should apply slight backward pressure to allow it to come off the ground.

C. A third common takeoff error is trying to fly the airplane before it has sufficient flying speed. It is easy to rotate the airplane off the ground too early and fly in the ground effect.

    1. Ground effect is the increased lift/decreased drag available within one wingspan of the ground. At these very low levels, there is nowhere for the wingtip vortices and the wing downwash to go, i.e., the air is firmer near the surface and there is more lift/decreased drag for the plane. Thus, airplanes can fly at a slower airspeed in ground effect than above ground effect.

2. If you fly through (above) ground effect at this lower airspeed, you may settle back to the ground. Thus, it is very important that you have sufficient flying speed before you attempt to execute the initial climb.

D. A fourth common takeoff error is overcontrolling during the latter part (faster speeds) of the takeoff roll.

1. As an airplane moves faster, progressively smaller control corrections (pressures) change the direction of the airplane.

2. Student pilots frequently have trouble adjusting to the increased sensitivity of the controls as the airplane accelerates during takeoff.

E. Other common takeoff errors, especially by student pilots.

1. Failure to scan the horizon for obstacles and traffic.

2. No crosswind drift correction while in the air (especially in the traffic pattern).

3. Taking too long to apply power, resulting in a longer takeoff roll.

4. Pushing the throttle in too fast, resulting in engine backfire or propeller surges.

5. Failure to plan where the airplane is going after takeoff, i.e., what heading you will turn to.

6. Taking too long to get on the runway and go.

7. Telling tower "ready for takeoff" when not ready to go and/or not up to hold line.

8. Failure to execute a standard traffic pattern departure unless told to "turn on course approved" by ATC.

9. Attempting to do other things before the airplane is trimmed for climb and under control.

F. Errors in short-field takeoffs.

1. Engaging full power too abruptly.

2. Attempting to pull the airplane into the air prior to V_x.

3. Not maintaining V_x after liftoff, i.e., allowing airspeed to increase above V_x.

4. Dropping the nose too soon and/or too crisply over an obstacle with the possibility of sinking into the obstacle.

G. Errors in soft-field takeoffs:

1. Stopping on the runway, i.e., not keeping the airplane rolling.

2. Not using fullback pressure on controls from inception of power.

3. Not using recommended flap settings.

4. Excessive back pressure on the controls once a nose-up attitude is attained, i.e., an excessive nose-up attitude.

5. Climbing out of ground effect too early, before reaching V_x.

CHAPTER SEVEN
BASIC FLIGHT MANEUVERS

The first phases of your flight instruction emphasize basic flight maneuvers, which are

1. Straight-and-level flight
2. Turns
3. Climbs
4. Descents

Basic flight maneuvers are used in the day-to-day operation of a plane (unlike specific proficiency maneuvers such as stalls and ground reference maneuvers, which are discussed in Chapters 9 and 10). Proficiency in the basic flight maneuvers is essential to achieving a recreational pilot certificate and safe flying. If you cannot fly your plane straight and level, in turns, and up and down, you are in real trouble. As simple as they may seem, the importance of the basic flight maneuvers cannot be over-emphasized.

Remember to always look for other traffic before beginning any flight maneuver. Clearing turns are usually two 90° turns in opposite directions (S turn) or a full 180° turn with the purpose of a complete and careful vigilance for other traffic. Make sure the area is clear.

This chapter covers 1 of the 34 "Tasks" in the FAA Practical Test Standards (PTSs). It is Constant-Altitude Turns.

INTEGRATED FLIGHT INSTRUCTION

A. In the integrated method of flight instruction, the instructor introduces the student to the two references for controlling the airplane: visual and instrument.

1. One is the outside or visual reference. The horizon is the best reference for determining the attitude of the airplane and where it is in a bank.

2. The inside references for controlling the airplane are the flight instruments.

3. The pilot controls the airplane by the sole use of either of these references or by combining them.

B.   The integrated method of flight instruction introduces both references from the very beginning. The instructor demonstrates a maneuver, such as straight-and-level flight, a climb, a descent, or a turn.

   1.   The maneuver is first demonstrated by visual references, looking outside.

   2.   Next, a view-limiting device (e.g., a hood) is placed on the student, who is only allowed to view the flight instruments. In this way, the student can see what a turn, a climb, or a descent looks like on the flight instruments.

C.   The purpose of integrated instruction is not to make the student an instrument pilot, but to allow the student to integrate both sets of references. Pilots should not look only outside or only inside, but rather should use both sets of references.

D.   Note: the recreational pilot certificate requires no instrument training, and thus integrated flight instruction is NOT recommended for recreational pilots. Nonetheless, recreational pilots should be aware of flight instruments and their use.

   1.   See "Flight Instruments" in Chapter 2, beginning on page 45.

E.   Review the following basic aeronautical concepts which are discussed in Chapter 2.

   Categories of Aircraft
   Axes of Rotation
   Flight Controls and Control Surfaces
   Controlling Yaw, Pitch, and Roll
   Forces Acting on the Airplane in Flight
   Lift
   Gravity (Weight)
   Thrust
   Drag
   Stalls
   Relationships Between Lift, Weight, Thrust, Drag, and Angle of Attack
   Ground Effect
   How Airplanes Turn
   Turning Tendency (Torque Effect)
   Airplane Stability
   Loads and Load Factors

STRAIGHT-AND-LEVEL FLIGHT

A.   Straight-and-level flight is the most common flight configuration.

   1.   Level flight refers to flight in which the airplane is neither climbing nor descending.

   2.   Straight flight refers to the airplane maintaining a constant heading with 0° of bank.

B.   Straight-and-level flight can be performed at many altitudes, headings, airspeeds, and power settings. Assuming you are above the best angle-of-climb speed:

   1.   To maintain level flight at lower power settings, the airspeed will be slower and the nose must be pitched slightly higher.

   2.   To maintain level flight at higher power settings the airplane's nose may be pitched slightly lower.

C. The pitch attitude for level flight (constant altitude) is usually maintained by selecting some portion of the airplane's nose as a reference point, and then keeping that point in a fixed position relative to the horizon.

   1. That position should be cross-checked occasionally against the altimeter to determine if the pitch attitude is correct.

   2. If altitude is changing, the pitch attitude should be readjusted in relation to the horizon and then the altimeter rechecked to determine if altitude is now being maintained.

   3. The application of forward or back elevator pressure is used to control this attitude.

   4. The term "increase the pitch attitude" implies raising the nose in relation to the horizon. The term "decreasing the pitch" means lowering the nose.

D. To achieve straight flight (constant heading), the pilot selects two or more outside visual reference points directly ahead of the airplane (such as fields, towns, lakes, or distant clouds) to form points along an imaginary line and keeps the airplane's nose headed along that line.

   1. Roads and section lines on the ground also offer excellent references. Straight flight can be maintained by flying parallel or perpendicular to them.

   2. While using these references, an occasional check of the heading indicator should be made to determine that the airplane is actually maintaining flight in a constant direction.

   3. Both wingtips should be equidistant above or below the horizon (depending on whether the airplane is a high-wing or low-wing type). Any necessary adjustments should be made with the ailerons, noting the relationship of control pressure and the airplane's attitude.

      a. Observing the wingtips helps divert the pilot's attention from the airplane's nose, prevents a fixed stare, and automatically expands the radius of visual scanning (for other aircraft).

      b. Any time the wings are banked, even though very slightly, the airplane will turn.

      c. Thus, attention should be given to the attitude indicator to detect small indications of bank, and to the heading indicator to note any change of direction.

   4. When the wings are approximately level, straight flight can be maintained by simply exerting the necessary forces on the rudder in the desired direction.

      a. This technique is good only for very small changes in heading.
      b. See the next sideheading, "Turns."

   5. Refer to the heading indicator or directional gyro in order to judge the accuracy of performing straight flight.

6.   Examples of instrument references:

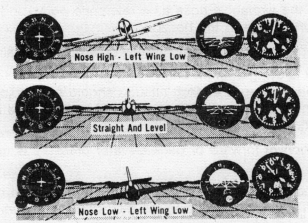

Nose High - Left Wing Low

Straight And Level

Nose Low - Left Wing Low

E.   Straight-and-level flight requires almost no application of control pressure if the airplane is properly trimmed and the air is smooth.

1.   Trim the airplane so it will fly straight and level without assistance.

a.   This is called "hands-off flight."

b.   The trim controls, when correctly used, are aids to smooth and precise flying.

c.   Improper trim technique usually results in flying that is physically tiring, particularly in prolonged straight-and-level flight.

2.   The airplane should be trimmed by first applying control pressure forward or backward to the control yoke or stick to establish the desired attitude, and then adjusting the trim tab by moving the trim wheel so that the airplane will maintain that attitude without control pressure in "hands-off flight."

F.   The airspeed will remain constant in straight-and-level flight with a constant power setting.

1.   Significant changes in airspeed as a result of power changes will require you to change pitch attitude and pitch trim to maintain altitude.

2.   Changes of pitch attitude and trim will also be necessary as the flaps are lowered.

TURNS

A.   A turn is a basic flight maneuver used to change from or return to the desired heading. It involves close coordination of all three flight controls: aileron (bank), rudder (yaw), and elevator (pitch).

1.   Shallow turns are those in which the bank is so shallow (less than approximately 20°) that the inherent stability of the airplane is acting to level the wings unless some control force is used to maintain the bank.

2.   Medium turns are those resulting from a degree of bank (approximately 20° to 45°) at which the airplane tends to hold a constant bank without control force on the ailerons.

3.   Steep turns are those resulting from a degree of bank (more than approximately 45°) at which the "overbanking tendency" of an airplane overcomes stability, and the bank tends to increase unless pressure is applied to the aileron controls to prevent it.

B.   When an airplane is flying straight and level, the total lift is acting perpendicular to the wings and to the earth. As the airplane is banked into a turn, the lift then becomes the resultant of two components:

1.   One, the vertical component, continues to act perpendicular to the earth and opposes gravity.

2.   The other, the horizontal component, acts <u>parallel</u> to the earth's surface and opposes centrifugal force caused by the turn.

3.   These two lift components act at right angles to each other, causing the resultant lifting force to act perpendicular to the banked wings of the airplane (see the diagram on page 124).

4.   It is this lifting force that actually turns the airplane, not the rudder.

C.   When applying aileron to bank the airplane, the depressed or lowered aileron (on the rising wing) produces a greater drag than the raised aileron (on the lowering wing).

1.   This increased aileron drag tends to yaw the airplane toward the rising wing, or opposite to the desired direction of turn, while the banking action is taking effect.

a.   The adverse yaw produced by aileron drag has been a major consideration in design of the controls, and in most modern airplanes has been significantly reduced. This is accomplished by providing greater up travel than down travel of the ailerons.

2.   To counteract the yawing tendency, rudder pressure must be applied simultaneously in the desired direction of turn. This produces a coordinated turn.

3.   After a medium bank has been established, all pressure on the aileron control may be relaxed. The airplane will remain at the bank selected with no further tendency to yaw since there is no longer a deflection of the ailerons.

a.   As a result, pressure may also be relaxed on the rudder pedals, and the rudder allowed to streamline itself with the direction of the air passing by it.

b.   The tendency to yaw and/or change bank must be controlled in very shallow and very steep banks.

D.   When entering turns, pressure should be applied on the ailerons and the rudder progressively. Apply the pressure smoothly and gradually, then gradually relax the pressure just before the desired degree of bank is attained.

1.   The rotation of the airplane about its longitudinal axis (bank) when entering a turn should be accomplished in such manner that a pitch attitude is also maintained which will produce flight at a constant altitude.

a.   To prevent a decrease in the vertical lift component, the angle of attack required to maintain altitude will be slightly higher than in straight-and-level flight.

b.   Consequently, sufficient back pressure must be applied to the elevator control. The steeper the bank, the greater the increase in required angle of attack; therefore, more back pressure is needed.

c.   Also, since the greater angle of attack in the turn causes more drag, an increase in power will be needed to maintain a constant airspeed.

2.   An explanation of why back pressure and increased power are needed in turns.

a.   In straight-and-level flight, lift equals weight.

b.   As an airplane enters a bank, the lift produced by the wings is divided between

1)   Vertical lift to maintain altitude.
2)   Horizontal lift to turn the airplane.

c.   In order to maintain altitude, the vertical component of lift must remain the same. Therefore, total lift must increase in a turn.

1)   This is usually accomplished by increasing the angle of attack (pulling the nose up a little). Raising the nose will cause a slight airspeed decrease.

d.   If constant airspeed is desired, power can be added to offset the otherwise resulting decrease in airspeed.

e.   The following diagram illustrates the vertical and horizontal components of lift in a turn.

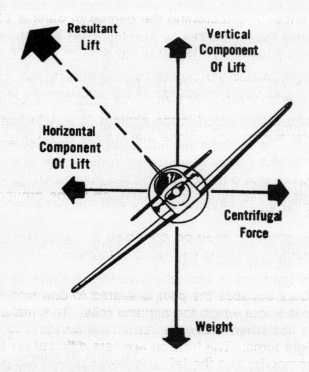

3. As soon as the airplane rolls from the wings-level attitude, the nose should also start to move along the horizon, increasing its rate of travel proportionately as the bank is increased. Any variation from this will indicate the particular control that is being misused.

   a. If the nose starts to move before the bank starts, rudder is being applied too soon.

   b. If the bank starts before the nose starts turning, or the nose moves in the opposite direction, the rudder is being used too late.

   c. If the nose moves up or down when entering a bank, excessive or insufficient back elevator pressure is being applied.

4. As the desired angle of bank is established, aileron and rudder pressures should be released. This will stop the bank from increasing since the aileron control surfaces will be neutral in their streamlined position.

   a. The back elevator pressure should not be released but should be held constant or sometimes increased to maintain a constant altitude.

   b. Throughout the turn, you should cross-check the references and occasionally include the altimeter to determine whether the pitch attitude is correct.

   c. If gaining or losing altitude, adjust the pitch attitude in relation to the horizon and then recheck the altimeter and vertical speed indicator to determine if altitude is now being maintained.

E. The best outside reference for establishing the degree of bank is the angle formed by the raised wing of low-wing airplanes (the lowered wing of high-wing airplanes) and the horizon, or the angle made by the top of the engine cowling and the horizon.

1. Since on most light planes the engine cowling is fairly flat, its horizontal angle to the horizon will give some indication of the approximate degree of bank.

2. The pilot's posture while seated in the airplane is very important in all maneuvers, particularly during turns, since that will affect the alignment of outside visual references.

   a. The beginning student may lean to the side when rolling into the turn in an attempt to remain upright in relation to the ground rather than "ride" with the airplane.

      1) This tendency must be corrected at the outset if the student is to learn to properly use visual references.

      2) This tendency is also characteristic in airplanes with side-by-side seats because the pilot is seated to one side of the longitudinal axis about which the airplane rolls. This makes the nose appear to rise when making a correct left turn and to descend in correct right turns. The horizon appears different on the right side in comparison to the left side because you (as pilot in command) are sitting in the left seat.

3. Information obtained from the attitude indicator will show the angle of the wings in relation to the horizon. This will help you learn to judge the degree of bank based on outside references.

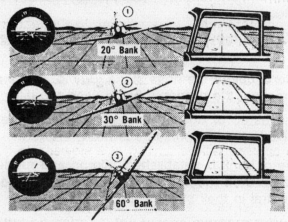

F. To make a precision 90° turn using outside references, align the airplane with a road or section line on the ground and then turn so that the airplane will be perpendicular to the road or line.

1. In the absence of any ground reference, select a point on the horizon directly off the wingtip, then turn the airplane until it is headed to that point.

G. The rollout from a turn is similar to the roll-in except that control pressures are used in the opposite direction. Aileron and rudder pressure are applied in the direction of the rollout or toward the high wing.

1. As the angle of bank decreases, the elevator pressure should be released smoothly as necessary to maintain altitude. Remember, when the airplane is no longer banking, the vertical component of lift increases.

2. Since the airplane will continue turning as long as there is any bank, the rollout must be started before reaching the desired heading.

   a. The time to begin rollout in order to lead the heading will depend on the rate of turn and the rate at which the rollout will be made.

      1) To roll out on the desired heading from a shallow bank turn, begin your smooth rollout 5° to 10° ahead of your desired heading.

      2) From a medium bank turn, start 15° to 20° ahead.

      3) From a steep bank turn, start 25° to 30° ahead.

3. The yaw effect will often be more apparent when rolling out of than into a turn. This is due to the higher angle of attack.

4. As the wings become level, the control pressures should be gradually and smoothly released so that the controls are neutralized as the airplane resumes straight-and-level flight.

5. As the rollout is completed, attention should be given to outside visual references as well as to the attitude indicator and heading indicator to determine that the wings are leveled precisely and the turn stopped.

H. The relationship between airspeed, bank, and radius of turn determines the rate of turn.

    1. The rate of turn at any given airspeed depends on the amount of the sideward force causing the turn, that is, the horizontal lift component.

    2. The horizontal lift component varies in proportion to the amount of bank. Thus, the rate of turn at a given airspeed increases as the angle of bank is increased.

    3. On the other hand, when a turn is made at a higher airspeed at a given bank angle, the inertia (to go straight ahead) is greater but the turning force of the horizontal lift component is the same, hence a slower turning rate.

    4. At a given angle of bank, a higher airspeed will make the radius of the turn larger because the airplane will be turning at a slower rate.

I. Slips and skids in turns occur when rudder and aileron use is not coordinated.

    1. A slip or skid means the airplane is flying sideways (the ball is not centered in the turn coordinator instrument).

    2. The rudder keeps the airplane lined up with the airstream.

    3. An airplane rolled left with no rudder will yaw right, i.e., a slip.

        a. But with too much rudder, it will yaw left, i.e., skid.

    4. If the ball of the turn-and-slip indicator or the turn coordinator is to the right of center, right rudder is needed to turn to the right to line up the airplane with the airstream and to center the ball.

SLIP   SKID   SLIP

    5. If pressure is maintained on the rudder after the turn is established, the airplane will tend to skid.

J. When changing from a shallow bank to a medium bank, the airspeed of the wing on the outside of the turn increases in relation to the inside wing as the radius of turn decreases. But the force (lift) created exactly balances the force of the inherent lateral stability (tendency to fly level) of the airplane, so that at a given speed no aileron pressure is required to maintain that bank.

    1. As the radius decreases further when the bank progresses from a medium bank to a steep bank, the lift differential overbalances the lateral stability. Counter-active pressure on the ailerons is then necessary to keep the bank from steepening.

    2. As the radius of the turn becomes smaller, a significant difference develops between the speed of the inside wing and the speed of the outside wing.

        a. The wing on the outside of the turn travels a longer circuit than the inside wing, yet both complete their respective circuits in the same length of time.

    b.   Therefore, the outside wing must travel faster than the inside wing and as a result it develops more lift. This creates a slight differential between the lift of the inside and outside wings and tends to further increase the bank.

CONSTANT-ALTITUDE TURNS (STEEP TURNS)

A.   The FAA Practical Test Standards require a "constant altitude turn" at a 40°-50° bank, which is a steep turn.

B.   Before starting the maneuver, be sure to be clear of traffic. Execute (a) clearing turn(s), and scan carefully for traffic.

    1.   Outside references are

       a.   To the nose's relation to the horizon (for pitch and bank control).

       b.   To roads, railroad tracks, lines of farm fields, etc. for directional (turn) control.

    2.   Instrument references are

       a.   The altimeter for pitch control.

       b.   The directional gyro for directional control.

       c.   The artificial horizon for bank control.

    3.   You must keep scanning all references as you execute the maneuver.

C.   Before rolling into a steep turn, have yourself in straight-and-level flight with a 90° cardinal heading: north, east, south, or west. Try to predetermine the amount of turn, e.g., 180°, 270°, or 360°.

    1.   As you roll into a 45° bank, increase back pressure and note the airplane nose's relationship to the horizon.

       a.   Scan the altimeter and adjust back pressure for any increase or decrease in altitude (noting the change of the airplane nose in relation to the horizon).

       b.   Use trim as appropriate to your airplane.

    2.   As you turn, keep track of your heading by calling each 90° change (out loud or silently), keeping in mind the desired rollout direction.

    3.   Begin your rollout to straight-and-level flight by 25° (one-half of your bank) before your desired heading. If your desired heading from a left-hand turn is 180°, begin your rollout at 205°.

    4.   As you roll out, decrease back pressure as appropriate to maintain a constant altitude.

    5.   A good practice maneuver is to rollout from one direction to the opposite direction at prespecified headings.

       a.   This permits practice of both the start of the rollout and the return to straight flight.

       b.   It also emphasizes the change needed in back pressure on the flight controls.

D. During steep turns, considerably more back elevator pressure is required to maintain altitude than in shallow and medium turns. Additional power may also be needed to maintain a safe airspeed.

   1. There is a tendency for the airplane's nose to lower, resulting in a loss of altitude.

   2. To recover from an unintentional nose-low attitude during a steep turn, first reduce the angle of bank with coordinated aileron and rudder pressure.

      a. Then use back elevator pressure to raise the airplane's nose to the desired pitch attitude.

      b. After accomplishing this, reestablish the desired angle of bank.

      c. Attempting to raise the nose first by increasing back elevator pressure will usually cause a tight descending spiral, and in extreme circumstances could lead to overstressing the airplane.

   3. Steep turns with 40° to 50° of bank should be practiced with rollouts on prespecified headings.

CONSTANT-ALTITUDE TURNS PTS

TASK: CONSTANT-ALTITUDE TURN (ASEL)
   PILOT OPERATION - 5
   REFERENCE: AC 61-21.

Objective. To determine that the applicant:

1. Exhibits knowledge by explaining the performance factors associated with constant-altitude turns, including increased load factors, power required, and overbanking tendency.

2. Selects an altitude that will allow the maneuver to be performed no lower than 1,500 feet AGL.

3. Establishes an airspeed which does not exceed airplane design maneuvering airspeed.

4. Enters a 360° turn, maintaining a bank angle of 40° to 50°, in coordinated flight.

5. Divides attention between airplane control and orientation.

6. Rolls out at the desired heading, ±10°.

7. Maintains the desired altitude, ±200 ft.

CLIMBS

A. Climbs and climbing turns are basic flight maneuvers in which the pitch attitude and power result in a gain in altitude. In a straight climb, the airplane gains altitude while traveling straight ahead. In climbing turns, the airplane gains altitude while turning.

   As with the other maneuvers, climbs should be performed by using both outside visual references and flight instruments.

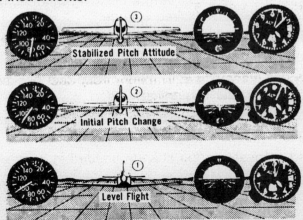

B. As a climb is started, adjust pitch by the relationship of the airplane nose with respect to the outside horizon, and crosscheck to your attitude indicator.

1. Airspeed will gradually diminish. This reduction in airspeed is gradual rather than immediate because of the momentum of the airplane.

2. The thrust required to maintain straight-and-level flight at a given airspeed is not sufficient to maintain the same airspeed in a climb.

3. Consequently, the engine power controls must be advanced to a higher power setting or airspeed will diminish to an unacceptable level.

4. When the climb is established, back elevator pressure must be maintained to keep the pitch attitude constant. As the airspeed decreases, the elevators will try to return to their neutral or streamlined position.

5. The pilot should cross-check the airspeed indicator and the pitch attitude by looking outside, then compare with that shown on the attitude indicator to determine if the pitch attitude is correct.

6. At the same time, a constant heading should be held with the wings level if a straight climb is being performed, or a constant angle of bank if in a climbing turn.

7. Once airspeed has stabilized, the trim should be adjusted to relieve the back pressure on the elevator control.

C. The effects of torque at the climb power setting are a primary factor in climbs.

1. Since the climb airspeed is lower than cruising speed, the airplane's angle of attack is relatively high.

2. With these conditions, torque and asymmetrical loading of the propeller will cause the airplane to have a tendency to roll and yaw to the left.

3. To counteract this, right-rudder pressure must be used. During the early practice of climbs and climbing turns, this may make coordination of the controls feel awkward. But after a little practice the correction for torque effects will become instinctive.

D. Trim is also a very important consideration during a climb.

1. After the climbing attitude, power setting, and airspeed have been established, the airplane should be trimmed to relieve all pressures from the controls.

2. If further adjustments are made in the pitch attitude, power, or airspeed, the airplane must be retrimmed.

E. To return to straight-and-level flight from a climbing attitude, it is necessary to start the level-off a few feet below the desired altitude.

1. Start to level off a distance below the desired altitude equal to about 10% of the aircraft's vertical speed.

a. EXAMPLE. If you are climbing at 500 feet per minute, start to level off 50 feet below your desired altitude.

2. To level off, the wings should be leveled and the nose lowered.

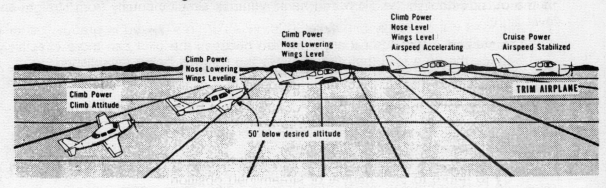

3. The nose must be lowered gradually, however, because a loss of altitude will result if the pitch attitude is decreased too abruptly before allowing the airspeed to increase adequately.

    a. As the nose is lowered and the wings leveled, retrim the airplane.

    b. When the airspeed reaches the desired cruise speed, reduce the throttle setting to appropriate cruise power setting, adjust the mixture control to the manufacturer's recommended setting, and trim the airplane for "hands-off" flight.

4. Acceptable performance for the climb is ±100 feet of the desired altitude.

F. Climbing turns. The following factors should be considered:

    1. With a constant power setting, the same pitch attitude and airspeed cannot be maintained in a bank as in a straight climb due to the decrease in effective lift and airspeed during a turn.

    2. The loss of vertical lift becomes greater as the angle of bank is increased, so shallow turns must be used to maintain an efficient rate of climb. If a medium- or steep-banked turn is used, the airplane will not climb so rapidly.

    3. The degree of bank should be neither too steep nor too shallow. Too steep a bank intensifies the effect mentioned in 2. above. If too shallow, the angle of bank may be difficult to maintain because of the inherent stability of the airplane.

    4. Once you enter a climbing turn, you should maintain a constant airspeed, a constant rate of turn, and a constant angle of bank. The coordination of all controls is likewise a primary factor to be stressed and developed.

    5. The airplane will have a greater tendency towards nose-heaviness than in a straight climb, due to the decrease in effective lift characteristic of all turns.

    6. As in all maneuvers, attention should be diverted from the airplane's nose and divided among all references equally.

    7. Proficiency should be developed in turns to the right as well as to the left.

    8. Note that while in a shallow climbing left turn, the airplane may still require right rudder pressure due to torque, even in the left turn.

        a. This is because the torque effect is stronger than the effect of the left turn.

G. There are two ways to establish a climbing turn: either establish a straight climb and then turn, or establish the pitch and bank attitudes simultaneously from straight-and-level flight.

1. The second method is usually preferred because the pilot can more effectively check the area for other aircraft while the climb is being established.

DESCENTS

A. A descent (or glide) is a basic maneuver in which the airplane loses altitude in a controlled manner.

B. As in straight-and-level flight, turns, and climbs, the pilot should perform descents by reference to both outside visual references and flight instruments.

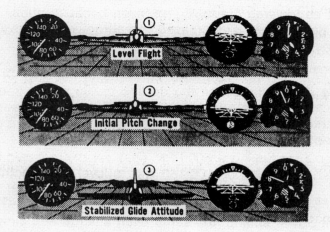

C. To enter the glide, the pilot should close the throttle. A constant altitude should be held with back pressure on the elevator control until the airspeed decreases to the desired glide speed. Then the pitch attitude should be allowed to decrease to maintain that gliding speed.

1. When the speed has stabilized, retrim the airplane for "hands-off flight."

2. When the approximate gliding pitch attitude is established, check the airspeed indicator.

a. If the airspeed is higher than the desired speed, the pitch attitude is too low. If the airspeed is lower than desired, the pitch attitude is too high. Therefore, readjust the pitch attitude accordingly.

b. After the adjustment has been made, it is important to retrim the airplane so that it will maintain this attitude without the need to hold pressure on the elevator control.

3. When the proper glide has been established, flaps may be used, but then the pitch attitude will have to be lowered to maintain the desired glide speed. Again, the pitch attitude should be adjusted first, then the airspeed checked after it has had time to stabilize.

D. The glide ratio of an airplane is the distance the airplane will, with power off, travel forward in relation to the altitude it loses.

    1. If an airplane travels 10,000 feet forward while descending 1,000 feet, its glide ratio is 10 to 1.

    2. The most efficient gliding speed will vary with the gross weight of the airplane, the configuration of landing gear and flaps, and the wind-milling of the propeller.

        a. Under different conditions of flight, the drag factors may be varied through the operation of the landing gear and/or flaps. When the landing gear or the flaps are lowered, the drag is greater and the airspeed will decrease unless the pitch attitude is lowered.

        b. As the pitch attitude is lowered, the glidepath steepens and reduces the distance traveled forward.

        c. With the power off, a windmilling propeller also creates considerable drag, retarding the airplane's forward movement.

E. The level off from a glide must be started before reaching the desired altitude because of the airplane's downward inertia.

    1. The amount of lead depends upon the rate of descent and the pilot's control technique.

        a. For example, assuming a 500-FPM (feet per minute) rate of descent, the altitude must be led by 100-150 feet to level off smoothly.

    2. At the lead point, add power to the appropriate level flight cruise setting so the desired airspeed will be attained at the desired altitude.

        a. Note that the nose will tend to rise as the airspeed increases.

    3. The pilot should smoothly control the pitch attitude to attain the level flight attitude so that the level off is completed at the desired altitude.

F. Acceptable performance for descents is ±100 feet from the desired altitude.

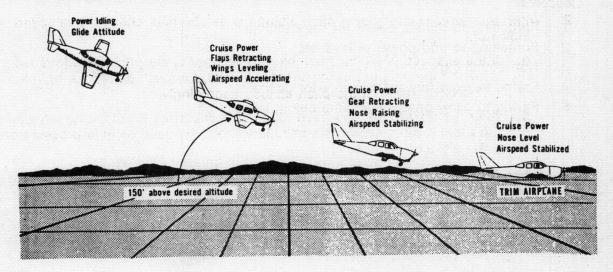

COMMON BASIC FLIGHT MANEUVER ERRORS

A. General

1. Poor scanning technique for other aircraft.

2. Staring at the instruments (many CFIs cover instruments to break this habit).

3. Forgetting to use the rudder in turns, climbs, and when moving ailerons to correct for turbulence.

4. Not understanding the ball in the turn coordinator.

5. Staring straight ahead (tunnel vision). You should look around and take in the whole picture.

B. Turns

1. Forgetting to look before turning. This is as dangerous as changing lanes on a freeway without looking first.

2. Letting the nose fall in steep turns.

3. Not using trim in steep turns (steep 720° turns take a while - don't fight it the whole time).

4. Staring straight ahead, at the bank indicator, or at the altimeter.

5. Not using rudder during rollout.

6. Holding rudder after bank is established.

C. Climbs

1. Forgetting to add power (when entering climb from cruise flight).
2. Not checking for traffic straight ahead (lower nose or make shallow turns).
3. Reducing power too early when leveling off.
4. Not using trim.
5. Failing to allow proper lead time before leveling off.

D. Descents

1. Forgetting to reduce power for the descent.
2. Forgetting to add power at level-off.
3. Not retrimming.
4. Failing to exert forward pressure for descents.
5. Failing to allow proper lead time before leveling off.

CHAPTER EIGHT
LANDINGS

Landing the airplane is the hardest flight maneuver for student pilots to master. Therefore, more time will be spent learning and practicing this flight procedure than any other. Landing consists of six steps: downwind, base leg, final approach, roundout (flare), touchdown, and after-landing roll.

1. The downwind step consists of entering the airport traffic pattern. The downwind portion of the traffic pattern is parallel to the active runway but in the opposite direction.

2. The base leg is that portion of the airport traffic pattern along which the airplane proceeds from the downwind leg to the final approach leg and begins the descent to a landing. While on the base leg the pilot must accurately judge the distance which the airplane must descend to the landing point and correct for wind drift so the ground track remains perpendicular to the extension of the centerline of the landing runway.

3. The final approach is the last part of the traffic pattern during which the airplane is aligned with the landing runway or area and a straight line descent is made to the point of touchdown. The descent rate (descent angle) is governed by the airplane's height and distance from the intended touchdown point and the airplane's speed over the ground.

4. The roundout, or flare as it is sometimes called, is that part of the final approach in which the airplane makes a transition from the approach attitude to the touchdown or landing attitude.

5. The touchdown is the actual contact or touching of the main wheels of the airplane on the landing surface. The full weight of the airplane is transferred from the wings to the wheels.

6. The after-landing roll, or rollout, is the forward roll of the airplane on the landing surface after touchdown while the airplane decelerates to a normal taxi speed or a stop.

This chapter outlines each of the six steps above after discussing airport traffic patterns. The chapter concludes with discussion of slips, go-arounds, and other special landing situations (crosswind, gusty wind, soft field, short field, etc.).

This chapter covers 5 of the 34 "Tasks" in the FAA Practical Test Standards (PTSs). They are

1. Traffic Pattern Operation
2. Normal and Crosswind Landing
3. Go-Around
4. Short-Field Landing
5. Soft-Field Landing

TRAFFIC PATTERN OPERATION

A. Established airport traffic patterns ensure that air traffic flows into and out of an airport in an orderly manner. Airport traffic patterns establish

1. The direction and placement of the pattern.
2. The altitude at which the pattern is to be flown.
3. The procedures for entering and leaving the pattern.

B. There is a basic rectangular airport traffic pattern which you should use unless modified by air traffic control or by approved visual markings at the airport. Thus, all you need to know is

1. The basic rectangular traffic pattern,
2. Visual markings and typical ATC clearances which modify the basic rectangular pattern, and
3. Reasons for modifying the basic pattern.

C. Regarding the basic rectangular airport traffic pattern:

1. The traffic pattern altitude is usually 1,000 ft above the elevation of the airport surface (some smaller airports use 800 ft). The use of a common altitude at a given airport is the key factor in minimizing the risk of collisions at nontower airports.

2. At all airports, the direction of traffic flow (in accordance with FAR Part 91) is always to the left (counterclockwise when seen from the air), unless right turns are indicated by approved light signals, visual markings on the airport, or control tower instructions.

3. Within airport traffic areas (up to 3,000 ft AGL and a 5-mile radius of the control tower), which you cannot fly in as a recreational pilot, the maximum speed (safety permitting) is

    a. 156 kts (180 MPH) for reciprocating engine aircraft.

    b. 200 kts (230 MPH) for turbine-powered airplanes.

    c. Also, speed should be adjusted when practicable, so that it is compatible with the speed of other aircraft in the pattern.

    d. In terminal control areas (TCAs), the speed limit is 250 kts because all airplanes are positively controlled and the controller can regulate airspeed.

4. The basic rectangular traffic pattern consists of five "legs" positioned in relation to the runway in use as illustrated below.

    a. Upwind.

    b. Crosswind.

    c. Downwind.

    d. Base.

    e. Final approach (note that the upwind leg and the final leg are on the same side of the "rectangle").

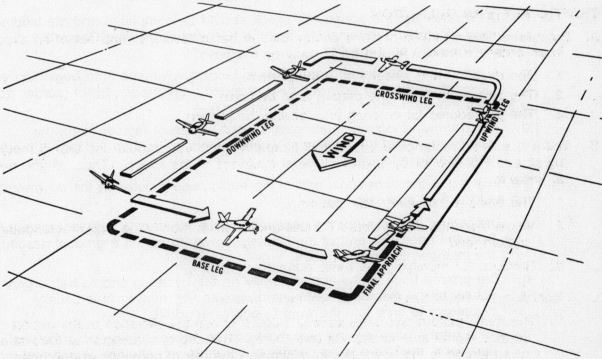

D. The four sides of the airport traffic pattern rectangle:

    1. The upwind leg of the rectangular pattern is a straight course aligned with, and leading from, the takeoff runway.

        a. This leg begins at the point the airplane leaves the ground and continues until the 90° turn onto the crosswind leg is started.

        b. After takeoff, you should continue climbing straight ahead until reaching a point beyond the departure end of the runway and within 500 ft of traffic pattern altitude.

   c. At that point, a left turn (assuming the standard left-hand traffic pattern) should be made to the crosswind leg if you are going to stay in the traffic pattern. If you are going to leave the pattern, see H. on page 141.

2. The crosswind leg is horizontally perpendicular to the extended centerline of the takeoff runway. It is entered by making a 90° left turn from the upwind leg.

   a. On the crosswind leg, the airplane proceeds to the downwind leg position.

   b. Since in most cases the takeoff is made into the wind, the wind now will be approximately perpendicular to the airplane's flightpath. As a result, the airplane will have to be crabbed or headed slightly into the wind while on the crosswind leg to maintain a ground track that is perpendicular to the runway centerline extension.

   c. After reaching the prescribed altitude for the traffic pattern and when in the proper position to enter the downwind leg, a level medium banked 90° turn should be made into the downwind leg.

3. The downwind leg is a course flown parallel to the landing runway, but in a direction opposite to the intended landing direction.

   a. This leg should be approximately ½ to 1 mile out from the landing runway, and at the specified traffic pattern altitude.

   b. During this leg, the prelanding check should be completed and the landing gear extended if retractable. See the "General Prelanding Checklist" sideheading on page 141.

   c. A consistent descent and approach to landing will result from beginning your descent on the late downwind leg at a point directly abeam of (across from) your intended landing point on the runway.

   d. The downwind leg continues past a point abeam of (across from) the approach end of the runway to where a medium banked 90° turn is made onto the base leg.

4. The base leg is the transitional part of the traffic pattern between the downwind leg and the final approach leg.

   a. Depending on the wind, the base leg is established at a sufficient distance from the approach end of the landing runway to permit a gradual descent to the intended touchdown point.

   b. The ground track of the airplane while on the base leg should be perpendicular to the extended centerline of the landing runway (it is usually necessary to crab into the wind to counteract drift).

   c. While on the base leg the pilot must ensure, before turning onto the final approach, that there is no danger of colliding with another aircraft that may already be on the final approach.

5. The final approach leg is a descending flightpath starting from the completion of the base-to-final turn and extending to the point of touchdown.

   a. Here the pilot's judgment and technique must be keenest to accurately control the airspeed and descent angle while approaching the intended touchdown point.

E. At a controlled airport (i.e., with a control tower), the controller will direct when and where you should enter the traffic pattern. Remember that you may enter an Airport Traffic Area only with proper authorization from a CFI. Your pilot-in-command privileges as a recreational pilot do not include operation in ATAs.

1. Remember, you are required to contact the control tower (or approach control) 5 miles out from the airport. It is recommended to contact them 10 miles out for more efficient entrance into the traffic pattern.

2. The controller may request that you perform some maneuvers for better traffic spacing. These may consist of

   a. Cutting the downwind leg short.
   b. Extending the downwind leg.
   c. Slowing down.
   d. A 360° turn to provide spacing ahead of you.

F. To enter the traffic pattern at an airport without a control tower, inbound pilots are expected to observe other aircraft already in the pattern and to conform to the traffic pattern in use.

1. If no other aircraft are in the pattern, then traffic indicators on the ground and wind indicators must be checked to determine which runway and traffic pattern direction should be used.

   a. Wind socks or wind cones indicate the direction from which the wind is blowing. The open hole in the sock or cone nearest the pole to which it is attached points to the direction the wind is coming from. That is the direction in which you should land, runways permitting, i.e., into the wind.

   b. Tetrahedrons indicate the direction in which you should land, i.e., in the same direction that the point of the tetrahedron is pointing. Tetrahedrons can swing freely to point into the wind or can be secured to indicate the desired direction of landing. In any event, land toward the direction that the small end (point) is pointing.

   c. Landing tees are wind indicators. Land such that your airplane points in the same direction (or as near as possible depending on the available runways) as the wind tee seems to be pointing. Note that the wind tee has a shape similar to an airplane, i.e., with wings and a tail (but no nose).

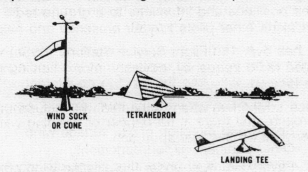

WIND SOCK OR CONE   TETRAHEDRON   LANDING TEE

2. Many airports have L-shaped traffic pattern indicators displayed with a segmented circle adjacent to the runway.

   a. The short member of the L shows the direction in which the traffic pattern turns should be made when using the runway parallel to the long member.

   b. Always look at the L as if you were flying a base leg (if landing) or taking off to determine the traffic pattern.

c.   For example, the airplane in the figure below appears to be on final in the process of landing. The pilot should have flown a right-hand pattern, e.g., turned right onto base and turned right onto final.

1)   Note that if the wind were from the opposite direction (note the tetrahedron), it would be a left-hand pattern.

d.   These indicators should be checked while at a distance well away from any pattern that might be in use, or while at a safe height well above generally used pattern altitudes.

e.   When the proper traffic pattern direction has been determined, the pilot should then proceed to a point well clear of the pattern before descending to the pattern altitude.

3.   Generally when approaching an airport for landing, you should enter the traffic pattern at a 45° angle to the downwind leg and headed toward the midpoint of the runway to be used for landing.

a.   Arriving airplanes should always be at the proper traffic pattern altitude before entering the pattern, and should stay clear of the traffic flow until established on the entry leg.

b.   The entry leg should be of sufficient length to provide a clear view of the entire traffic pattern.

4.   The FAA PTSs require maintaining traffic pattern altitude to ±100 ft and traffic pattern airspeed to within ±10 kts.

G.   Pilots operating at uncontrolled airports should use the communications radio to announce their positions and intentions to a ground radio station located at those airports. This alerts other pilots to your presence and helps avoid midair collisions.

1.   The FAA has over 180 Flight Service Stations (FSSs) which provide, on a designated radio frequency, advisory information concerning the airport at which they are located.

a.   These advisories, when requested, will include the

1)   Speed and direction of the surface wind.
2)   Other pertinent airport conditions.
3)   Favored runway under the existing wind condition.
4)   Observed or reported traffic in the traffic pattern or in the vicinity.

b.   Make your radio calls on the FSS frequency.

2.   When there is no FAA facility on the airport, use the UNICOM.

3.   If there is no ground station, broadcast anyway on the air-to-air frequency 122.9 (MULTICOM).

H. Departing from a traffic pattern.

1. The general procedure at either a controlled or an uncontrolled airport is to make a 45° left turn from the upwind leg after takeoff at approximately the point one would turn crosswind if one were staying in the traffic pattern.

   a. Make a 45° right turn for a right-hand pattern.

2. At controlled airports, a straight-out, right turn, or downwind departure may be requested.

   a. This request should be made when requesting takeoff clearance.

   b. A departure from the downwind leg should be made by a 45° turn out or by simply climbing to cruise altitude.

3. At uncontrolled airports, straight-out departures are common.

   a. However, there are no FAA rules regarding departures. Check for local airport rules.

   b. Make your intentions known by announcing to the other traffic your departure direction so there is no confusion.

TRAFFIC PATTERN OPERATION PTS

TASK: **TRAFFIC PATTERN OPERATION** *(ASEL)*
PILOT OPERATION - 2
REFERENCES: AC 61-21, AC 61-23; AIM.

Objective. To determine that the applicant:

1. Exhibits knowledge by explaining traffic pattern procedures at uncontrolled airports, including collision and wind-shear avoidance.

2. Follows the established traffic pattern procedures according to instructions or rules.

3. Corrects for wind drift to follow the appropriate ground track.

4. Maintains proper spacing from other traffic.

5. Maintains traffic pattern altitude, ±100 feet.

6. Maintains desired airspeed, ±10 knots.

7. Completes the prelanding cockpit checklist.

8. Maintains orientation with the runway in use.

9. Completes a turn to final approach at least one-fourth mile from the approach end of the runway.

GENERAL PRELANDING CHECKLIST

Prior to or as you enter the airport traffic pattern (usually on the downwind leg), you should conduct a prelanding checklist to be sure that you and your airplane are ready to land. Generally, such a checklist includes:

1. Seat belts fastened.
2. Gas fullest tank, or both tanks.
3. Carburetor heat on (before power reduction).
4. Mixture set (usually full rich in case you have to "go around," i.e., use full power).
   a. Electric fuel boost pump on also (if applicable).
5. Speed reduced to lower approach flaps.
6. Approach flaps partially down.
7. Landing gear down, if retractable.

BEFORE-LANDING CHECKLIST FOR A BEECH SKIPPER

1. Seat Belts and Shoulder Harnesses - FASTENED
2. Fuel Selector - CHECK ON
3. Fuel Boost Pump - ON
4. Mixture - FULL RICH (or as required by field elevation)
5. Carburetor Heat - FULL HOT or FULL COLD, AS REQUIRED

6. Landing Light - AS REQUIRED

   CAUTION: Do not use the landing light if Battery Switch is OFF, battery power is lost, or battery circuit breaker is open.
7. Wing Flaps - FULL DOWN (90 KTS MAXIMUM)
8. Airspeed - ESTABLISH NORMAL LANDING APPROACH SPEED (63 KTS)

NOTE: In the event of a go-around, carburetor heat shall be in the FULL COLD position after full throttle application.

BEFORE-LANDING CHECKLIST FOR A CESSNA 152

1. Seats, Seat Belts, Shoulder Harnesses -- ADJUST and LOCK
2. Mixture -- RICH
3. Carburetor Heat -- ON (apply full heat before reducing power)
4. Airspeed -- 60-70 KIAS (flaps UP)

5. Wing Flaps -- AS DESIRED (below 85 KIAS)
6. Airspeed -- 55-65 KIAS (flaps DOWN)
7. Touchdown -- MAIN WHEELS FIRST
8. Landing Roll -- LOWER NOSEWHEEL GENTLY
9. Braking -- MINIMUM REQUIRED

BEFORE-LANDING CHECKLIST FOR A PIPER TOMAHAWK

1. Fuel selector - PROPER TANK
2. Seat backs - ERECT
3. Belts/harness - FASTEN
4. Electric fuel pump - ON
5. Mixture - SET
6. Flaps - SET (89 KIAS max)

7. Trim to 70 KIAS
8. Final approach speed -

   Full flaps (Outboard Flow Strips Installed) - 62 KIAS

   Full flaps (Outboard and Inboard Flow Strips Installed) - 67 KIAS

NORMAL APPROACH AND LANDING

A. This type of approach and landing involves techniques for what is considered a "normal" situation.

   1. Engine power is available.

   2. The wind is light or the final approach is made directly into the wind.

   3. The final approach path has no obstacles.

   4. The landing surface is firm and of ample length to gradually bring the airplane to a stop.

   5. The PTS for normal and cross-wind landings appears on page 159.

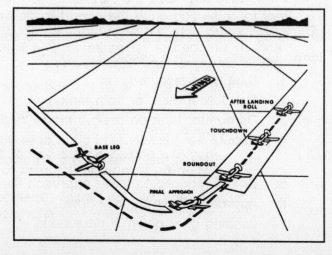

B.   Other types of landings.

   1.   Go-arounds (rejected landings).

   2.   Crosswind.

   3.   Turbulent air.

   4.   Short field.

   5.   Soft field.

   6.   Tailwheel.

   7.   Emergency (discussion of emergency landings appears in Chapter 13 on page 229).

C.   The normal approach and landing is explained in the next five sideheadings.

BASE LEG

A.   Note the explanation of upwind, crosswind, and downwind segments of the airport traffic pattern explained in the first sideheading of this chapter. These segments precede the base leg and final portions of the landing sequence.

B.   The placement of the base leg is one of the more important judgments to be made by the pilot in any landing approach. The placement of the base leg refers to at what point you turn from downwind to base leg, i.e., how far you extend your downwind beyond the end of the active runway. The pilot must accurately judge the altitude and distance from which a gradual descent will result in landing at the desired spot.

   1.   The distance will depend on

      a.   The altitude of the base leg.

      b.   The effect of wind.

      c.   The amount of wing flaps used.

   2.   When there is a strong wind on final approach or the flaps will be used to produce a steep angle of descent, you should either:

      a.   Adjust the glideslope by adding power, or

      b.   The base leg may be positioned closer to the approach end of the runway than would be required with a light wind or no flaps.

   3.   Normally, the before-landing check should be completed prior to reaching the base leg. See the sideheadings for before-landing checklists on page 142.

C.   After turning onto the base leg, the pilot should start the descent with reduced power and an airspeed of approximately 1.4 times V_{so}. (V_{so} is the stalling speed with power off, landing gear and flaps down.)

   1.   EXAMPLE. If V_{so} is 60 kts, the speed should be 1.4 times 60, or 84 kts.

   2.   Your airplane operating manual may also provide the recommended airspeeds on downwind, base, and final.

      a.   Also, depending on the size of the traffic pattern, descents may be started when on downwind adjacent to the end of the runway.

   3.   Landing flaps may be partially lowered if desired at this time. Full flaps are not recommended until the final approach is established and the landing assured.

4. Drift correction should be established and maintained to follow a ground track perpendicular to the extension of the centerline of the runway on which the landing is to be made (i.e., the active runway).

    a. Since the final approach and landing will normally be made into the wind, there will be somewhat of a crosswind during the base leg.

    b. This requires that the airplane be angled (crabbed) sufficiently into the wind to prevent drifting farther away from the intended landing spot.

D. The base leg should be continued to the point where a medium to shallow banked turn will align the airplane's path directly with the centerline of the landing runway.

    1. This descending turn should be completed at a safe altitude which will be dependent upon the height of the terrain and any obstructions along the ground track.

    2. The turn to the final approach should also be sufficiently above the airport elevation to permit a final approach long enough for the pilot to accurately estimate the point of touchdown, while maintaining the proper approach airspeed.

        a. This will require careful planning as to the starting point and the radius of the turn.

            1) Normally, it is recommended that the angle of bank not exceed a medium bank because the steeper the angle of bank, the higher the airspeed at which the airplane stalls.

            2) Be very careful to keep the nose down and the airspeed up. You will already be at an airspeed relatively close to stalling speed.

    3. If an extremely steep bank is needed to prevent overshooting the proper final approach path, it is advisable to discontinue the approach, go around, and plan to start the turn earlier on the next approach rather than risk a hazardous situation.

FINAL APPROACH

A. Immediately after the base-to-final approach turn is completed, the longitudinal axis of the airplane should be aligned with the centerline of the runway or landing surface, so that drift (if any) will be recognized immediately.

    1. On a normal approach with no wind drift, the longitudinal axis should be kept aligned with the runway centerline throughout the approach and landing.

    2. The proper way to correct for a crosswind is explained under a subsequent sideheading, "Crosswind Landings," beginning on page 153.

B. After aligning the airplane with the runway centerline, complete the final flap setting and adjust the pitch attitude as required for the desired rate of descent (descent angle).

    1. Slight adjustments in pitch and power may be necessary to maintain the descent attitude and the desired approach airspeed.

        a. If the descent (pitch) angle and flap settings are both correct but the airspeed is high, then reduce power, holding pitch constant (this will require slight back pressure and retrimming to hold).

        b. If airspeed is too low, it should be corrected immediately by lowering pitch; then add power, readjust pitch to the desired level, and recheck airspeed.

2. In the absence of the manufacturer's recommended airspeed, a speed equal to 1.3 times V_{so} should be used.

    a. EXAMPLE. If V_{so} is 60 kts, the speed should be 78 kts.

    b. The FAA PTSs require you to maintain ±5 kts of the desired airspeed.

3. When the pitch attitude and airspeed have been stabilized, retrim the airplane to relieve the pressure required to hold the controls.

4. The descent angle should be controlled throughout the approach so that the airplane will land in the center of the first third of the runway. Many flight instructors have their students aim to land on the "numbers," i.e., the runway numbers at the very beginning of the runway, to allow more runway room for touch and goes, etc. Landing on the "numbers" also provides a specific visible target.

    a. The descent angle is affected by all four fundamental forces that act on an airplane (lift, drag, thrust, and weight).

    b. The wind also plays a prominent part in the gliding distance over the ground. Naturally, the pilot has no control over the wind but may correct for its effect on the airplane's descent by appropriate pitch and power adjustments.

5. At a given pitch attitude there is only one power setting for one airspeed, one flap setting, one wind condition, and one targeted landing point.

    a. A change in any one of these variables will require an appropriate coordinated change in the other controllable variables.

    b. EXAMPLE. If the pitch attitude is raised too high without an increase of power, the airplane will settle very rapidly and touch down short of the desired spot.

        1) Never try to stretch a glide by applying back elevator pressure alone to reach the desired landing spot.

        2) This will shorten the gliding distance if power is not added simultaneously. It will also result in a lower airspeed and a serious risk of a stall.

    c. Therefore, the proper angle of descent and airspeed should be maintained by coordinating pitch attitude changes and power changes.

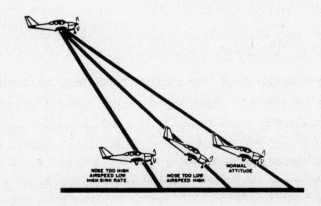

C. The objective of a good final approach is to descend at an angle and airspeed that will permit the airplane to reach the desired touchdown point at an airspeed which will result in a minimum of floating just before touchdown.

1. To accomplish this, it is essential that both the descent angle and the airspeed be accurately controlled.

    a. On a normal approach the power should be adjusted as necessary to control the airspeed.

    b. Adjust the pitch attitude simultaneously to control the descent angle or to attain the desired altitudes along the approach path.

2. By lowering the nose and reducing power to keep approach airspeed constant, a descent at a higher rate can be made to correct for being too high in the approach.

    a. This is one reason for performing approaches with partial power.

3. When the approach is too low, add power and raise the nose.

4. On the other hand, if the approach is extremely high or low, it is advisable to reject the landing and execute a go-around. This procedure is explained later in this chapter, beginning on page 160.

D. The lift/drag factors may also be varied by the pilot to adjust the descent through the use of the landing flaps.

1. When the flaps are lowered, the airspeed will decrease unless the power is increased or the pitch attitude lowered.

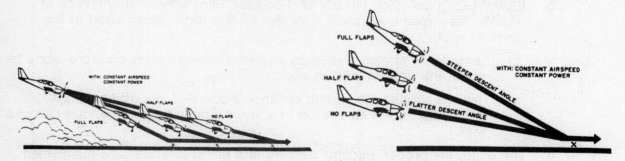

2. After starting the final approach, the pilot must estimate where the airplane will land by judging the descent angle.

    a. If it appears that the airplane is going to overshoot or land slightly beyond the desired spot, more flaps may be used if not already fully extended, or the power may be reduced further.

        1) In either case, the pitch attitude must be lowered.

    b. This will result in a steeper approach without increasing the airspeed.

    c. If the spot is being undershot and a shallower approach is needed, the power and the pitch attitude should be increased to readjust the descent angle and the airspeed.

    d. Never retract the flaps to correct for undershooting since that will suddenly decrease the lift and cause the airplane to sink even more rapidly.

E. See the "Visual Approach Slope Indicator" sideheading on page 168.

F. With reduced power and a slower airspeed, the airflow produces less lift on the wings and less downward force on the horizontal stabilizer, resulting in a significant nose-down tendency. Therefore, the elevator must be trimmed more "nose-up."

G. The roundout, touchdown, and landing roll are much easier to accomplish when they are preceded by a proper final approach with precise control of airspeed, attitude, power, and drag resulting in a stabilized descent angle.

H. During the approach, roundout, and touchdown, vision is of prime importance.

   1. To provide a wide scope of vision and to foster good judgment of height and movement, the pilot's head should assume a natural, straight-ahead position.

   2. The pilot's visual focus should not be fixed on any one side or any one spot ahead of the airplane, but should be changing slowly from a point just over the airplane's nose to the desired touchdown zone and back again, while maintaining a deliberate awareness of distance from either side of the runway within the pilot's peripheral field of vision.

   3. Speed blurs objects at close range.

      a. Most everyone has noted this in an automobile moving at high speed.

      b. Nearby objects seem to merge together in a blur, while objects farther away stand out clearly. An automobile driver subconsciously focuses the eyes sufficiently far ahead to see objects distinctly.

      c. Similarly, the distance at which the pilot's vision is focused should be proportionate to the speed at which the airplane is traveling over the ground.

      d. Thus, as speed is reduced during the roundout, your focus should be brought closer.

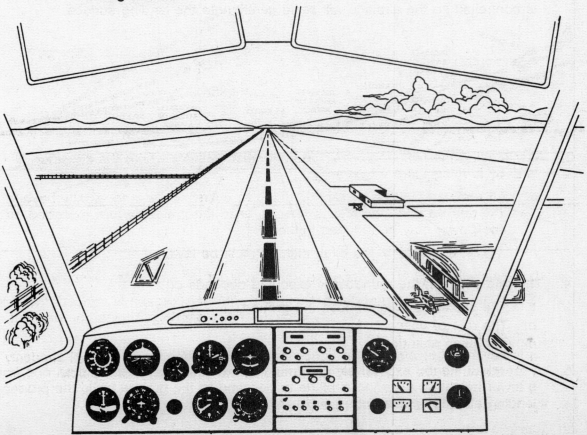

4. If the focus is changed gradually, being brought progressively closer as speed is reduced, the time interval and the attendant pilot reaction times will be reduced and the entire landing process smoothed out.

ROUNDOUT (FLARE)

A. The roundout is a slow, smooth transition from a normal approach attitude to a landing attitude. When the airplane (in a normal descent) approaches within what appears to be about 10 to 20 ft above the ground, the roundout or flare should be started. Then it should be a continuous process until the airplane touches down on the ground.

1. As the airplane reaches 10 to 20 ft above the ground, back elevator pressure should be gradually applied to slowly increase the pitch attitude and angle of attack.

2. This will cause the airplane's nose to gradually rise toward the desired landing attitude.

3. The angle of attack should be increased at a rate that will allow the airplane to continue settling slowly as forward speed decreases.

B. When the angle of attack is increased, lift is momentarily increased, which decreases the rate of descent.

1. Since power normally is reduced to idle during the roundout, the airspeed will also gradually decrease.

2. This, in turn, causes lift to decrease again. It must be controlled by raising the nose and further increasing the angle of attack.

3. During the roundout, the airspeed is decreased to touchdown speed while the lift is controlled so the airplane will settle gently onto the landing surface.

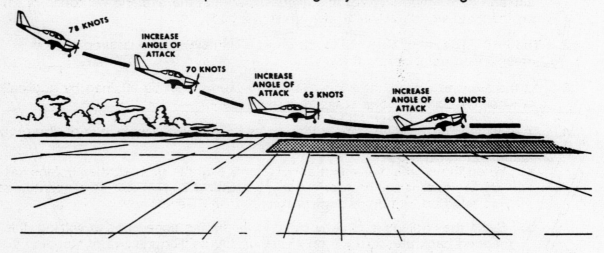

4. The rate at which the roundout is executed depends on

a. The airplane's height above the ground,

b. The rate of descent, and

c. The pitch attitude.

5. A roundout started excessively high must be executed more slowly than one from a lower height to allow the airplane to descend to the ground while the proper landing attitude is established.

6. The rate of rounding out must also be proportionate to the rate of closure with the ground. That is, when the airplane appears to be descending very slowly, the increase in pitch attitude must be made at a correspondingly slow rate.

7. The pitch attitude of the airplane in a full-flap approach is considerably lower than in a no-flap approach.

    a. The use of flaps increases the wings' angle of attack without increasing the pitch attitude of the airplane.

    b. Therefore, to attain the proper landing attitude before touching down, the nose must be raised more when flaps are fully extended.

    c. Since the roundout is usually started at approximately the same height above the ground regardless of the degree of flaps used, the pitch attitude must be increased (i.e., nose raised) at a faster rate when full flaps are used.

8. Once the actual process of rounding out is started, the elevator control should not be pushed forward.

    a. If too much back pressure has been exerted, this pressure should be either slightly relaxed or held constant, depending on the degree of the error.

9. If the roundout is too high or if anything else occurs that may interfere with a successful landing, you should "go around," i.e., abort the landing attempt (see the "Go-Arounds" (Rejected Landings) sideheading on page 160).

TOUCHDOWN

A. The touchdown is the gentle settling of the airplane onto the landing surface.

    1. The roundout and touchdown should be made with the engine idling, and the airplane at minimum controllable airspeed, so that the airplane will touch down on the main wheels at just above stalling speed.

    2. The FAA PTSs require you to touch down within 500 ft of a desired and/or prespecified point on the runway.

    3. As the airplane settles, the proper landing attitude must be attained by application of whatever back elevator pressure is necessary.

    4. An ideal landing is to try to hold the airplane's wheels a few inches off the ground as long as possible with the elevators.

        a. When the wheels are within about 2 or 3 ft of the ground, the airplane will still be settling too fast for a gentle touchdown. This rate of descent must be retarded by further back pressure on the elevators.

        b. Since the airplane is already close to its stalling speed and is settling, this added back pressure will only slow up the settling instead of stopping it.

    5. Remember and recognize "ground effect." Near the surface (10-15 ft), your airplane will seem to have more lift and fly easier due to the "effect of the ground" beneath the airplane. The air under the airplane has little room to compress and thus provides more lift and less drag.

        a. This contributes to the airplane's "floating" and explains the hesitation prior to touchdown.

B. Nosewheel-type airplanes should contact the ground in a tail-low attitude, with the main wheels touching down first so that no weight is on the nosewheel.

   1. After the main wheels make initial contact with the ground, back pressure on the elevator control should be held to maintain a positive angle of attack for aerodynamic braking and to hold the nosewheel off the ground until the airplane decelerates.

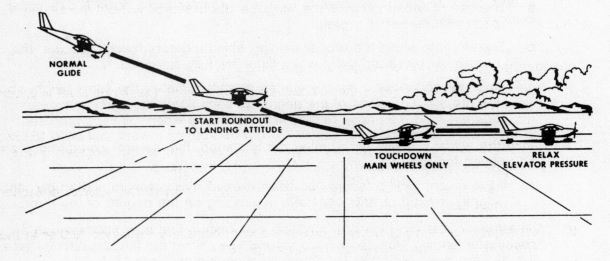

NORMAL GLIDE

START ROUNDOUT TO LANDING ATTITUDE

TOUCHDOWN MAIN WHEELS ONLY

RELAX ELEVATOR PRESSURE

   2. As the airplane's momentum decreases, back pressure may be gradually relaxed to allow the nosewheel to gently settle onto the runway. This will permit prompt steering with the nosewheel if it is of the steerable type. This will cause:

      a. A low angle of attack and negative lift on the wings to prevent floating or skipping, and

      b. The full weight of the airplane to rest on the wheels for better braking action.

      c. An alternative approach is to hold full back pressure and keep the nose-wheel off the ground to utilize aerodynamic braking.

   3. The airplane should never be "flown on" the runway with excess speed.

C. In the event you miscalculate and hit the runway too hard, the airplane will "bounce" right back in the air.

   1. This is very dangerous and can lead to a stall and another "bounce" on the runway.

   2. If this happens, you must immediately apply full power to correct for a hard bounce, and simultaneously smoothly apply forward pressure to lower the nose.

      a. This should be an automatic reaction.

   3. You can then go around or land again if the runway is long enough.

AFTER-LANDING ROLL

A. The landing process must never be considered complete until the airplane decelerates to the normal taxi speed during the landing roll.

B. Loss of directional control may lead to an aggravated, uncontrolled, tight turn on the ground (in a nosewheel-equipped airplane), or a "ground loop" (in a tailwheel-equipped airplane).

C. The rudder serves the same purpose on the ground as it does in the air. It controls the yawing of the airplane.

1. The effectiveness of the rudder, however, is dependent on the airflow, which depends on the speed of the airplane.

2. As the speed decreases and the nosewheel or tailwheel has been lowered to the ground, the steerable nosewheel or tailwheel provides more positive directional control than the rudder.

D. The ailerons, too, serve the same purpose on the ground as they do in the air. They change the lift and drag components of the wings.

1. During the after-landing roll they should be used to keep the wings level in much the same way they were used in flight.

2. If a wing starts to rise, aileron control should be applied toward that wing to lower it. The amount required will depend on speed because as the airspeed of the airplane decreases, the ailerons will become less effective.

a. The slower the airplane is moving, the larger the corrective aileron deflection must be.

3. Techniques for using ailerons in crosswind conditions are explained further in the "Crosswind Landings" sideheading on page 153.

E. The brakes of an airplane serve the same primary purpose as the brakes of an automobile. They reduce speed on the ground.

1. In airplanes, brakes may also be used as an aid in directional control when more positive control is required than could be obtained with rudder, nosewheel steering, or tailwheel steering alone. However, brakes should only be used at extremely slow speeds.

SLIPS

A. A slip is a maneuver usually used on a landing approach, and involves lowering one wing while simultaneously applying opposite side rudder to prevent a turn. It may be used for either of two purposes, or both of them combined.

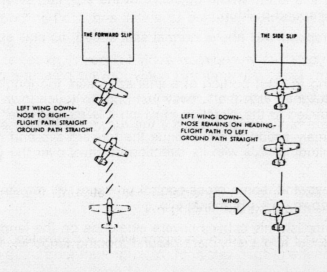

1. A slip may be used to steepen the approach path without increasing the airspeed, i.e., a forward slip.

   a. A dive can also be used to steepen the approach path, but it will increase airspeed.

2. A slip can also be used to make the airplane move sideways through the air to counteract the drift which results from a crosswind, i.e., a side slip.

B. Years ago, forward slips were used as a normal means of controlling landing descents to short or obstructed fields.

   1. With the installation of wing flaps on modern airplanes, the use of forward slips to steepen or control the angle of descent is no longer a common procedure.

   2. Pilots still need skill in the performance of forward slips to correct for possible errors in judging the landing approach.

C. The primary purpose of "forward slips" is to dissipate altitude without increasing the airplane's speed, particularly in airplanes not equipped with flaps. There are many circumstances requiring the use of forward slips, such as in a landing approach over obstacles and in making forced landings, when it is always wise to allow an extra margin of altitude for safety in the original estimate of the approach.

   1. Assuming that the airplane is originally in straight flight, the wing on the side toward which the slip is to be made should be lowered by use of the ailerons.

      a. In the previous illustration, the left wing down means the slip is to the left.

      b. Forward slips are normally performed with the wing dropped on the upwind side of the airplane if there is a crosswind. This eases the conversion to a side-slip for landing.

   2. Simultaneously, the airplane's nose must be yawed in the opposite direction by applying opposite rudder so that the airplane's longitudinal axis is at an angle to its original flightpath.

   3. The degree to which the nose is yawed in the opposite direction from the bank should be such that the original ground track is maintained.

   4. The nose should be lowered as necessary to maintain airspeed.

      a. Pilots are reluctant to put the nose into a steep nose-down attitude. However, this is the whole objective of the slip, i.e., steep descent angle without airspeed buildup.

      b. Use an airspeed well above normal stall speed, as stall speed increases in a slip.

D. If a slip is used during the last portion of a final approach, the longitudinal axis of the airplane must be realigned with the runway just prior to touchdown so that the airplane will land pointed in the direction in which it is moving over the runway.

   1. This requires timely action to discontinue the forward slip and realign the airplane's longitudinal axis with its direction of travel over the ground before touchdown.

   2. If there is a crosswind, some cross-control pressure will remain to counteract wind drift for touchdown. This is a side slip.

   3. Failure to accomplish this causes severe sideloads on the landing gear and, in the case of a tailwheel airplane, violent ground looping tendencies.

E. In the absence of a crosswind, discontinuing the slip is accomplished by leveling the wings and simultaneously releasing the rudder pressure while readjusting the pitch attitude to the normal glide attitude.

1. If the pressure on the rudder is released abruptly, the nose will swing too quickly into line and the airplane will tend to acquire excess speed.

a. Also, momentum may carry the nose of the airplane past straight ahead. Recovery should be smooth.

F. Because of the location of the pitot tube and static vents, airspeed indicators in some airplanes may have considerable error when the airplane is in a slip.

G. Forward slips with wing flaps extended should not be attempted in airplanes in which the manufacturer's operating instructions prohibit such operation.

H. In a side slip, as distinguished from a forward slip, the airplane's longitudinal axis remains parallel to the original flightpath, but the flightpath changes direction according to the steepness of the bank. The side slip is important in counteracting wind drift during crosswind landings and is discussed under the "Crosswind Landings" side-heading below.

I. The FAA PTSs require touchdowns from a forward slip at just above stalling speed within 500 ft of a desired point. Directional control must be maintained.

CROSSWIND LANDINGS

A. Many runways or landing areas necessitate that you land while the wind is blowing across rather than parallel to the direction you are landing.

1. All pilots should be well prepared to execute crosswind landings.

2. The same basic principles and factors involved in a normal approach and landing apply to a crosswind approach and landing.

3. The only additional technique required is correcting for wind drift.

4. Crosswind landings are a little more difficult to perform than are crosswind takeoffs, mainly due to problems in maintaining accurate control of the airplane while its speed is decreasing rather than increasing as on takeoff.

B. The crosswind landing is the maneuver that students and private pilots alike have more trouble with than any other. It requires a high degree of judgment and skill because so many variables come into play:

1. Drift
2. Alignment
3. Slip (cross control inputs)
4. Airspeed
5. Power
6. Flaps
7. Gusty turbulence
8. Variable wind direction
9. Roundout/flare
10. Ground roll

C. It is especially difficult for students to grasp crosswind techniques since they are usually just learning the roundout and flare, and the additional variables really complicate matters.

D. There are two usual methods of accomplishing a crosswind approach and landing: the crab method and the wing-low method (side slip).

1. Although the crab method may be easier for the pilot to maintain during final approach, it requires a high degree of judgment and timing in removing the crab immediately prior to touchdown.

2. The wing-low method is recommended in most cases although a combination of both methods may be used.

E. The crab method is executed by establishing a heading (crab) toward the wind with the wings level so that the airplane's ground track remains aligned with the centerline of the runway.

1. This crab angle is maintained until just prior to touchdown, when the longitudinal axis of the airplane must be quickly aligned with the runway to avoid sideways contact of the wheels with the runway.

2. If a long final approach is flown, the pilot may use the crab method until just before the roundout is started and then smoothly change to the wing-low method for the remainder of the landing.

3. If the crab method of drift correction has been used throughout the final approach and roundout, the crab must be removed the instant before touchdown by applying rudder to align the airplane's longitudinal axis with its direction of movement. This requires timely and accurate action.

a. Failure to accomplish this realignment results in severe sideloads on the landing gear and, in the case of a tailwheel-equipped airplane, ground looping tendencies.

F. The wing-low method (side slip) will compensate for a crosswind from any angle. Most important, it enables the pilot to keep the airplane's ground track and the longitudinal axis simultaneously aligned with the runway centerline throughout the final approach, roundout, touchdown, and after-landing roll.

1. This prevents the airplane from touching down in a sideward motion and imposing damaging side loads on the landing gear.

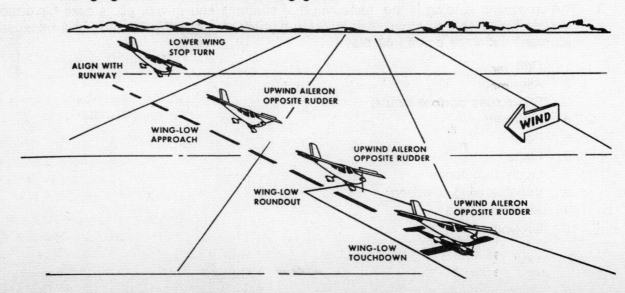

2. To use the wing-low method, the pilot aligns the airplane's heading with the centerline of the runway, notes the rate and direction of drift, then promptly applies drift correction by lowering the upwind wing.

    a. The amount the wing must be lowered depends on the rate of drift.

    b. When the wing is lowered, the airplane will tend to turn in that direction.

    c. Simultaneously, it is necessary to apply sufficient opposite rudder pressure to prevent the turn and keep the airplane's longitudinal axis aligned with the runway.

3. The drift is controlled with aileron and the heading with rudder.

    a. The airplane will now be side slipping into the wind just enough so that both the resultant flightpath and the ground track are aligned with the runway.

    b. Airspeed will drop. Be prepared to lower pitch or add power. With side slip, pitch attitude is slightly lower.

    c. If the crosswind diminishes, this crosswind correction (side slip) must be reduced accordingly or the airplane will begin slipping away from the desired path.

4. To correct for a very strong crosswind, the slip into the wind must be increased by lowering the upwind wing a considerable amount. As a consequence, this results in a greater tendency for the airplane to turn. Since turning is not desired, considerable opposite rudder must be applied to keep the airplane's longitudinal axis aligned with the runway.

5. Some airplanes may not have sufficient rudder travel available to compensate for the strong turning tendency caused by the steep bank.

    a. If the required bank is so steep that full opposite rudder will not prevent a turn, the wind is too strong to safely land the airplane on that particular runway with those wind conditions.

    b. Since the airplane's capability would be exceeded, it is imperative that the landing be made on a more favorable runway either at that airport or at an alternate airport.

6. Flaps can and should be used during most approaches since they tend to have a stabilizing effect on the airplane. Flaps also lower stall speed, giving a greater margin above stall.

    a. However, the degree to which flaps should be extended will vary with the airplane's handling characteristics, as well as the amount of turbulence.

    b. In higher or gusty winds, less flaps should be used as explained in the "Gusty Winds and Turbulence" sideheading on page 159.

    c. Full flaps may be used as long as the crosswind component is not in excess of the airplane's capability or unless the manufacturer recommends otherwise.

7.   Generally, the roundout can be made as in a normal landing approach but the application of a crosswind correction must be continued as necessary to prevent drifting.

   a.   Do not level the wings. Keep the upwind wing down throughout the roundout.

      1)   If the wings are leveled, the airplane will begin drifting and the touch-down will occur while drifting.

      2)   Remember, the primary objective is to land the airplane without subjecting it to any side loads resulting from touching down while drifting and to prevent ground looping during the landing.

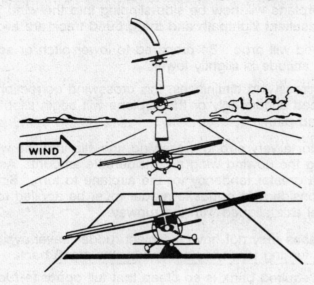

   b.   Since the airspeed decreases as the roundout progresses, the flight controls gradually become less effective. As a result, the crosswind correction being held would become inadequate.

      1)   It is necessary to gradually increase the deflection of the rudder and ailerons to maintain the proper amount of drift correction.

G.   The crosswind correction (aileron into the wind and opposite rudder) should be maintained throughout the roundout, and the touchdown should be made on the upwind main wheel.

   1.   Continue to hold your crosswind correction position until the airplane settles onto the downwind main wheel by itself.

   2.   As the forward momentum decreases after initial contact, the weight of the airplane will cause the downwind main wheel to gradually settle onto the runway.

   3.   In those airplanes having nosewheel steering interconnected with the rudder, the nosewheel may not be aligned with the runway as the wheels touch down because opposite rudder is being held in the crosswind correction.

   a.   To prevent swerving in the direction the nosewheel is offset, the corrective rudder pressure must be diminished as the downwind (second) main wheel settles. Thus, the nosewheel will already be closely aligned as the nose-wheel settles.

H. During gusty or high wind conditions, prompt adjustments (increasing or decreasing the crosswind adjustments) must be made in the crosswind correction to assure that the airplane does not drift as the airplane touches down.

I. Particularly during the after-landing roll, give special attention to maintaining directional control by use of rudder, or nosewheel/tailwheel steering, while keeping the upwind wing from rising by use of aileron.

   1. When an airplane is airborne it moves with the air mass in which it is flying regardless of the airplane's ground track and groundspeed.

   2. When an airplane is on the ground it is unable to move with the air mass (crosswind) because of the resistance created by ground friction on the wheels.

   3. An airplane has a greater profile, or side area, behind the main landing gear than forward of it.

      a. With the main wheels acting as a pivot point and the greater surface area exposed to the crosswind behind that pivot point, the airplane on the ground will tend to turn or "weathervane" into the wind.

      b. This means the opposite rudder used during the side slip will have to be continued on the ground, but with less pressure.

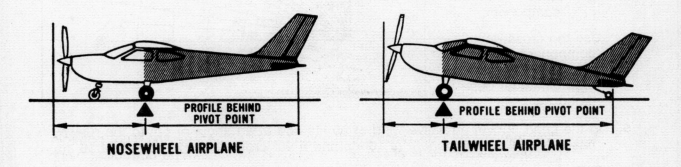

NOSEWHEEL AIRPLANE   TAILWHEEL AIRPLANE

   4. While the airplane is decelerating during the after-landing roll, more and more aileron must be applied to keep the upwind wing from rising.

      a. Since the airplane is slowing down, there is less airflow around the ailerons and they become less effective.

      b. At the same time, the relative wind is becoming more of a crosswind and exerting a greater lifting force on the upwind wing.

      c. Consequently, when the airplane is coming to a stop, the aileron control must be held fully toward the wind.

J. Computing crosswind components.

1. Each airplane, due to its design, has a maximum crosswind in which it can be safely landed.

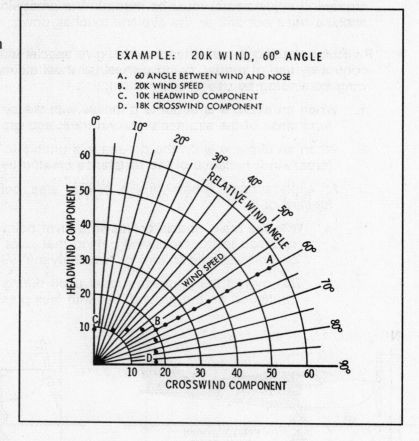

EXAMPLE: 20K WIND, 60° ANGLE

A. 60 ANGLE BETWEEN WIND AND NOSE
B. 20K WIND SPEED
C. 10K HEADWIND COMPONENT
D. 18K CROSSWIND COMPONENT

2. Wind blowing from a 90° angle to the runway is a direct crosswind.

3. Wind blowing from a 0° to 90° angle to the runway is not a direct crosswind, but the wind can be divided into

    a. Headwind component.

    b. Crosswind component.

4. Use the crosswind component chart in your airplane operating manual as illustrated here.

5. In the chart above, a relative wind at 20 kts and at an angle of 60° to the runway has a headwind component of 10 kts and a 90° crosswind component of 18 kts.

6. FARs require that all airplanes type-certificated since 1962 have safe ground handling characteristics with a 90° crosswind component equal to 0.2 times V_{so}.

    a. Thus, an airplane that stalls at 55 kts in the landing configuration must have no uncontrollable ground looping (weathervaning) tendencies with a 90° crosswind component of 11 kts (0.2 x 55). The fractions are usually rounded.

    b. Examples of 20% of V_{so}

        Beechcraft Skipper   47 kts V_{so} x .20 = 9.5 kt crosswind component
        Cessna 152   35 kts V_{so} x .20 = 7   kt crosswind component
        Piper Tomahawk   49 kts V_{so} x .20 = 10   kt crosswind component

    c. Each airplane exceeds the above requirement with the following demonstrated crosswind component

        Beechcraft Skipper . . . . 15 kts
        Cessna 152 . . . . 12 kts
        Piper Tomahawk . . . . 15 kts

K. It is imperative that pilots determine the maximum crosswind component of each airplane they fly and avoid operations in wind conditions that exceed the capability of the airplane.

L. If you cannot align your airplane with the runway with full rudder before or during roundout due to crosswinds, you must go around, i.e., you risk an accident (aircraft damage and personal injury) by attempting to land.

1. Since the wind is stronger 200 to 300 ft in the air than it is close to the ground, your decision to go-around due to excessive crosswind will normally be made just before touchdown, assuming good runway alignment up to that point.

2. Wind velocity often changes in gusts, making a last minute decision to go around necessary. You should not be embarrassed or hesitate to go around if inclined to do so. In fact, a go around is an important maneuver to develop.

M. The FAA PTSs require a crosswind landing such that you

1. Maintain recommended approach airspeed ±5 kts.
2. Touch down smoothly at just above stalling speed within 500 ft of desired point.
3. Maintain directional control.

NORMAL AND CROSSWIND LANDING PTS

*TASK: **NORMAL AND CROSSWIND LANDING** (ASEL)*
*   PILOT OPERATION - 8*
*   REFERENCES: AC 61-21.*

Objective. To determine that the applicant:

1. Exhibits knowledge by explaining the elements of normal and crosswind landings, including crosswind limitations, airspeeds, configurations, and related safety factors.

2. Maintains the proper ground track on final approach.

3. Establishes the approach and landing configuration and power required.

4. Maintains the recommended approach airspeed, ±5 knots.

5. Makes smooth, timely, and correct control application during the final approach and transition from the approach to landing roundout.

6. Touches down smoothly at approximate stalling speed, beyond and within 500 feet of a specified point, with no appreciable drift, and airplane longitudinal axis aligned with the runway centerline.

7. Maintains directional control, increasing aileron deflection into the wind, as necessary, during the after-landing roll.

GUSTY WINDS AND TURBULENCE

A. For landing in significantly turbulent air, power-on approaches at an airspeed slightly above the normal approach speed should be used.

1. This provides for more positive control of the airplane in strong horizontal wind gusts or up and downdrafts.

2. The angle of descent is controlled primarily by pitch adjustments.

3. The airspeed is controlled primarily by changes in power.

4. Coordinated combination of both pitch and power adjustments is required.

5. The proper approach attitude and airspeed require a minimum roundout or flare and should result in little or no floating during the landing.

6. To maintain good control, the approach in turbulent air with a gusty crosswind may require the use of only partial wing flaps.

   a. With less than full flaps, the airplane will be in a higher nose-up attitude during the approach.

   b. Thus, it will require less of a pitch change to establish the landing attitude (i.e., a less dramatic roundout).

   c. The touchdown will also be at a higher airspeed to ensure more positive control.

   d. Also, using a reduced flap setting in turbulence means less secondary control surface area exposed to the airstream, which reduces the net effect of the turbulence.

7. These landing approaches are usually performed at the normal approach speed plus ½ the wind gust factor.

   a. EXAMPLE. If the normal speed is 70 kts and the wind gusts are of 15 kts, an airspeed of about 77 kts is appropriate.

   b. In any case, the airspeed and the amount of flaps should be according to the airplane manufacturer recommendations.

B. Adequate power should be used to maintain the proper airspeed throughout the approach. The throttle should be retarded to idling position only AFTER the main wheels contact the landing surface.

1. Care must be exercised in closing the throttle before the pilot is ready for touchdown. In this situation the sudden or premature closing of the throttle may cause a sudden increase in the descent rate, which could result in a hard landing.

2. Landings from power approaches in strong turbulence should be such that touchdown is made with the airplane in approximately level flight attitude.

GO-AROUNDS (REJECTED LANDINGS)

A. Occasionally it may be advisable for safety reasons to discontinue the landing approach and make another approach under more favorable conditions. These reasons include

1. Extremely low base-to-final turn.

2. Too high or too low final approach.

3. The unexpected appearance of hazards on the runway, e.g., another airplane. failing to clear the runway in time.

4. Wake turbulence from a preceding airplane.

5. Overtaking another airplane on final approach.

6. ATC instructions to "go-around."

B. The need to discontinue a landing may arise at any point in the landing process, but the most critical go-around is one started when very close to the ground. A timely decision must be made.

C. When the decision is made to discontinue an approach and perform a go-around, takeoff power should be applied immediately and the airplane's pitch attitude changed so as to slow or stop the descent.

   1. Adjust carburetor heat to OFF (cold) position.

   2. After the descent has been stopped, the landing flaps may be partially retracted or placed in the takeoff position, as recommended by the manufacturer.

      a. Caution must be used in retracting the flaps. Depending on the airplane's altitude and airspeed, it may be wise to retract the flaps intermittently in small increments to allow time for the airplane to accelerate progressively as the flaps are being raised.

      b. A sudden and complete retraction of the flaps at a very low airspeed could cause a loss of lift, resulting in the airplane settling onto the ground.

      c. Retract the landing gear (if so equipped) after a positive rate of climb has been established.

      d. Trim and climb at V_Y ±5 kts. Track the runway centerline until it is appropriate to turn to crosswind leg.

      e. Tell the control tower of your actions after you attain a positive rate of climb. Fly the airplane first, then communicate (not required if you initiated the go-around at the control tower's direction).

   3. When takeoff power is applied, it will usually be necessary to hold considerable forward pressure on the controls to maintain straight flight and a safe climb attitude.

      a. Since the airplane has been trimmed for the approach (a low power and airspeed condition), the nose will tend to rise sharply and veer to the left unless firm control pressures are applied.

      b. Forward elevator pressure must be applied to hold the nose in a safe climbing attitude. Right rudder pressure must be increased to counteract torque, or "P" factor, and to keep the nose straight.

      c. The airplane must be held in the proper flight attitude regardless of the amount of control pressure that is required. Frequently, this requires considerable pressure.

   4. While holding the airplane straight and in a safe climbing attitude, the pilot should retrim the airplane to relieve the heavy control pressures.

      a. Since the airspeed will build up rapidly with the application of take-off power and the controls will become more effective, this initial trim is to relieve the heavy pressures until a more precise trim can be made for the lighter pressures.

   5. If the pitch attitude is increased excessively in an effort to prevent the airplane from sinking onto the runway, it may cause the airplane to stall. This would be especially likely if no trim correction is made.

D. After a positive rate of climb is established, the airplane should be allowed to accelerate to the best rate of climb speed (V_Y) before the final flap retraction is accomplished.

   1. From this point on, the procedure is identical to that of a normal climb after takeoff. Climb to within 500 ft of traffic pattern altitude and turn onto the crosswind leg. Then continue around the traffic pattern.

GO-AROUNDS PTS

TASK: GO-AROUND (ASEL)
    PILOT OPERATION - 8
    REFERENCES: AC 61-21.

Objective. To determine that the applicant:

1. Exhibits knowledge by explaining the elements of the go-around procedure, including making timely decisions, recommended airspeeds, drag effect of wing flaps, and coping with undesirable pitch and yaw tendencies.

2. Makes a timely decision to go around from a rejected landing.

3. Applies takeoff power and establishes the proper pitch attitude to attain the recommended airspeed.

4. Retracts the wing flaps as recommended or at a safe altitude.

5. Trims the airplane and climbs at V_y ±10 knots, and tracks the appropriate traffic pattern.

SOFT-FIELD LANDINGS

A. Landing on fields that are rough or have soft surfaces (such as snow, sand, mud, or tall grass) requires special techniques. The objective of a soft-field landing is to land as softly as possible, with a nose-high attitude. This is to prevent getting bogged down and to prevent damage to the nose gear.

   1. Tailwheel airplane landings are slightly different and are discussed in H. below.

B. Elements of a soft-field landing.

   1. Normal approach assuming no obstacles are present.
   2. Some power left on all the way to touchdown.
   3. Full flaps.
   4. Slower than normal approach speed.
   5. Slow, patient roundout ensuring main gear touches down softly.

C. When landing on such surfaces, the pilot must control the airplane in a manner such that the wings support the weight of the airplane as long as practical. This minimizes drag and stresses on the landing gear from the rough or soft surface.

D. The approach for the soft field landing is similar to the normal approach used for long, firm landing areas.

E. The major difference between the two types of landings is that during the soft-field landing, the airplane is held 1 to 2 ft off the surface as long as possible to dissipate the forward speed sufficiently to allow the wheels to touch down gently at minumum speed.

   1. The use of flaps during soft-field landings will aid in touching down at minimum speed and is recommended whenever practical.

   2. In low-wing airplanes, however, the flaps may suffer damage from mud, stones, or slush thrown up by the wheels. In such cases, it may be advisable not to use flaps.

   3. If flaps are used, it is generally inadvisable to retract them during the after-landing roll because flap retraction usually is less important than the need for total concentration on maintaining full control of the airplane.

4. The FAA PTSs require the pilot to establish the manufacturer's recommended soft-field approach and landing configuration.

    a. Maintain recommended airspeed, ±5 kts, along centerline of landing site.

    b. Maintain directional control.

    c. Maintain proper position of flight controls and proper speed for taxiing on soft surface.

F. Touchdown on a soft or rough field should be made at the lowest possible airspeed with the airplane in a nose-high pitch attitude.

G. After the main wheels touch the surface, the pilot should hold sufficient back elevator pressure to keep the nosewheel off the ground until it can no longer aerodynamically be held off the field surface.

1. Let the nosewheel come down on its own. Maintain full up elevator (i.e., back pressure) at all times while on the soft surface (including while taxiing).

2. A slight addition of power during and immediately after touchdown usually will aid in easing the nosewheel down.

3. Brakes are not needed on a soft field. You should avoid using the brakes as this may tend to impose a heavy load on the nose gear due to premature or hard contact with the landing surface, causing the nosewheel to dig in.

    a. The soft or rough surface itself will provide sufficient reduction in the airplane's forward speed.

    b. Often, the pilot will need to increase power after landing on a very soft field to keep the airplane moving and prevent being stuck in the soft surface.

    c. Care must be taken not to taxi excessively fast because if you taxi onto a very soft area, the airplane may bog down and bend the landing gear and/or nose over.

H. In tailwheel airplanes, the tailwheel should touch down simultaneously with or just before the main wheels. The tailwheel should be held down by maintaining firm back elevator pressure throughout the landing roll. This will minimize any tendency for the airplane to nose over and will provide aerodynamic braking.

SOFT-FIELD LANDINGS PTS

TASK: *SOFT-FIELD LANDING (ASEL)*
PILOT OPERATION - 7
REFERENCES: AC 61-21.

Objective. *To determine that the applicant:*

1. *Exhibits knowledge by explaining the elements of a soft-field landing procedure, including airspeeds, configurations, operations on various surfaces, and related safety factors.*

2. *Evaluates obstructions, landing surface, and wind conditions.*

3. *Establishes the recommended soft-field approach and landing configuration and airspeed.*

4. *Maintains recommended airspeed, ±5 knots, along the extended runway centerline.*

5. *Touches down smoothly at minimum descent rate and groundspeed, with no appreciable drift and the airplane longitudinal axis aligned with runway centerline.*

6. *Maintains directional control during the after-landing roll.*

7. *Maintains proper position of flight controls and sufficient speed to taxi on soft surface.*

SHORT-FIELD LANDINGS

A. This maximum performance operation requires the use of procedures and techniques for the approach and landing at fields which have a relatively short landing area or where an approach must be made over obstacles which limit the available landing area. You must consider the landing surface and wind conditions.

    1. As in takeoff, short-field landing is one of the most critical maximum performance operations. It requires the pilot to fly the airplane at one of its critical performance capabilities while close to the ground in order to safely land within confined areas.

    2. This low-speed type of <u>power-on approach</u> is closely related to the performance of "flight at minimum controllable airspeeds."

B. The pilot must have precise, positive control over the rate of descent and airspeed to produce an approach that will clear any obstacles, result in little or no floating during the roundout, and bring the airplane to a stop in the shortest possible distance.

C. Elements of a short-field landing.

    1. Steeper than normal approach.
    2. Full flaps.
    3. Slower than normal approach speed.
    4. Little or no float at touchdown.

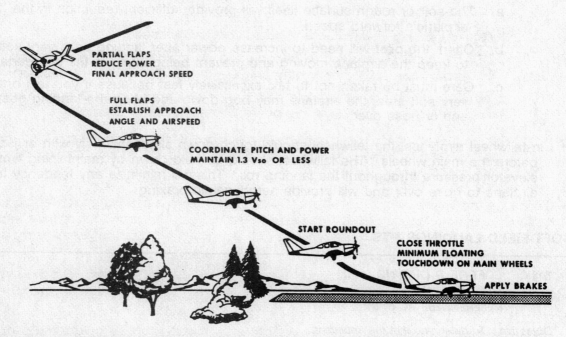

PARTIAL FLAPS
REDUCE POWER
FINAL APPROACH SPEED

FULL FLAPS
ESTABLISH APPROACH
ANGLE AND AIRSPEED

COORDINATE PITCH AND POWER
MAINTAIN 1.3 Vso OR LESS

START ROUNDOUT

CLOSE THROTTLE
MINIMUM FLOATING
TOUCHDOWN ON MAIN WHEELS

APPLY BRAKES

D. Use the procedures for landing in a short field or for landing approaches over 50-ft obstacles as recommended in the airplane operating manual.

    1. These procedures generally involve the use of full flaps and starting the final approach from an altitude of at least 500 ft higher than the touchdown area.

    2. In the absence of the manufacturer's recommended approach speed, a speed of not more than 1.3 times V_{so} should be used.

        a. EXAMPLE. In an airplane which stalls at 60 kts with power off and flaps and landing gear extended, the approach speed should be no higher than 78 kts.

        b. In gusty air, no more than ½ the gust factor should be added.

    c.   An excessive amount of airspeed could result in a touchdown too far from the runway threshold and an after-landing roll that exceeds the available landing area.

E.   After the landing gear and full flaps have been extended, the pilot should simultaneously adjust the power and the pitch attitude to establish and maintain the proper descent angle and airspeed.

   1.   The pitch attitude is adjusted as necessary to establish and maintain the desired rate or angle of descent. Power is adjusted to maintain the desired airspeed.

      a.   However, a coordinated combination of both pitch and power adjustments is required.

      b.   When this is done properly, very little change in the airplane's pitch attitude is necessary to make corrections in the angle of descent and only small power changes are needed to control the airspeed.

   2.   If it appears that the obstacle clearance is excessive and touchdown will occur well beyond the desired spot, leaving insufficient room to stop, power may be reduced while lowering the pitch attitude to increase the rate of descent.

   3.   If it appears that the descent angle will not ensure safe clearance of obstacles, power should be increased while simultaneously raising the pitch attitude to decrease the rate of descent.

   4.   Care must be taken to avoid an excessively low airspeed.

      a.   If the speed is allowed to become too slow, an increase in pitch and application of full power may only result in a further rate of descent.

      b.   This occurs when the angle of attack is so great and creates so much drag that the maximum available power is insufficient to overcome it.

   5.   Forward slips can be used for an even steeper descent angle if the airplane manufacturer approves of slips with flaps (see the "Slips" sideheading on page 151).

F.   Because the final approach over obstacles is made at a steep approach angle and close to the airplane's stalling speed, the beginning of the roundout or flare must be judged accurately to avoid either flying into the ground or stalling prematurely and sinking rapidly.

   1.   Touchdown should occur at the minimum controllable airspeed with the airplane in approximately the pitch attitude that will result in a power-off stall when the throttle is closed.

   2.   Care must be exercised to avoid closing the throttle rapidly before the pilot is ready for touchdown, as closing the throttle may result in an immediate increase in the rate of descent and a hard landing.

G.   Upon touchdown, the airplane should be held in this positive pitch attitude as long as the elevators remain effective. Tailwheel airplanes should be firmly held in a three-point attitude. This provides aerodynamic braking by the wings.

H.   Immediately upon touchdown and closing the throttle, the brakes should be applied evenly and firmly to minimize the after-landing roll. The airplane should be stopped within the shortest possible distance consistent with safety.

I.   The FAA PTSs require

    1.   Maintaining recommended airspeed ± 5 kts.
    2.   A touchdown beyond and within 200 ft of a specified point.
    3.   Applying brakes to stop in the shortest distance consistent with safety.
    4.   Maintaining directional control.

SHORT-FIELD LANDINGS PTS

TASK: SHORT-FIELD LANDING (ASEL)
PILOT OPERATION - 7
REFERENCES: AC 61-21.

Objective. To determine that the applicant:

1. Exhibits knowledge by explaining the elements of a short-field landing, including airspeeds, configurations, and related safety factors.

2. Considers obstructions, landing surface, and wind conditions.

3. Selects a suitable touchdown point.

4. Establishes the short-field landing configuration, airspeed, and descent angle.

5. Maintains control of the descent rate and the recommended airspeed, ±5 knots, along the extended runway centerline.

6. Touches down beyond and within 200 feet of a specified point, with minimum float and no appreciable drift and airplane longitudinal axis aligned with the runway centerline.

7. Maintains directional control during the after-landing roll.

8. Applies braking and controls, as necessary, to stop in the shortest distance, consistent with safety.

TAILWHEEL AIRPLANE LANDINGS

A.   The final approach and roundout for "normal" landings in tailwheel airplanes are the same as in a nosewheel airplane. The difference begins at touchdown and continues through the after-landing roll.

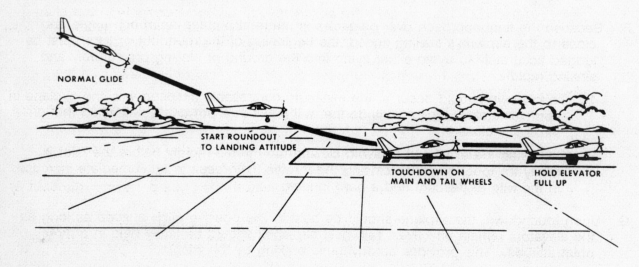

1.   The roundout and touchdown should be so timed that the wheels of the main landing gear and tailwheel touch down simultaneously (3-point landing). This requires fine timing, technique, and judgment of distance and altitude.

a. The tailwheel is at the very back of the airplane and is much less susceptible to damage than the main wheels. This situation is opposite to nosewheel airplanes, for which you must worry more about the nosewheel than the main wheels.

2. When the three wheels of a tailwheel airplane make contact with the ground, carefully ease the elevator control fully back to hold the tailwheel on the ground.

   a. This provides more positive directional control of the airplane equipped with a steerable tailwheel, and prevents any tendency for the airplane to nose over.

   b. If the tailwheel is not on the ground, easing back on the elevator control may cause the airplane to become airborne again because the change in attitude will increase the angle of attack and produce enough lift for the airplane to fly.

3. The pilot must be alert for directional control difficulties immediately upon and after touchdown due to the ground friction on the wheels.

   a. The friction creates a pivot point on which the airplane can swing to the side.

   b. This is especially true in tailwheel airplanes because, unlike nosewheel airplanes, the center of gravity (CG) is behind the main wheels. This means there is more fuselage and more weight on one side (rear) of the pivot point, which makes the airplane more likely to pivot or swing.

   c. Any difference between the direction in which the tailwheel airplane is traveling and the direction it is headed will cause the airplane to tend to swerve.

   d. Loss of directional control may lead to an aggravated, uncontrolled, tight turn on the ground, called a "ground loop."

   e. The combination of centrifugal force acting on the CG and ground friction of the main wheels resisting it during the ground loop may cause the airplane to tip or lean enough for the outside wingtip to touch the ground. It may even impose a sideward force strong enough to collapse the landing gear.

   f. Tailwheel airplanes are most susceptible to ground loops late in the after-landing roll because rudder effectiveness decreases with the decreasing flow of air along the rudder surface as the airplane slows.

B. **Wheel landings.** Wheel landings are made on the two main wheels, i.e., with the tailwheel off the ground.

   1. They are a difficult maneuver and should not be attempted by student pilots prior to supervision by a CFI.

   2. They should not be undertaken in crosswind situations due to the difficulty of directional control since the tailwheel is in the air.

   3. Tailwheel landings consist of flying the airplane to the ground, i.e., no roundout or a very slight roundout.

   4. The main wheels are kept on the ground by slight forward pressure. This is similar to holding an airplane on the ground beyond rotating speed on takeoff.

C. **Soft-field landings.** In tailwheel airplanes, the tailwheel should touch down simultaneously with or just before the main wheels. The tailwheel should be held down by maintaining firm back elevator pressure throughout the landing roll. This will minimize any tendency for the airplane to nose over and will provide aerodynamic braking.

VISUAL APPROACH SLOPE INDICATOR (VASI)

A.   The VASI at airports that have them provides a color-coded visual glidepath using a system of two or three light units positioned alongside the runway, near the designated touchdown point. It ensures safety by providing a visual glidepath which clears all obstructions in the final approach area.

    1.   The VASI is especially effective at night and during approaches over water or featureless terrain where other sources of visual reference are lacking or misleading.

    2.   Once the principles and color code of the lighting system are understood, flying the VASI is a simple matter of noting the lights' colors and adjusting the airplane's rate of descent to stay on the visual glide slope.

    3.   It provides optimum descent guidance for landing and minimizes the possibility of under- or overshooting the designated touchdown area.

B.   Each light unit projects a beam of light having a white segment in the upper part of the beam and a red segment in the lower part of the beam. Your position thus determines which color(s) you see.

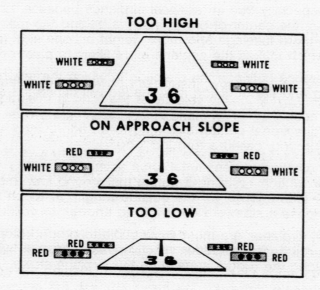

    1.   When on the proper glidepath, the pilot will overshoot the downwind bars and undershoot the upwind bars. Thus, the downwind bars will be seen as white and the upwind bars as red.

    2.   From a position below the glidepath the pilot will see all the light bars as red. From above the glidepath all the light bars will appear white.

    3.   Passing through the glidepath from a low position is indicated to the pilot by a transition in color from red to white. This will occur if you maintain or gain altitude.

    4.   Passing through the glidepath from a high position is indicated to the pilot by a transition in color from white to red. This will occur if you are above the VASI glidepath and your rate of descent is too great (i.e., exceeds the VASI glidepath).

C. Three-bar VASI installations provide two visual glidepaths.

    1. The lower glidepath is provided by the near and middle bars and is normally set at a 3° incline. The upper glidepath, provided by the middle and far bars, is normally ¼° higher. This higher glidepath is intended for use only by high cockpit aircraft to provide a sufficient threshold crossing height.

    2. When approaching a 3-bar VASI it is not necessary to use all three bars. The near and middle bars constitue a two-bar VASI for using the lower glidepath. Also, the middle and far bars constitute a 2-bar VASI for using the upper glidepath.

    3. Using the upper glidepath just means you will come in a little steeper and land a little longer. This is not a real problem as long as the runway is long enough.

D. The Tri-Color Approach Slope Indicator normally consists of a single light unit, projecting a three-color visual approach path into the final approach area of the runway upon which the system is installed.

    1. In this system, the below glidepath indication is red, the above glidepath indication is amber, and the on-path indication is green.

FAULTY APPROACHES AND LANDINGS

A. Low final approach.

    1. When the base leg is too low, insufficient power is used, landing flaps are extended prematurely, or the velocity of the wind is misjudged, sufficient altitude may be lost such that the airplane is well below the proper final approach path.

    2. In this situation, the pilot would have to apply considerable power to fly the airplane (at an excessively low altitude) up to the runway threshold.

    3. When you realize that the runway will not be reached unless appropriate action is taken, immediately apply power to maintain the airspeed while the pitch attitude is raised to increase lift and stop the descent.

    4. When the proper approach path has been intercepted, the correct approach attitude should be reestablished and the power reduced again.

    5. DO NOT increase the pitch attitude without increasing the power, since the airplane will decelerate rapidly. It may approach the critical angle of attack and stall.

B. Slow final approach.

    1. When the airplane is flown at too slow an airspeed on the final approach, the pilot's judgment of the rate of sink (descent) and the height of roundout may be defective.

    2. During an excessively slow approach, the wing is operating near the critical angle of attack and the airplane may stall or sink rapidly, hitting the ground hard.

    3. When you notice a slow-speed approach, apply power to accelerate the airplane and increase the lift to reduce the sink rate and to prevent a stall. You should NOT increase the angle of attack as this may cause a stall.

C. High roundout.

1. When the roundout has been made too rapidly, the airplane is flying level too high above the runway.

2. Continuing the roundout would further reduce the airspeed, resulting in an increase in angle of attack to the critical angle.

3. This would result in the airplane stalling and dropping hard onto the runway.

4. To prevent this, the pitch attitude should be held constant until the airplane decelerates enough to again start descending. Then the roundout can be continued to establish the proper landing attitude.

5. This technique should be used only when there is adequate airspeed and runway. It may be necessary to add a slight amount of power to keep the airspeed from decreasing excessively and to avoid losing lift too rapidly.

6. Be careful adding power near stall speed because this may result in uncoordination of flight controls.

    a. The result may be that the left wing stalls first, falling, and contacting the ground.

    b. Also, violent forward pitching may cause the airplane to hit the ground nose first, damaging both the propeller and the nosewheel.

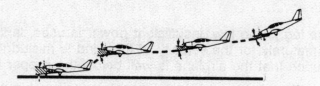

D. Late or rapid roundout.

1. Starting the roundout too late or pulling the elevator control back too rapidly to prevent the airplane from touching down prematurely can impose a heavy load factor on the wing and cause an accelerated stall.

2. Suddenly increasing the angle of attack and stalling the airplane during a roundout is a dangerous situation. It may cause the airplane to land very hard on the main landing gear and then bounce back into the air.

3. As the airplane contacts the ground, the tail will be forced down very rapidly by the back pressure on the elevator and by inertia acting downward on the tail.

4. Increased power and increased angle of attack may provide relief.

E. Floating during roundout.

1. If the airspeed on final approach is excessive, it will usually result in the airplane "floating." Before touchdown can be made, the airplane may be well past the desired landing point and the available runway may be insufficient.

2. When diving an airplane on final approach to land at the proper point, there will be an appreciable increase in airspeed. Consequently, the proper touchdown attitude cannot be established without producing an excessive angle of attack and lift. This will usually cause the airplane to "float" or even result in "ballooning."

3.   Usually, a go around is appropriate, especially if there is limited runway remaining.

F.   Ballooning during roundout.

1.   If the pilot misjudges the rate of descent during a landing and thinks the airplane is sinking faster than it should, there is a tendency to increase the pitch attitude and angle of attack too rapidly. This not only stops the descent, but actually starts the airplane climbing. This climbing during the roundout is known as "ballooning."

2.   Ballooning can be dangerous because the height above the ground increases and the airplane may rapidly approach a stall. The altitude gained in each instance will depend on the airspeed or the rapidity with which the pitch attitude is increased.

3.   When ballooning is slight, a constant landing attitude should be held and the airplane allowed to gradually decelerate and settle onto the runway.

4.   Depending on the severity of ballooning, the use of throttle may be helpful in cushioning the landing. By adding power, thrust can be increased to keep the airspeed from decelerating too rapidly and the wings from suddenly losing lift. But the throttle must be closed immediately after touchdown.

5.   When ballooning is excessive, it is best to EXECUTE A GO-AROUND IMMEDIATELY. DO NOT ATTEMPT TO SALVAGE THE LANDING. Power must be applied before the airplane enters a stall.

G.   Bouncing during touchdown.

1.   When the airplane contacts the ground with a sharp impact as the result of an improper attitude or an excessive rate of sink, it tends to "bounce" back into the air. Though the airplane's tires and shock struts provide some springing action, the airplane does not bounce as does a rubber ball. Instead, it rebounds into the air because the wing's angle of attack was abruptly increased, producing a sudden addition of lift.

2.   The abrupt change in angle of attack is the result of inertia instantly forcing the airplane's tail downward when the main wheels contact the ground sharply. The severity of the "bounce" depends on the airspeed at the moment of contact and the degree to which the angle of attack or pitch attitude was increased.

3.   The corrective action for a bounce is the same as for ballooning and similarly depends on its severity.

a.   When it is very slight and there is no extreme change in the airplane's pitch attitude, a followup landing may be executed by applying sufficient power to cushion the subsequent touchdown and smoothly adjusting the pitch to the proper touchdown attitude.

b.   Remember that addition of power requires immediate right rudder to preclude a yaw to the left. A yaw to the left means uncoordinated flight controls, which may result in the left wing stalling first and dropping to strike the ground.

H. Hard landing.

1. When the airplane contacts the ground during landing, its vertical speed is instantly reduced to zero. Unless provision is made to slow this vertical speed and cushion the impact of touchdown, the force of contact with the ground may be so great as to cause structural damage to the airplane.

2. The purpose of pneumatic tires, rubber or oleo shock absorbers, and other such devices is, in part, to cushion the impact and to increase the time it takes to stop the airplane's vertical descent.

a. The importance of this cushion may be understood from the computation that a 6-inch free fall on landing is roughly equal to a 340-ft per minute descent. Within a fraction of a second the airplane must be slowed from this rate of vertical descent to zero, without damage.

b. During this time, the landing gear together with some aid from the lift of the wings must supply whatever force is needed to counteract the force of the airplane's inertia and weight.

I. Touchdown in a drift or crab.

1. At times the pilot may correct for wind drift by crabbing on the final approach. If the roundout and touchdown are made while the airplane is drifting or in a crab as illustrated next, it will contact the ground while moving sideways. This will impose extreme side loads on the landing gear, and if severe enough, may cause structural failure.

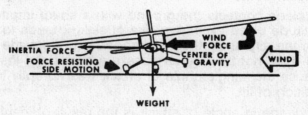

2. The most effective method to prevent drift in primary training aircraft is the "wing-low method" (illustrated on page 154). This technique keeps the longitudinal axis of the airplane aligned with both the runway and the direction of motion throughout the approach and touchdown.

3. There are three factors that will cause the longitudinal axis and the direction of motion to be misaligned during touchdown.

a. Drifting.
b. Crabbing.
c. A combination of both.

J. Ground loop.

1. A ground loop is an uncontrolled turn during ground operation that may occur while taxiing or taking off, but especially during the after-landing roll.

a. It is not always caused by drift or weathervaning, although one of these may cause the initial swerve.

b. Careless use of the rudder, an uneven ground surface, or a soft spot that retards one main wheel of the airplane may also cause a swerve.

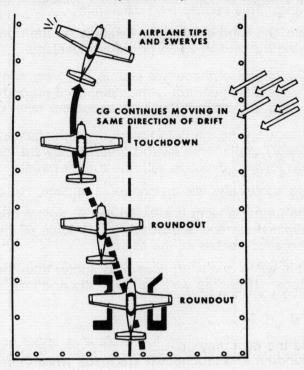

2. The initial swerve tends to make the airplane ground loop, whether it be a tailwheel or nosewheel airplane.

a. For airplanes equipped with a tailwheel, the forces that cause a ground loop increase as the swerve increases. The farther the airplane turns, the greater the angle between the path of the airplane (the direction in which it was moving before the problem began) and the direction the wheels are facing.

1) Since the CG is behind the main wheels, the tail tends to swing around, making this angle greater and greater. The wheels are not lined up with the direction they are moving (i.e., they are skidding sideways).

2) Thus, the wheels are gripping the pavement rather than rolling over it. The outside wheel becomes a pivot point, and the airplane could possibly tip over that point.

b. Airplanes with a nosewheel are somewhat less prone to ground loop. Since the center of gravity is located forward of the main landing gear on these airplanes, inertia acting on the center of gravity will tend to stop the swerving action when a swerve develops.

3. If the airplane touches down while drifting or in a crab, the pilot should apply aileron toward the high wing and stop the swerve with the rudder.

K. Wing rising after touchdown.

1. When landing in a crosswind there may be instances when a wing will rise during the after-landing roll. This may occur whether or not there is a loss of directional control, depending on the amount of crosswind and the degree of corrective action.

a.   When an airplane is rolling on the ground in a crosswind condition, the upwind wing is receiving a greater force from the wind than the downwind wing. This causes a lift differential.

b.   Also, the wind striking the fuselage on the upwind side may further raise the wing by tending to tip or roll the fuselage.

2.   When the effects of these two factors are great enough, one wing may rise even though directional control is maintained. If no correction is applied, it is possible that a wing will rise sufficiently to cause the other one to strike the ground.

3.   In the event a wing starts to rise during the after-landing roll, the pilot should immediately apply more aileron pressure toward the high wing and continue to maintain forward direction with the rudder pedals.

a.   The sooner the aileron control is applied, the more effective it will be.

b.   The further a wing is allowed to rise before taking corrective action, the more airplane surface is exposed to the force of the crosswind. This diminishes the effectiveness of the aileron.

c.   Also, when one wing rises or is lighter than the other, the wheel on that side does not grip as well, so it will slip and lose contact with the ground.

L.   Other Landing Errors.

1.   Talking on the radio before the airplane is under control as in a go-around, crosswind landing, etc., instead of: Aviate - Navigate - Communicate.

2.   Shoving the control yoke forward trying to force the airplane onto the ground. As the airplane begins to bounce or swerve, students often think they are anchoring the plane down.

3.   Relaxing crosswind control inputs before landing roll is complete.

4.   Leaving power on throughout touchdown and ground roll and wondering why the airplane floats.

5.   Adding flaps out of habit instead of necessity (if you had to extend your downwind, you may not need flaps on base this time).

6.   Staring at the runway and not watching pitch attitude, primary airspeed indicator, and traffic.

7.   Not listening for your airplane identification number, i.e., missing calls on the radio, especially during touch-and-go landings.

8.   Not flying rectangular airport traffic patterns, forgetting to correct for drift, or just sloppy directional control.

9.   Flying patterns too close or too wide.

10. Looking too close or too far. When you first turn final, you see the runway as a whole and as you get closer that focus comes to about 20 to 50 ft ahead just at touchdown. If you focus too closely, you see a motion blur.

11. Correcting for a nonexistent crosswind, e.g., correcting for crosswind on the last landing that has died down for the next landing.

CHAPTER NINE
SLOWFLIGHT, STALLS, AND SPINS

Slowflight, stalls, and spins each involve flight at very low airspeeds. The phenomena controlling these maneuvers are also discussed in Chapter 2, "Airplanes and Aerodynamics."

Slowflight is flight in the entire low-speed range at which a reduction in speed imposes more drag. It is flight at lower than best angle-of-climb airspeed. Slowflight wastes altitude.

Note some define slowflight as airspeeds where a reduction in speed imposes more drag. This is flight at lower than the speed for optimum glide and maximum range. This is also known as the "region of reverse command." In this book, we limit slowflight to airspeeds below V_x, because if you wish to gain altitude, especially in an emergency situation, you should use full power at V_x.

Minimum controllable airspeed is the airspeed below which flightpath control is impossible. Any angle-of-attack increase or power reduction will cause a stall. Speeds well below the lowest speeds attainable without power can be sustained with added power.

A *stall* occurs when the wings' angle of attack with respect to the relative wind exceeds the critical angle of attack and produces insufficient lift relative to the increasing drag. Inadvertent stalls result when pilots already in slowflight attempt to increase altitude by raising the plane's nose.

A *spin* is a descent along a spiral path of steep pitch and small radius in which the inner wing has more drag and less lift than the outer wing; i.e., the inner wing is more stalled than the outer wing. Skidding away from the center of the spiral while stalled characterizes the spin flightpath.

IMPORTANT: Whenever you are in slowflight, you will GAIN altitude by adding full power and slowly lowering the nose to increase airspeed to V_x (the best angle of climb) or to V_y (the best rate of climb). Remember to avoid the natural tendency to pull the controls back in slowflight situations where more altitude is needed. This is what contributes to most stall/spin accidents.

After sufficient dual instruction, you should practice slowflight and stalls (as well as all other flight maneuvers) during solo practice flight (obtain permission for each solo maneuver from your CFI).

This chapter covers 3 of the 34 "Tasks" in the FAA Practical Test Standards (PTSs). They are

1.   Stall - Power-On
2.   Stall - Power-Off
3.   Maneuvering During Slow Flight

STALLS

A.   A stall occurs when the smooth airflow over the airplane's wing is disrupted, as illustrated below. Lift degenerates and drag increases dramatically. Recall that lift (lower air pressure on top of the wing than on the bottom) is created by the top of the wing being curved and longer than the bottom, i.e., the air going over the top of the wing has further to go. The smooth airflow is disrupted (resulting in the loss of lift and an increase in drag) when the critical angle of attack is exceeded. The angle of attack is the angle between the relative wind and the chord line of the wing. See the "Definitions" sideheading in Chapter 2 of *PRIVATE PILOT HANDBOOK*.

1.   Stalls can occur AT ANY AIRSPEED, IN ANY ATTITUDE, WITH ANY POWER SETTING, but stall accidents usually occur when a pilot wishes to gain altitude.

2.   For the pilot trainee, the practice of stall recovery and the development of awareness of imminent stalls are of primary importance.

3.   The objectives in performing intentional stalls are

     a.   To familiarize the pilot with the conditions that produce stalls.
     b.   To assist in recognizing an approaching stall.
     c.   To develop the habit of taking prompt preventive or corrective action.

B.   Pilots must recognize the flight conditions conducive to stalls and know how to apply the necessary corrective action.

1.   Vision is useful in detecting a stall condition by noting the attitude of the airplane. This sense can be fully relied on only when the stall is the result of an intentional unusual attitude of the airplane.

2.   Hearing is also helpful in sensing a stall condition, since the tone level and intensity of sounds incident to flight decrease as the airspeed decreases.

3.   Kinesthesia, or the mind's sensing of changes in direction or speed of motion, is probably the most important and the best indicator to the trained and experienced pilot. If this sensitivity is properly developed, it will warn of a decrease in speed or the beginning of a settling or "mushing" of the airplane.

4.   The feeling of control pressures is also very important. As speed is reduced, the "live" resistance to pressures on the controls becomes progressively less.

     a.   The airplane controls become less and less effective as one approaches the critical angle of attack.

     b.   In a complete stall, all controls can be moved with almost no resistance and with little immediate effect on the airplane.

C. Intentional stalls should be performed at an altitude that will provide adequate height above the ground for recovery and return to normal level flight. This is usually several thousand feet AGL for the student pilot in trainer airplanes.

    1. The FAA PTSs require that you must not fly below 1,500 ft AGL; i.e., full recovery must be made above 1,500 ft AGL.

D. Several types of stall warning indicators, e.g., horns and lights, have been developed that warn the pilot of an approaching stall.

    1. The use of such indicators is valuable and desirable, but the reason for practicing stalls is to learn to recognize them without the benefit of warning devices in the event such devices become inoperative.

    2. Also, it is instructive that in many accidents (i.e., critical situations), pilots have ignored stall warning devices.

E. Most modern airplanes are designed so that the wings will stall progressively outward from the wing roots to the wingtips.

    1. The wings are designed so that the wingtips have less angle of incidence than the wing roots. Angle of incidence is the angle between the chord line of the wing and the longitudinal axis of the airplane.

    2. Thus, the tips of such wings have a smaller angle of attack than the wing roots during flight.

    3. Now is the time to review Chapter 2, "Airplanes and Aerodynamics," if you had difficulty understanding it previously.

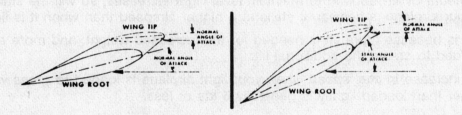

    4. Since a stall is caused by exceeding the critical angle of attack, the wing roots of an airplane will exceed the critical angle before the wingtips. Therefore, the roots will stall first. The wings are designed in this manner so that control of the ailerons (which are located toward the tips of the wings) will be available at high angles of attack (slow airspeed) and give the airplane more stable stalling characteristics.

F. Slow flight at minimum controllable airspeed (discussed as a separate sideheading on page 187) means flight at airspeed such that any further increase in the angle of attack or reduction in power will result in a stall.

G. Imminent stalls (discussed below as a separate sideheading on page 187) occur when the airplane is approaching a stall but is not allowed to completely stall, i.e., stall recovery techniques are implemented prior to a full stall.

    1. Conversely, when recovery techniques are not implemented until the stall occurs, the occurence is referred to as a "full stall," or just a "stall."

H. Landing stalls, also called power-off stalls (discussed below as a separate sideheading on page 184) occur when the airplane is in a landing configuration, i.e., with power off, gear down, and flaps down.

I. Departure stalls, also called power-on stalls (discussed below as a separate sideheading on page 181) occur when the airplane is in a takeoff configuration, i.e., with power at takeoff setting, gear down, and flaps to the takeoff setting.

J. Accelerated stalls occur at high indicated airspeeds when excessive maneuvering loads are imposed by steep turns, pull-ups, or other abrupt changes in the flightpath. If not corrected for immediately, they can result in complete loss of flight control (through excessive airspeed and/or "G" loads).

FACTORS AFFECTING STALL SPEED

A. As the amount of lift required to maintain level flight increases, so will the stall speed. When your airplane is heavier, it stalls at a higher airspeed than when it is lighter.

    1. This is because more lift is needed for the increased weight, and more airspeed is needed to create the additional lift.

    2. The increase in stall speed when your light airplane is loaded to gross weight rather than loaded lightly is generally 5 kts or less.

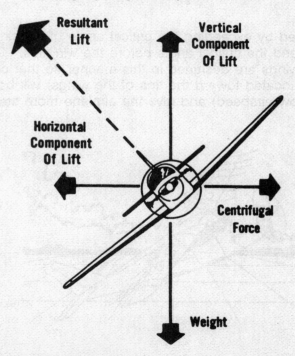

B. When your airplane is banked, it stalls at a higher airspeed than when it is in straight flight.

    1. The vertical component of lift must remain equal to weight to maintain a constant vertical speed (i.e., level flight).

    2. In a bank, the lift generated by the wings is separated into vertical lift and horizontal lift (the horizontal lift making the airplane turn).

    3. Therefore, more total lift is required when the airplane is banked to retain the same amount of vertical lift.

    4. Since more lift is required in a turn (bank), the critical angle of attack is reached at a higher airspeed than in straight-and-level flight (when the airplane is not banked).

    5. The steeper the bank angle, the more vertical lift is transferred horizontally to turn the airplane.

        a. Therefore, total lift must increase enough that the remaining vertical lift is still enough to counteract gravity, to maintain the same altitude.

        b. The presence of horizontal lift increases load factor because of centrifugal force.

        c. With this increased wing load, the critical angle of attack is reached earlier.

        d. A stall, therefore, occurs at a higher airspeed.

    6. Stall speed increases up to 10 kts at 40° banks and up to 15-20 kts at 60° banks in light trainer airplanes.

C. Another situation in which total lift required will be greater than weight occurs in pulling an airplane out of a dive (a pull-up). The lift force must not only support the weight of the airplane, but must also overcome its downward momentum. Since the required lift is greater, the stall speed is higher in a pull-up.

D. How an airplane is loaded also affects stall speed. If it is loaded with all the weight to the front, the wings bear more load and require more lift. This means a higher stall speed.

    1. If the weight is more toward the rear, the horizontal stabilizer has to exert less negative lift, which means the wings do not have to exert as much positive lift. This means a lower stall speed.

    2. Recall that the center of gravity is ahead of the center of lift which requires the horizontal stabilizer to exert negative lift. See the "Airplane Stability" sideheading in Chapter 2.

    3. The change in stall speed caused by moving the center of gravity from the rear CG limit to the forward CG limit is about 5 kts on most light airplanes.

E. The use of power affects stall speed. When the airplane is at a higher angle of attack and at high power settings, the thrust force of the propeller is slightly downward so the wings do not have to produce quite as much lift. Also, there is less tail "down force" at slow airspeeds and higher angles of attack. Thus, stall speed is slightly lower with high power settings.

F. Flaps increase lift (and drag) for any given airspeed or angle of attack. Thus, flaps lower your stall speed. Refer to your airplane operating manual for the effect of flaps on stall speed.

G. Summary of factors affecting stall speed.

    1. Gross weight.

    2. Turns.

    3. Pull-ups.

    4. CG location.

    5. Power.

    6. Flaps.

STALL RECOVERY FUNDAMENTALS

A. The real objective is not to learn how to stall an airplane but rather how to recognize an imminent stall and take prompt corrective action.

    1. However, to demonstrate having met this objective on the FAA practical test, the applicant must be able to "perform" all the stalls.

    2. The required stalls are described in the subsequent sideheadings.

B. Stall recovery consists of THREE STEPS which must be taken in a COORDINATED manner.

    1. First, at the indication of a stall, the pitch attitude and angle of attack must be decreased positively and immediately.

        a. Since the basic cause of a stall is always an excessive angle of attack, first eliminate the cause by releasing the back elevator pressure (move the elevator control forward) that created that angle of attack.

        b. This lowers the nose and returns the wing to an effective angle of attack.

        c. The amount of elevator control pressure or movement used depends on the airplane's design. In some airplanes a moderate movement of the elevator control, perhaps slightly forward of neutral, is enough. In others, a forcible push to the full forward position may be required.

        d. The object is to reduce the angle of attack, but only enough to allow the wings to regain lift. Remember, you want to minimize your altitude loss.

    2. Second, the maximum allowable power should be applied to increase the altitude.

        a. Generally, the throttle should be promptly but smoothly advanced to the maximum allowable power setting.

        b. Usually, the greater the power applied, the less the loss in altitude.

        c. As always, never allow the RPM to exceed the red line (maximum allowable RPM) marked on the tachometer.

        d. Although stall recoveries should be practiced with and without the use of power, in most actual stalls the application of power is an integral part of the stall recovery.

    3. Third, regain straight-and-level flight with coordinated use of all controls.

C. CFIs teach and demonstrate stalls in many different ways:

1. For some, the first few practices should include only approaches to stalls, with recovery initiated as soon as the first buffeting or partial loss of control is noted. In this way the pilot can become familiar with the indications of an imminent stall without actually stalling the airplane.

2. For other CFIs, the best approach is to demonstrate and recover from a full stall cleanly and quickly with confidence. This is followed by multiple executions by the student pilot. The intent is to teach and practice stalls as any other flight maneuver, i.e., not one to be apprehensive about.

STALL - POWER-ON

A. Power-on stall recoveries are practiced from straight climbs and climbing turns with 10° to 30° banks to simulate an accidental stall occurring during takeoffs and departure climbs.

1. Airplanes equipped with flaps and/or retractable landing gear normally should be in the takeoff configuration.

2. You should also practice power-on stalls with the airplane in a clean configuration (flaps and/or gear retracted), as in departure and normal climbs.

B. After establishing the takeoff or departure configuration, the airplane should be slowed to the normal lift-off speed while clearing the area for other air traffic. You can reduce power to help reduce airspeed.

1. Reach an altitude that will allow full recovery to be completed no lower than 1,500 ft AGL.

2. CLEARING TURNS ARE REQUIRED PRIOR TO INITIATING A DEPARTURE STALL.

   a. Clearing turns are at least two distinct 90° turns during which you either complete a 180° turn or regain your original direction.

      1) The FAA does not require a specific procedure.

      2) Accordingly, procedures vary with the area, CFIs, etc. For instance, a 360° turn is acceptable.

   b. Clearing turns provide you with an opportunity to observe nearby traffic.

      1) Clearing turns also increase the probability of nearby traffic observing you.

      2) Your airspeed, altitude, etc. should be such that you are ready and able to execute your stall upon completion of your second 90° turn and with recovery complete no lower than 1,500 ft AGL.

3. The purpose of reducing the speed to lift-off speed before the throttle is advanced to the recommended setting is to avoid an excessively steep nose-up attitude for a long period before the airplane stalls (and to avoid a stall at an excessively steep nose-up attitude).

4. When the desired speed (i.e., lift-off speed) is attained, raise the nose and increase the throttle to takeoff power for the takeoff stall or to the recommended climb power for the departure stall.

    a. Once you have begun to enter the power-on stall, you should not reduce power to induce the stall.

    b. The stall is induced by increasing back pressure on the flight controls.

C. After the takeoff or climb attitude is established, the pitch attitude is increased to an attitude obviously impossible for the airplane to maintain and is held at that attitude until the full stall occurs. Maintain coordinated flight.

1. In most airplanes, after attaining the stalling attitude, the elevator control must be moved progressively further back as the airspeed decreases until, at the full stall, it will have reached its limit and cannot be moved back any more.

2. Flightpath of a power-on stall.

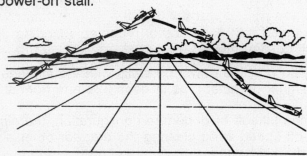

D. Diagram of a power-on stall.

1. At point A, power is temporarily reduced to help slow the airplane while pitch is increased, maintaining the same altitude during the entry. At about V_x, climb power is added and a climb is begun.

2. During interval B, the angle of attack is increasing with respect to the relative wind. Note that airspeed is decreasing.

3. At point C, the critical angle of attack is exceeded, resulting in a loss of lift, i.e., the stall occurs.

4. At point D, the pitch attitude has decreased due to a lack of lift, but the angle of attack has not decreased since the airplane is now dropping almost straight down. The pilot must release back pressure on the control yoke.

5. At point E, the pitch attitude has been decreased sufficiently so that the air is flowing smoothly over the wings, i.e., the airplane is flying. All that remains for recovery is a smooth return to straight-and-level flight.

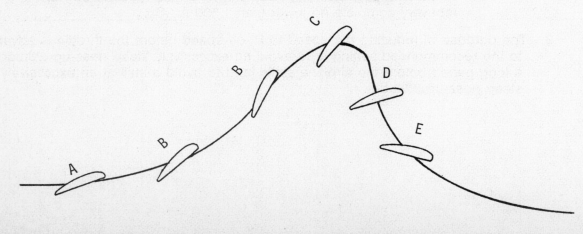

E. Always measure your pitch attitude with respect to the horizon. In entering a departure (power-on) stall, be careful not to pull the elevator back too abruptly. This could result in a vertical attitude with respect to the horizon. Rather than stalling forward, the airplane may enter a "tailslide."

  1. The airplane never actually "stalls" since the critical angle of attack is never exceeded. Rather, the airplane falls backward into a tailslide.

  2. This can result in the loss of use of the rudder or elevator and is extremely dangerous!

F. Recovery from the power-on stall should be accomplished by immediately reducing the angle of attack. You must release back elevator pressure, i.e., move the control yoke forward. If in a departure climb at less than full power, smoothly advance the throttle to maximum allowable power.

  1. The nose should be lowered as far as necessary to increase speed.

  2. Then the airplane should be returned to the normal straight-and-level flight attitude.

G. When in normal level flight, the throttle should be returned to cruise power setting.

STALL - POWER-ON PTS

TASK: **STALL - POWER-ON** *(ASEL)*
  PILOT OPERATION - 5
  REFERENCE: AC 61-21.

Objective. *To determine that the applicant:*

1. *Exhibits knowledge by explaining the aerodynamic factors and flight situations that may result in stalls - power-on, including proper recovery procedures, and hazards of stalling during uncoordinated flight.*

2. *Selects an entry altitude that will allow a recovery to be completed no lower than 1,500 feet AGL.*

3. *Establishes takeoff or normal climb configuration.*

4. *Establishes takeoff or climb airspeed before applying takeoff or climb power (reduced power may be used to avoid excessive pitch-up during entry only.)*

5. *Establishes and maintains a pitch attitude straight ahead that will induce a stall.*

6. *Establishes and maintains a pitch attitude that will induce a stall in a turn with a bank angle of 20°, ±10°.*

7. *Applies proper control to maintain coordinated flight.*

8. *Recognizes the indications of a stall and promptly recovers with a minimum loss of altitude by simultaneously decreasing the angle of attack, leveling the wings, and adjusting the power, as necessary, to regain normal flight attitude.*

9. *Avoids secondary stall.*

10. *Retracts the wing flaps and establishes straight-and-level flight.*

STALL - POWER-OFF

A. Power-off (landing) stalls occur when the airplane is in a landing configuration.

   1. Flaps and gear down.
   2. Power at idle and carburetor heat on.

B. Select an altitude that will allow recoveries to be completed no lower than 1,500 ft AGL.

C. CLEARING TURNS ARE REQUIRED PRIOR TO INITIATING A LANDING STALL.

   1. Clearing turns are at least two distinct 90° turns during which you either complete a 180° turn or regain your original direction.

      a. The FAA does not require a specific procedure.

      b. Accordingly, procedures vary with the area, CFIs, etc. For instance, a 360° turn is acceptable.

   2. Clearing turns provide you with an opportunity to observe nearby traffic.

      a. Clearing turns also increase the probability of nearby traffic observing you.

      b. Your airspeed, altitude, etc. should be such that you are ready and able to execute your stall upon completion of your second 90° turn.

D. To execute the stall, smoothly raise the airplane's pitch attitude to an attitude which will induce a stall.

   1. Directional control should be maintained with the rudder.

   2. The wings may also be held level by use of the ailerons, but the rudder is most important.

   3. A constant pitch attitude should be maintained with the elevator until the full stall occurs.

E. The full stall will be evidenced by such clues as

   1. Full up-elevator (i.e., control yoke all the way back) and high sink rate.
   2. Possible buffeting and uncontrollable nose-down pitching.

F. Recovery from the stall should be accomplished by

   1. Reducing the angle of attack (releasing back elevator pressure).

   2. Advancing the throttle to maximum allowable power.

   3. Rudder pressure as necessary for directional control. Right rudder pressure is frequently necessary to overcome the engine torque effects as power is advanced.

G. Diagram of a power-off stall.

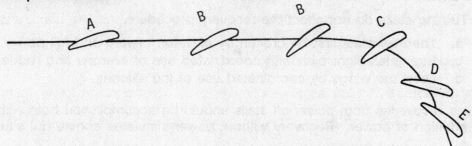

1. At point A, power is reduced. The pilot then applies back pressure to maintain constant lift, and airspeed decreases.

2. During interval B, the pilot continues to increase the angle of attack (maintaining constant lift) until point C, and airspeed continues to decrease.

3. At point C, the angle of attack exceeds the critical angle of attack and lift diminishes while drag increases. This results in a downward flightpath with the nose pitching down.

4. At point D, the nose is down but the angle of attack is still excessive due to the downward flightpath, so the pilot reduces back pressure to lower the nose and align the chord line of the wings with the relative wind.

5. At point E, the angle of attack has been sufficiently reduced to reestablish lift.

H. Recovery from power-off stalls should also be practiced from moderately banked turns (20°-40°) to simulate an accidental stall during a turn from base leg to final approach.

1. During the practice of power-off turning stalls, care should be taken to see that the turn continues at a constant bank until the complete stall occurs.

  a. It is also very important that the turn be coordinated, i.e., ball centered, or the airplane may enter a spin.

2. If the power-off turn is not properly coordinated while approaching the stall, wallowing may result when the stall occurs. Or if the airplane is in a slip, the outer wing may stall first and whip downward abruptly.

  a. EXAMPLE. Assume you are in a left turn, approaching the critical angle of attack, and the airplane is slipping "down."

    1) This means you do not have enough left rudder or you have too much right rudder, i.e., the ball will be to the left.

    2) With right uncoordinated rudder, the nose and fuselage of the airplane disrupt the airflow over the root of the right wing because the airplane is cocked to the right with respect to the relative wind.

    3) This disruption of airflow over the root of the right wing causes the right wing to stall first.

    4) The same thing is true with respect to the left wing in turns to the right.

  b. Always remember that at critical angles of attack, the airplane will usually break (fall) to the side that has excessive rudder. In the above example, even though the airplane was banked to the left in a left turn, the stall broke to the right (right wing stalled first) because excessive right rudder was used (i.e., not enough left rudder).

    c. Stalls will usually break straight ahead when the controls are coordinated.

   3. Turning stalls do not affect the recovery procedure.

    a. The stall must first be broken by elevator forward and full power.
    b. Straighten flight path with coordinated use of ailerons and rudder.
    c. Level the wings by coordinated use of the ailerons.

I.   Practice recoveries from power-off stalls should be accomplished both with and without the addition of power. Recovery without power simulates engine out situations.

STALL - POWER-OFF PTS

> **TASK:** *STALL - POWER-OFF (ASEL)*
> *PILOT OPERATION - 5*
> *REFERENCE: AC 61-21.*
>
> ***Objective.*** *To determine that the applicant:*
>
> *1. Exhibits knowledge by explaining the aerodynamic factors and flight situations that may result in stalls - power-off, including proper recovery procedures, and hazards of stalling during uncoordinated flight.*
>
> *2. Selects an entry altitude that will allow a recovery to be completed no lower than 1,500 feet AGL.*
>
> *3. Establishes the normal approach or landing configuration and airspeed with the throttle closed or at a reduced power setting.*
>
> *4. Establishes a straight glide or a gliding turn with a bank angle of 30°, ±10°, in coordinated flight.*
>
> *5. Establishes and maintains a landing pitch attitude that will induce a stall.*
>
> *6. Recognizes the indications of a stall and promptly recovers with a minimum loss of altitude by simultaneously decreasing the angle of attack, leveling the wings, and adjusting the power as necessary to regain normal flight attitude.*
>
> *7. Avoids a secondary stall.*
>
> *8. Retracts the wing flaps and establishes straight-and-level flight.*

SECONDARY STALLS

A. A secondary stall may occur if your stall recovery technique is incomplete or deficient in a primary stall.

   1. This stall usually occurs when the pilot becomes too anxious to return to straight-and-level flight after a stall or spin recovery.

B. A secondary stall is caused by attempting to hasten completion of a stall recovery (return to straight-and-level flight) before the airplane has realigned itself with the flightpath (relative wind).

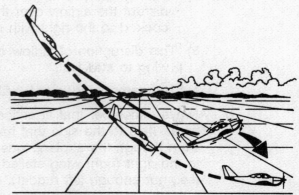

   1. The increase in angle of attack (back pressure) occurs too soon and the critical angle of attack is exceeded a second time.

C. When this stall occurs, the back elevator pressure should again be released just as in a normal stall recovery. When the angle of attack has been reduced and sufficient airspeed has been regained, the airplane can be returned to straight-and-level flight.

IMMINENT STALLS

A. An imminent stall is one in which the airplane is approaching a stall but is not allowed to stall completely.

    1. This stall maneuver is primarily for practice in retaining (or regaining) full control of the airplane immediately upon recognizing that it is almost in a full stall or that a full stall is likely to occur if timely preventive action is not taken.

B. These maneuvers require flight with the airplane just on the verge of a stall and recovery initiated before a full stall occurs.

C. CLEARING TURNS ARE REQUIRED.

    1. As in all manuevers that involve significant changes in altitude or direction, the pilot must ensure that the area is clear of other air traffic before executing the maneuver.

    2. See the procedures for clearing turns previously discussed under "Stalls - Power-On" and "Stalls - Power-Off."

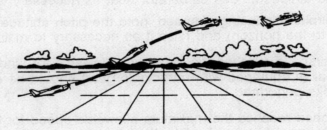

D. Instead of allowing a full stall, when the first buffeting or decay of control effectiveness is noted, recovery action is taken.

    1. The angle of attack must be reduced immediately by releasing the elevator back pressure.

    2. The airplane is not completely stalled, so control effectiveness will be quickly regained. However, the complete recovery procedure should be followed.

    3. The pilot must promptly recognize the indications of an imminent stall and take timely, positive control action to prevent a full stall.

MANEUVERING DURING SLOWFLIGHT

A. Slowflight is flight at airspeeds less than best climb speed (V_x). Your instructor may have you fly at 60, 70, 80, etc. kts to practice maintaining direction, altitude, etc. at various airspeeds.

    1. Some refer specifically to "flight at minimum controllable airspeed" as slowflight rather than minimum controllable airspeed.

        a. Minimum controllable airspeed is the airspeed at which any further increase in angle of attack will cause a stall.

      b. This critical airspeed, i.e., just above stall speed, will depend upon

          1) Gross weight.
          2) CG location of the airplane.
          3) Maneuvering load imposed by turns and pull-ups.
          4) Flap setting.
          5) Power setting.

    2. Practicing slowflight develops the pilot's sense of feel and ability to use the controls correctly. It also improves proficiency in performing maneuvers in which very low airspeeds are required.

B. Maneuvering at minimum controllable airspeed should be performed using both instrument indications and outside visual references.

C. As in all manuevers that involve significant changes in altitude or direction, the pilot must ensure that the area is clear of other air traffic before and while executing the maneuver.

    1. Select an entry altitude that will allow flight to be performed no lower than 1,500 ft AGL.

    2. Clearing turns are required.

D. To begin the maneuver, gradually reduce the throttle from cruising position and raise the nose to lose airspeed. Use carburetor heat as necessary.

    1. While the airplane is losing airspeed, note the pitch attitude (position of the nose in relation to the horizon) and raise it as necessary to maintain altitude.

    2. When the airspeed reaches the maximum allowable for landing gear operation, the landing gear (if equipped with retractable gear) should be extended and all gear-down checks performed.

    3. As the airspeed reaches the maximum allowable speed for flap operation, lower full flaps or partial flaps and adjust the pitch attitude. Slowflight should also be practiced with flaps up.

    4. During these changing flight conditions, it is important to retrim the airplane as often as necessary to compensate for changes in control pressures.

    5. Additional power will be required as the speed further decreases to maintain altitude at high-drag airspeed just above a stall.

      a. If too much speed is lost or too little power is used, further back pressure on the elevator control may result in a stall.

    6. When the desired pitch attitude and minimum control airspeed have been established, it is important to continually cross-check the attitude indicator, altimeter, and airspeed indicator, as well as outside references, to ensure that accurate control is being maintained.

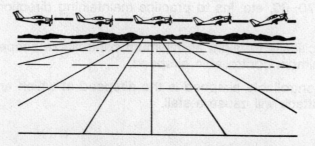

E. When the attitude, airspeed, and power have been stabilized in straight flight, turns should be practiced to determine the airplane's controllability characteristics at this minimum speed.

 1. During the turns, power may need to be increased to maintain the airspeed and altitude. More lift is needed in a turn but it cannot be obtained by increasing the angle of attack due to the accompanying increase in drag.

 2. If an excessively steep turn is made, the loss of vertical lift may result in a descent. If you try to prevent it by pulling back on the control yoke, i.e., increasing the angle of attack, a stall will occur because the airplane is already at the critical angle of attack.

 a. Thus, the steeper the bank, the more power is required.
 b. As you decrease the bank, decrease the power.

 3. A stall may also occur as a result of abrupt or rough control movements when flying at this critical airspeed. Abruptly raising the flaps while at minimum controllable airspeed will also result in sudden loss of lift, causing the airplane to lose altitude and/or perhaps stall.

F. Once flight at minimum controllable airspeed is set up properly for level flight, a descent or climb at minimum controllable airspeed can be established by

 1. Reducing or adding power to maintain the desired airspeed, and

 2. Simultaneously lowering or raising the pitch attitude to maintain the desired rate of descent or climb.

MANEUVERING DURING SLOWFLIGHT PTS

TASK: MANEUVERING DURING SLOW FLIGHT (ASEL)
PILOT OPERATION - 5
REFERENCE: AC 61-21.

Objective. To determine that the applicant:

1. *Exhibits knowledge by explaining the flight characteristics and controllability associated with maneuvering during slow flight.*

2. *Selects an entry altitude that will allow the maneuver to be performed no lower than 1,500 ft AGL.*

3. *Establishes and maintains slow flight during coordinated straight and turning flight in various configurations and bank angles.*

4. *Maintains the desired altitude, ±100 ft.*

5. *Maintains the specified heading during straight flight, ±10°.*

6. *Maintains the specified bank angle, ±10°, during turning flight.*

7. *Maintains an airspeed of 10 kts above stall speed, ±5 kts.*

SPINS

A. A spin is a continuing stall in which the airplane follows a corkscrew path in a downward direction.

   1. While both wings are stalled, one wing is producing some lift and the airplane spirals downward (see the diagram on page 193).

   2. Spins result from stalling your airplane while the controls are uncoordinated, i.e., with improper use of the rudder.

   3. Spins continue because recovery procedures are not undertaken.

      a. Many airplanes require special procedures to get the airplane to spin, i.e., they are spin resistant.

      b. Also, in most cases airplanes must be kept in spins, i.e., if the controls are released the airplane will recover from the spin itself.

   4. Fear of spins is deeply rooted in the public's mind, and many pilots have a subconscious (or even conscious) aversion to them.

   5. Learning the cause of a spin and the proper techniques to prevent and/or recover from the spin removes mental anxiety and many causes of unintentional spins.

B. Though instruction in spins is not required of applicants for the recreational pilot certificate, applicants for a flight instructor certificate with an airplane or glider instructor rating may be asked to demonstrate that they can recognize and recover from spin situations that might be encountered in poorly executed maneuvers during student training flights.

   1. Spins must be done under the supervision of a CFI.

C. The INTENTIONAL SPINNING of an airplane for which the spin maneuver is not specifically approved is NOT encouraged and is not authorized either by this study manual or by FARs.

   1. Official sources for determining if the spin maneuver is approved for a specific airplane are

      a. The airplane's Type Certificate and Data Sheets;

      b. On a placard located in clear view of the pilot in the airplane, e.g., "NO ACROBATIC MANEUVERS INCLUDING SPINS APPROVED"; and

      c. The maneuvers section of the airplane operating manual.

   2. Some pilots reason that the airplane was spin tested during its certification process and therefore no problem should result from demonstrating or practicing spins.

      a. Actually, certification in the "normal" category requires only that the airplane recover from a one-turn spin in not more than one additional turn or three seconds, whichever takes longer.

      b. This same test of controllability can also be used in certificating an airplane in the "utility" category (FAR 23.221(b)).

   3. THE PILOT OF AN AIRPLANE PLACARDED AGAINST INTENTIONAL SPINS SHOULD ASSUME THAT THE AIRPLANE MAY BECOME UNCONTROLLABLE IN A SPIN.

D. This is how a spin develops. Often a wing will drop at the beginning of a stall. When this happens, the nose will attempt to move (yaw) in the direction of the low wing.

1. Whenever an airplane is flying slightly sideways, it is said to be uncoordinated. An uncentered "ball" on the turn-and-slip indicator or the turn coordinator indicates an uncoordinated condition. In the drawing below, the ball would be to the right, indicating a need for right rudder to align the longitudinal axis with the relative wind.

a. If the airplane stalls while in an uncoordinated condition, one wing (the left wing in this example) will stall first. Airflow over the root of the left wing is partially blocked by the fuselage and is disrupted sooner.

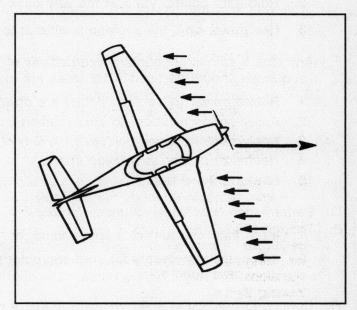

b. As the airplane turns toward the low wing, the angle of attack on the stalled wing increases while the angle of attack on the unstalled wing (the right wing in the diagram) decreases and continues producing lift.

c. The wing producing lift pulls the airplane around, keeping it uncoordinated as long as back pressure is maintained. Remember, the airplane must be in a stalled condition to spin.

d. The airplane's right (less-stalled) wing will come up and over, so that the airplane is temporarily inverted. However, the nose quickly comes down and under, thus normally establishing the spin in a non-inverted condition.

e. The stall condition remains. The uncoordination feeds on itself, and around it goes. With one wing completely stalled, the nose appears pointed almost directly at the ground (even though it is not).

f. This is a very alarming situation, causing the unknowing pilot to panic and pull the wheel back in an attempt to raise the nose. This only keeps the aircraft in the stall configuration.

g. Another factor contributing to the problem is that as one wing drops when entering the spin, pilots attempt to yank it back up with the ailerons. This produces adverse yaw in the same direction as the already existing uncoordination, and contributes further to the spin condition.

2. This is where use of the rudder is important during a stall. The correct amount of opposite rudder must be applied to keep the nose from yawing toward the low wing. By maintaining directional control and not allowing the nose to yaw toward the low wing, the wing will not drop any more before the stall is broken. Thus, a spin will be averted.

E.   How to induce a spin.

1.   Stall your airplane with uncoordinated rudder.

a.   The airplane will usually spin in the direction of excessive rudder.

b.   If you completely cross control and stall, the airplane will enter the spin by the low wing dropping and the high wing going up and over, i.e., a flip over.

2.   Hold your control yoke all the way back to maintain the spin.

3.   Use power-on if the airplane is difficult to get into a spin with power off.

F.   Any time a spin is encountered, regardless of the conditions, the normal spin recovery sequence should be used. The steps are elaborated in H. below.

1.   Retard power (raise flaps if they are down).

2.   Apply opposite rudder to stop rotation.

3.   Apply positive forward-elevator movement as necessary to break the stall.

4.   Neutralize rudder as rotation stops.

5.   Return to level flight.

G.   Performance is considered unsatisfactory if

1.   More than one turn of a spin occurs, or

2.   It becomes necessary for your instructor to take control of the airplane to avoid a fully developed spin.

H.   Continued practice in stalls will help the pilot develop a more instinctive and prompt reaction in recognizing an approaching spin. It is essential to learn to apply immediate corrective action any time it is apparent that the airplane is nearing spin conditions. If an unintentional spin can be prevented, it should be.

1.   The first corrective action taken during any power-on spin is to close the throttle.

a.   Power aggravates the spin characteristics and causes an abnormal loss of altitude in the recovery.

2.   To recover from the spin the pilot should apply full opposite rudder.

a.   Opposite rudder should be maintained until the rotation stops. Then the rudder should be neutralized. Continue to use the rudder for directional control.

b.   If the rudder is not neutralized at the proper time, the ensuing increased airspeed acting upon the fully deflected rudder will cause an excessive and unfavorable yawing effect. This places great strain on the airplane and may cause a secondary spin in the opposite direction.

3.   After the rotation stops, apply brisk, positive straight-forward movement of the elevator control (forward of the neutral position).

a.   The control should be held firmly in this position.

b.   The forceful movement of the elevator will decrease the excessive angle of attack and will break the stall.

4. When the stall is broken, use back pressure as required to control airspeed and minimize altitude loss.

    a. First, forward control yoke pressure is used to break the stall. Then back control yoke pressure is used to regain level flight.

CLOSE THROTTLE
FULL OPPOSITE RUDDER
BRISK FORWARD ELEVATOR

HOLD ELEVATOR FORWARD
NEUTRALIZE RUDDER

EASE ELEVATOR BACK
TOWARD NEUTRAL

COMMON SLOWFLIGHT, STALL, AND SPIN ERRORS

A. Slowflight.

1. Forgetting clearing turns.

2. Ignoring altitude loss, i.e., not adding power as necessary.

3. Fighting the control yoke, i.e., not letting trim help. Use of trim is very important.

4. Locking onto one variable. You need to monitor airspeed, pitch attitude, power, altitude, heading, traffic, etc.

B. Power-off stall.

1. Forgetting clearing turns.

2. Not knowing procedures. These should be memorized on the ground.

3. Taking too long on one item, e.g., power reduction or flap lowering. Just execute them immediately.

4. Forgetting to maintain a constant pitch attitude. This requires an increasing back pressure on the control yoke as airspeed decreases. The typical error is to put the nose in the stall attitude and freeze the yoke. As airspeed and lift decrease, the nose falls and the stall never occurs.

5. Raising the flaps abruptly during stall recovery. Flap retraction should be accomplished very slowly to prevent settling or a secondary stall.

C. Power-on stall.

1. The above power-off stall errors apply here except the last one, because power-on stalls are performed without flaps.

2. Putting the nose too high. Remember to avoid a tailslide. Monitor your pitch attitude with respect to the horizon.

3. Not putting the nose high enough. You need to realize when the stall is not occurring and raise the nose of the airplane.

4. Uncoordination is the biggest problem with power-on stalls. This results from not using right rudder to counteract torque and P-factor encountered in a climb.

    a. Rather than using the rudder to correct the uncoordinated flight attitude, students frequently lower the right wing to stop the left turn.

    b. The airplane stalls in an uncoordinated condition. The left wing drops. The pilot tries to pick it up with aileron control and fails to use rudder to stop the yaw. This describes the entry into a spin.

D. Spin errors.

1. Releasing elevator back pressure prematurely, which causes the airplane to enter a spiral dive. Hold elevator back pressure until opposite rudder stops the spin.

2. Not pulling out of the dive quickly when recovering. This allows too much airspeed to build up.

3. Pulling out of the dive too fast, which results in too great a G load. Note that you have to balance the excessive airspeed and excessive G load hazards.

4. Sloppy entry--some airplanes, like Cessna 172s, are spin resistant. You need to enter the stall rather abruptly and fully uncoordinated (or with power) to enter a spin.

    a. Forgetting clearing turns.

CHAPTER TEN
GROUND REFERENCE MANEUVERS

General Description of Ground Reference Maneuvers 195
Rectangular Course 197
Rectangular Course, PTS 200
Turns Around a Point 200
Turns Around a Point PTS 202
"S-Turns" Across a Road 202
"S-Turns" Across a Road PTS 205
Common Ground Reference Maneuver Errors 205

Ground reference maneuvers are intended to help you develop a high degree of pilot skill. Although these maneuvers are not practiced in normal, everyday flight, they aid the pilot in analyzing the effect of wind and other forces acting on the airplane. Ground reference maneuvers also help develop control touch, coordination, and division of attention for accurate and safe maneuvering of your airplane.

This chapter covers 3 of the 34 "Tasks" in the FAA Practical Test Standards (PTSs). They are

1. Rectangular Course
2. Turns Around a Point
3. "S-Turns" Across a Road

GENERAL DESCRIPTION OF GROUND REFERENCE MANEUVERS

A. Ground reference maneuvers are maneuvers performed with reference to objects on the ground. All ground reference maneuvers are performed at or near pattern altitude, 600 ft AGL to 1,000 ft AGL, and at cruise power.

B. Ground reference maneuvers require

1. Planning.
2. Maintaining orientation in relation to the ground.
3. Flying appropriate headings to follow a desired ground track.
4. Being aware of other traffic in the immediate area.

C. The low altitude used for ground reference maneuvers requires you to be on the lookout continually for appropriate landing sites in case of an engine failure or other in-flight emergency.

D. Wind is probably the most important factor in performing a proper ground reference maneuver. Since an airplane is free from the ground, it is affected by the medium in which it is surrounded. The wind must be taken into consideration at all times.

1. All ground reference maneuvers are started with the wind, i.e., downwind, not into the wind.

2. Beginning a maneuver downwind offers the pilot a good place to start, in that there is no tendency for the airplane to weathervane into the wind, or to fly a course that differs from the airplane's heading.

E.   The heading of an airplane is the direction in which the airplane is pointed.

   1.   The course of the airplane is the track on which the airplane flies along the ground.

   2.   When the wind is blowing from either side of the airplane, other than from straight ahead or directly behind, you must use a technique known as crabbing.

      a.   Crabbing requires heading an airplane slightly more into the wind to avoid being blown off the desired course.

      b.   The amount of crab angle or the angle between the course and the heading of the airplane will vary depending on the strength of the wind. The stronger the wind, the greater that angle.

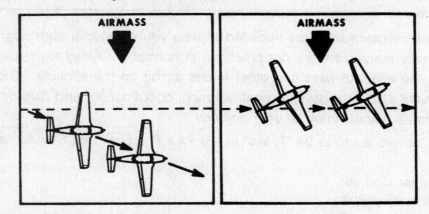

   3.   The effect of wind on turns is illustrated below.

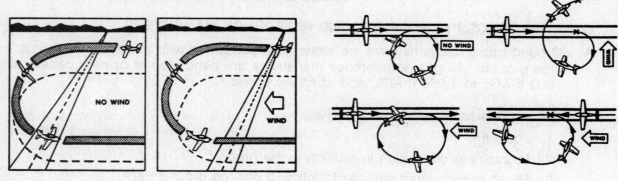

F.   To fly a specific ground track, the rate of turn must be proportional to groundspeed.

   1.   Therefore, when groundspeed is higher (tailwind), the rate of turn must be greater to maintain the desired track. To get a greater rate of turn, use a steeper bank.

   2.   Headwind results in a slower groundspeed, so use a lower rate of turn, i.e., less bank.

G.   When flying ground reference maneuvers, remember that all downwind turns, i.e., turns with a tailwind, require the steepest amount of bank. Since the wind is blowing directly behind the airplane, the groundspeed is greater than the true airspeed of the airplane.

   1.   When in the traffic pattern flying at low airspeeds (e.g., turning from downwind leg to base leg), a critical situation can arise if you do not maintain the airplane's **airspeed** because you are paying too much attention to the airplane's **groundspeed**.

2. In contrast to entering turns with a tailwind, all turns that are begun into the wind should be shallow. This will keep the airplane from blowing back into the pattern that is being flown.

H. Visualizing the desired ground track plays a very important part in ground reference maneuvers; i.e., it is important for you to visualize the track on the ground along which you wish to fly. Select ground reference points to mark your desired path over the ground.

RECTANGULAR COURSE

A. The "rectangular course" is a practice maneuver in which the ground track of the airplane is equidistant from all sides of a selected rectangular area on the ground.

1. While performing the maneuver, the altitude (±100 ft) and airspeed (±10 kts) should be held constant. Bank angle should not exceed 45°.

2. As with other ground track maneuvers, one of the objectives is to develop an appropriate division of attention between the flightpath, flight instruments, flight controls, ground references, and other aircraft in the vicinity.

3. Another objective is to develop recognition of drift toward or away from a line parallel to the intended ground track.

   a. This will be helpful in recognizing drift toward or from an airport runway during the various legs of the airport traffic pattern.

B. For this maneuver, a square or rectangular field (or an area bounded on four sides by section lines or roads), the sides of which are approximately 1 mile in length, should be selected well away from other air traffic.

1. The altitude flown should be approximately 600 to 1,000 ft AGL (1,000 ft is the altitude usually required for airport traffic patterns).

2. The airplane should be flown parallel to and at a uniform distance (about ¼ mile away) from the field boundaries.

   a. The flightpath should be positioned outside the field boundaries just far enough that they may be easily observed from either pilot seat by looking out the side of the airplane.

   b. If you try to fly directly above the edges of the field, you will have no usable reference points to start and complete the turns.

   c. The closer the track of the airplane is to the field boundaries, the steeper the bank necessary at the turning points.

   d. You will experience more difficulty with a right-hand course when seated on the left side because you must look across the airplane to see the field. However, the distance of the ground track from the edge of the field should be the same whether flying left or right course.

      1) If you have picked a good rectangular field, after establishing the maneuver, you may use the edge on the opposite side to tell you about your ground track, if you cannot readily see the near edge at the recommended ¼ mile from the near edge.

3. All turns should be started when the airplane is just ahead of or abeam the corners of the field boundaries and the bank normally should not exceed 45°.

4. Although the rectangular course may be entered from any direction, this discussion assumes entry on a downwind heading.

    a. This provides you with your fastest groundspeed.

    b. No crabbing is required either.

C. While the airplane is on the downwind leg (similar to the downwind leg of an airport traffic pattern), observe the next field boundary as it approaches to plan the turn onto the crosswind leg.

1. Since you have a tailwind on this leg, it increases the airplane's groundspeed. During the turn onto the crosswind leg, the wind will tend to drift the airplane away from the field.

2. The roll-in to the turn must therefore be fast and the bank relatively steep to counteract the tailwind. Also, begin the roll-in a little early, i.e., anticipate.

3. As the turn progresses, the tailwind component decreases, and the groundspeed decreases.

4. Consequently, the bank angle and rate of turn must be decreased gradually to ensure that, upon completion of the turn, the crosswind ground track will continue the same distance from the edge of the field.

5. Completion of the turn with the wings level should be accomplished at a point aligned with the upwind corner of the field, i.e., when you can look straight down the side of the field that you just flew, your wings should roll level.

6. Simultaneous with rolling the wings level, the proper drift correction must be established with the airplane crabbed into the wind.

    a. This requires that the turn be more than a 90° change in heading.

    b. If the turn has been made properly, the field boundary will again appear to be ¼ mile away.

7. While on the crosswind leg, the crab angle should be adjusted as necessary to maintain a uniform distance from the field boundary.

8. Note that this crosswind leg is similar to the base leg of an airport traffic pattern as the wind is blowing you away from the field.

D. As the next field boundary approaches, you should plan the turn from the crosswind leg onto the upwind leg.

1. Since a crab angle is being held into the wind and toward the field while on the crosswind leg, this next turn requires a turn of less than 90°.

2. Since the crosswind will become a headwind, causing the groundspeed to decrease during this turn, the bank initially must be medium and must progressively decrease as the turn proceeds.

3. To complete the turn, the rollout must be timed so that the wings become level at a point aligned with the crosswind corner of the field just as the longitudinal axis of the airplane again becomes parallel to the field boundary.

4. The distance from the field boundary should again be one-quarter mile from the side of the field.

E. As the upwind field boundary is approached, plan the turn from the upwind leg to the next crosswind leg. This crosswind leg is similar to the crosswind in an airport traffic pattern in which the wind blows you toward the field.

1. On the upwind leg, the wind is a headwind and results in a decreased ground-speed. Consequently, the turn onto the crosswind leg must be entered with a fairly slow rate of roll-in to a relatively shallow bank.

2. As the turn progresses, the bank angle must be increased gradually because the headwind component is diminishing, resulting in an increasing groundspeed.

3. During and after the turn onto this leg (the equivalent of the crosswind leg in a traffic pattern), the wind will tend to drift the airplane toward the field boundary.

4. To compensate for the drift, the amount of turn must be less than 90°.

5. The rollout from this turn must be such that, as the wings become level, the airplane is crabbed slightly away from the field and into the wind to correct for drift.

6. The airplane should again be the same distance from the field boundary, and at the same altitude, as on other legs.

F. The crosswind leg should be continued until you approach the boundary of the downwind leg (the leg you started with). Once more, you should anticipate drift and turning radius.

1. Since drift correction was held on the crosswind leg, it is necessary to turn more than 90° to align the airplane parallel to the downwind leg.

2. This turn should be started with a medium bank angle gradually increasing to a steep bank as the turn progresses.

3. The rollout should be timed so as to parallel the boundary of the field as the wings become level.

G. The diagram below illustrates the above discussion.

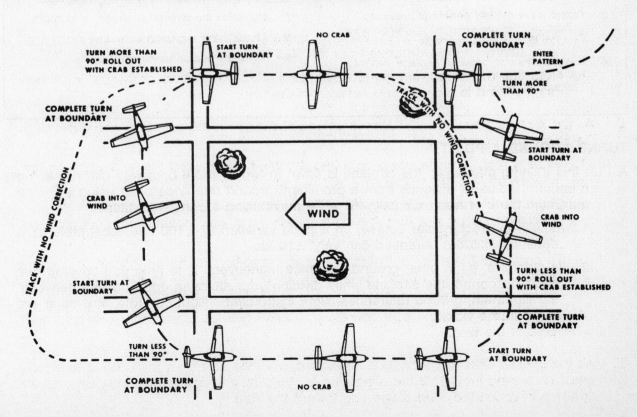

H. Usually drift should not be encountered on the upwind or the downwind leg, but it may be difficult to find a situation in which the wind is blowing exactly parallel to the field boundaries.

1. This would make it necessary to crab slightly on all the legs.

2. It is important to anticipate the turns to correct for groundspeed, drift, and turning radius.

3. With a tailwind, the turn must be faster and steeper. With a headwind, the turn must be slower and shallower.

4. These same techniques apply to flying in airport traffic patterns.

I. You should practice reversing the course on the same field or switch over to a nearby field with the opposite direction around the course (right versus left turn).

1. This will reverse your wind adjustments on each side of the field.

RECTANGULAR COURSE PTS

TASK: **RECTANGULAR COURSE** (ASEL)
        PILOT OPERATION - 3
        REFERENCE: AC 61-21.

Objective. To determine that the applicant:

1. Exhibits knowledge by explaining wind-drift correction in straight and turning flight and the relationship of the rectangular course to airport traffic patterns.

2. Selects a suitable reference area.

3. Enters a left or right pattern at a desired distance from the selected reference area and at 600 to 1,000 feet AGL.

4. Divides attention between airplane control and ground track, and maintains coordinated flight control.

5. Applies the necessary wind-drift corrections during straight and turning flight to track a uniform distance outside the selected reference area.

6. Maintains the desired altitude, ±100 feet.

7. Maintains the desired airspeed, ±10 knots.

8. Avoids bank angles in excess of 45°.

9. Reverses course as directed by the examiner.

TURNS AROUND A POINT

A. In this training maneuver, the airplane is flown in two or more complete circles each of a uniform radius or distance from a prominent ground reference point using a maximum bank of approximately 45° while maintaining a constant altitude.

1. As with the rectangular course, an altitude variation of ±100 ft is acceptable as a constant altitude. Airspeed can vary ±10 kts.

2. Its objective, as in other ground reference maneuvers, is to help you develop the ability to control the airplane while dividing your attention appropriately between the flightpath, ground references, flight instruments, flight controls, and other air traffic in the vicinity.

B.   As in other ground track maneuvers, a constant radius around a point will, if any wind exists, require a constantly changing angle of bank and angle of crab.

  1.   The closer the airplane is to a direct downwind heading, on which the ground-speed is greatest, the steeper the bank and the faster the rate of turn required to establish the proper crab.

  2.   The more nearly the plane is to a direct upwind heading, on which the ground-speed is least, the shallower the bank and the slower the rate of turn required to establish the proper crab.

C.   The point selected for turns around a point should be prominent, easily distinguished by the pilot, and yet small enough to present a precise reference.

  1.   Isolated trees, crossroads, or other similar small landmarks are usually suitable.

  2.   The point should, however, be in an area away from communities, livestock, or groups of people on the ground to prevent possible annoyance or hazard.

  3.   Since the maneuver is performed at a relatively low altitude (but not less than 600 ft), the area selected should also afford an opportunity for a safe emergency landing if necessary.

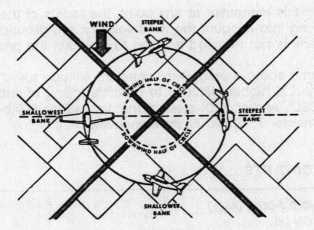

D.   To enter turns about a point, the airplane should be flown on a downwind heading to one side of the selected point at a distance equal to the desired radius of turn. One-quarter to one-fifth of a mile works well.

  1.   In a high-wing airplane, the distance from the point must permit the pilot to see the point throughout the maneuver even with the wing lowered in a bank. If the radius is too large, the lowered wing will block the pilot's view of the point.

E.   When any significant wind exists, it will be necessary to roll into the initial bank at a rapid rate so that the steepest bank is attained abeam of the point at which the airplane is headed directly downwind.

  1.   By entering the maneuver while heading directly downwind, the steepest bank can be attained immediately.

  2.   Thereafter, the bank must be shallowed gradually until the point is reached at which the airplane is headed directly upwind.

  3.   At this point, the bank should be gradually steepened until the steepest bank is again attained when heading downwind at the initial point of entry.

F. During the downwind half of the circle, the airplane's nose must be progressively crabbed toward the inside of the circle.

   1. During the upwind half, the nose must be progressively crabbed toward the outside.

   2. This crabbing is fairly hard to visualize since the direction of flight is constantly changing.

      a. What we are doing in practice is watching the ground track and adjusting the bank to keep the ground track as we want it.

      b. Although in theory we are crabbing, it may be confusing if someone tries to crab as (s)he did on a straight path with a crosswind. Just adjust bank to maintain the desired track.

      c. Your turns must be coordinated, i.e., ball centered. Do not try to shape the circle by cheating with the rudder.

G. As the pilot becomes experienced in performing turns about a point and has a good understandng of the effects of wind drift, entry into the maneuver may be from any point.

   1. When entering this maneuver at any point, the radius of the turn must be carefully selected, taking into account the wind velocity and groundspeed so that an excessive bank is not required later on to maintain the proper ground track.

H. Do not confuse turns about a point with "constant altitude turns" or steep turns. Steep turns are performed at higher altitudes to practice rolling in and out and maintaining altitude in 180°, 360°, and/or 720° steep turns, i.e., 40° to 50° bank. See the "Turns" sideheading in Chapter 7, "Basic Flight Maneuvers."

TURNS AROUND A POINT PTS

TASK: TURNS AROUND A POINT (ASEL)
PILOT OPERATION - 3
REFERENCE: AC 61-21.

Objective. To determine that the applicant:

1. *Exhibits knowledge by explaining the procedures associated with turns around a point and wind-drift correction throughout the maneuver.*

2. *Selects a suitable ground reference point.*

3. *Enters a left or right turn at a desired distance from the selected reference point at 600 to 1,000 feet AGL.*

4. *Divides attention between airplane control and ground track, and maintains coordinated flight control.*

5. *Applies the necessary wind-drift corrections to track a constant radius turn around the selected reference point.*

6. *Maintains the desired altitude, ±100 feet.*

7. *Maintains the desired airspeed, ±10 knots.*

"S-TURNS" ACROSS A ROAD

A. An "S-turn across a road" is a practice maneuver in which the airplane's ground track describes semicircles each of an equal radius on each side of a selected straight line on the ground.

   1. The straight line may be a road, fence, railroad, or section line which lies perpendicular to the wind. It should be of sufficient length for making a series of turns.

2. A constant altitude (±100 ft) should be maintained throughout the maneuver. Airspeed may vary ±10 kts and bank should not exceed 45°.

3. The altitude should be low enough to easily recognize drift but in no case lower than 500 ft above the highest obstruction.

   a. The area selected should also afford an opportunity for a safe emergency landing, if necessary.

B. The objectives are to develop the ability to

   1. Compensate for drift during turns.
   2. Orient the flightpath with ground references.
   3. Divide your attention between the flightpath, ground references, flight instruments, flight controls, and other traffic.

C. Before starting the maneuver, a straight ground reference line or road that lies 90° to the direction of the wind (i.e., perpendicular) should be selected, then the area checked to ensure that no obstructions or other aircraft are in the immediate vicinity.

   1. The road (or the ground reference line) should be approached from the upwind side, 600 to 1,000 ft AGL on a downwind heading.

   2. When directly over the road, the first turn should be started immediately.

   3. With the airplane headed downwind, the groundspeed is greatest and the rate of departure from the road will be rapid. Therefore, the roll into the steep bank must be fairly rapid to attain the proper crab angle.

   4. This prevents the airplane from flying too far from the road and from establishing a ground track with an excessive radius.

   5. During the latter portion of the first 90° of turn, when the airplane's heading is changing from a downwind heading to a crosswind heading, the groundspeed becomes less and the rate of departure from the road decreases.

   6. The crab angle will be at the maximum when the airplane is headed directly crosswind.

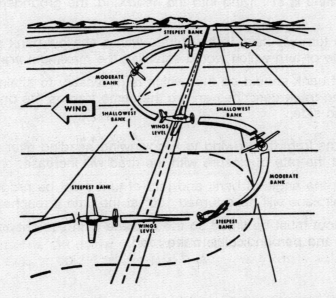

D. This maneuver consists of initially crossing the road at a 90° angle and immediately beginning a series of 180° turns each of a uniform radius in opposite directions, recrossing the road at a 90° angle just as each 180° turn is completed.

   1. Since turns to effect a constant radius ground track require a changing roll rate and angle of bank to establish the crab needed to compensate for the wind, both roll rate and bank angle will increase or decrease as groundspeed increases or decreases.

   2. The bank must be steepest when beginning the turn on the downwind side of the road and must be shallowed gradually as the turn progresses from a downwind heading to an upwind heading.

   3. On the upwind side, the turn should be started with a relatively shallow bank and then gradually steepened as the airplane turns from an upwind heading to a downwind heading.

E. Roll the airplane from one bank directly into the opposite just as you cross the reference line on the ground.

F. After turning 90°, the airplane's heading becomes more and more an upwind heading, the groundspeed will decrease, and the rate of closure with the road will become slower.

   1. If a constant steep bank were maintained, the airplane would turn too quickly for the slower rate of closure with the road, and would be headed perpendicular to the road prematurely.

   2. Because of the decreasing groundspeed and rate of closure with the road while approaching the upwind heading, it will be necessary to gradually shallow the bank during the remaining 90° of the semicircle. The crab angle is removed completely and the wings become level as the 180° turn is completed at the moment the road is reached.

G. At the instant the road is being crossed again, a turn in the opposite direction should be started.

   1. Since the airplane is still flying into the headwind, the groundspeed is relatively slow.

   2. Therefore, the turn will have to be started with a shallow bank so as to avoid an excessive rate of turn which would establish the maximum crab angle too soon.

   3. The degree of bank should be that which is necessary to attain the proper crab so the ground track describes an arc the same size as the one established on the downwind side.

H. As the airplane turns from the upwind to a downwind heading after turning 90°, the groundspeed and the rate of closure with the road will increase.

   1. Consequently, the angle of bank and rate of turn must be progressively increased so that the airplane will have turned 180° at the time it reaches the road.

   2. Again, the rollout must be timed so the airplane is in straight-and-level flight directly over and perpendicular to the road.

I. When the wind is not perpendicular to the road, it will be difficult to begin the maneuver with a tailwind. A tailwind requires the steepest turn and once you have made the steepest turn, subsequent turns cannot be steeper. If you started upwind and your first turn is too steep, a dangerously steep turn may be required on subsequent turns.

1. Accordingly, explain the problem to your CFI and FAA examiner if you are forced into entering any of the ground reference maneuvers on other than a downwind.

2. If you ever execute an upwind entry, be sure to make your initial turn very shallow so your subsequent turn to downwind will not have to be too steep.

"S-TURNS" ACROSS A ROAD PTS

TASK: *"S-TURNS" ACROSS A ROAD (ASEL)*
PILOT OPERATION - 3
REFERENCE: AC 61-21.

Objective. To determine that the applicant:

1. *Exhibits knowledge by explaining the procedures associated with "S-turns," and wind-drift correction throughout the maneuver.*

2. *Selects a suitable ground reference line.*

3. *Enters perpendicular to the selected reference line at 600 to 1,000 feet AGL.*

4. *Divides attention between airplane control and ground track, and maintains coordinated flight control.*

5. *Applies the necessary wind-drift correction to track a constant radius turn on each side of the selected reference line.*

6. *Reverses the direction of turn directly over the selected reference line.*

7. *Maintains the desired altitude, ±100 feet.*

8. *Maintains the desired airspeed, ±10 knots.*

9. *Avoids bank angles in excess of 45°.*

COMMON GROUND REFERENCE MANEUVER ERRORS

A. Ground reference maneuvers are primarily maneuvers for developing

1. Coordination.
2. Judgment.
3. Division of attention.
4. Awareness of wind drift.
5. Correction of wind drift.

B. Errors are inevitable since ground reference maneuvers are designed to iron out errors in other areas of training (especially in the traffic pattern). The most common weak area is division of attention. You should be watching three things during these maneuvers:

1. Path over the ground.
2. Altitude.
3. Traffic.

C. Most students tend to stare out the side, watch the ground track, allow pitch attitude to vary as bank varies, and forget to watch for traffic.

1. Watching for traffic is an extremely important habit to learn early so it becomes automatic in the traffic pattern.

D. Two other common weaknesses are

1. Not adequately judging the direction of the wind either before or during the maneuver.

a. Look for blowing smoke, dust, laundry on a line, etc.
b. Remember the winds from takeoff.

2. Not properly determining how to enter the maneuver.

E. Most students have relatively little trouble flying the actual maneuver. The difficulties are in determining the wind direction, picking references accordingly, and entering the maneuver correctly. Practice by drawing the maneuvers until you can do each of them without looking at the diagram (and pick wind from all four directions).

F. Common errors in rectangular courses:

1. Picking too small a field.
2. Flying too close to the edge of the field.
3. Over or under crabbing (or forgetting it altogether).
4. Allowing pitch to vary as bank varies (and therefore allowing altitude to vary).
5. Forgetting to use rudder coordination in turns.
6. Exceeding 45° of bank.
7. Not watching for other traffic.

G. Common errors in turns around a point.

1. Staring at the point.
2. Not planning how the wind will affect flight path.
3. Allowing bank to exceed 45° maximum.
4. Too small a radius.
5. Not watching for traffic.
6. Forgetting to keep the rudder coordinated, or intentionally using rudder to affect the circle.

H. Common errors in "S-turns" across a road.

1. Determining wind direction incorrectly (should be across the road).
2. Not entering with wind.
3. Radius too small.
4. Not watching for traffic.
5. Forgetting to keep the rudder coordinated, or intentionally using rudder to affect the outcome of the turn.

CHAPTER ELEVEN
SOLO FLIGHT

Your solo flight is your first flight as the sole occupant of the airplane. After your instructor is confident that you are capable of flying the airplane yourself and if the weather (usually surface winds) and traffic permit, you will fly the airplane yourself (usually for three takeoffs and landings while remaining in the traffic pattern). The purpose of this chapter is to explain how to prepare for your solo flight and what to expect during that flight.

Your first solo flight is a "big event" in your flight training program. A traditional procedure is to cut off the tail of the shirt you "soloed" in. Your name and date of solo will be painted on the shirt tail and it will be hung on the wall of the fixed base operator (FBO) where you soloed. Subsequently, your flight training program will include 15 hours of solo (practice) flight.

PRE-SOLO FLIGHT INSTRUCTION

A. You will probably receive 10 to 12 hours of dual flight instruction before your first solo flight. This will depend on many variables. It is a flight instructor's discretion as to when a student should solo. Some student pilots solo after 6 to 8 hours of dual flight.

B. Most students do not feel ready when it comes time to solo. This is usually due to lack of confidence and the inability and inexperience of students in judging their own performance.

C. Your flight training before solo will include ground and flight instruction in at least the following procedures and operations:

   1. Flight preparation procedures, including preflight inspections, engine operation, and aircraft systems.

   2. Taxiing or surface operations, including runups.

   3. Takeoffs and landings, including normal and crosswind.

   4. Straight-and-level flight, shallow, medium, and steep banked turns in both directions.

   5. Climbs and climbing turns.

   6. Airport traffic patterns including entry and departure procedures and collision and wake turbulence avoidance.

   7. Descents with and without turns using high and low drag configurations.

8.   Flight at various airspeeds from cruising to minimum controllable airspeed.

9.   Emergency procedures and equipment malfunctions.

10.   Ground reference maneuvers.

11.   Approaches to the landing area with engine power at idle and with partial power.

12.   Slips to a landing.

13.   Go-arounds from final approach and from the landing flare in various flight configurations including turns.

14.   Forced landing procedures initiated on takeoff, during initial climb, cruise, descent, and in the landing pattern.

15.   Stall entries from various flight attitudes and power combinations with recovery initiated at the first indication of a stall, and recovery from a full stall.

INSTRUCTOR ADMINISTERED WRITTEN TEST REQUIRED PRIOR TO SOLO

FAR 61.97b requires that your flight instructor give you a written test on appropriate portions of FAR Parts 61 and 91 and also on the flight characteristics and operational limitations of your airplane, i.e., *Pilot's Operating Handbook* (POH) data. The following 25 questions are illustrative of the type of questions you may encounter.

1. Do the Federal Aviation Regulations specifically prohibit the operation of an aircraft in a careless or reckless manner?

Yes. *(91.9)*

2. Are deviations from control tower instructions allowed in the case of an emergency?

Yes, but <u>only</u> in an emergency. *(91.75)*

3. Which aircraft has the right-of-way when two or more aircraft at different altitudes, but not on final approach, are approaching an airport for the purpose of landing?

The lower aircraft. *(91.67)*

4. What are the restrictions on the proximity of one aircraft to another in flight?

No person may operate an aircraft so close to another aircraft as to create a collision hazard. *(91.65)*

5. When aircraft are approaching each other head-on, in which direction should each pilot alter course?

To the right. *(91.67)*.

6. Is an intentional maneuver that exceeds a bank of 60° considered an acrobatic maneuver?

Yes. *(91.71)*

7. If an airplane is converging with a glider at approximately the same altitude, which has the right-of-way?

Glider. It is the least maneuverable. *(91.67)*

8. What is the minimum safe altitude over congested areas as established by regulations?

1,000 ft AGL. *(91.79)*

9. What is the standard direction for all turns for an airplane approaching to land at an airport without a control tower?

To the left. *(91.89)*

10. Is buzzing or intentionally flying in close proximity to the ground, other than for takeoff or landing, considered to be careless or reckless operation?

Yes. *(91.79)*

11. Assume there is no altimeter setting available at your airport. What setting would you use for a local flight?

Field elevation. Ultimately you set your altimeter to field elevation. The difference is that when an altimeter setting is available you can check the calibration error in your altimeter, note the magnitude of that error, and then set the altimeter to the field elevation. *(91.81)*

12. Except when necessary for takeoff or landing, what is considered to be a minimum safe altitude for all flight situations?

An altitude allowing an emergency landing without undue hazard to persons or property on the surface. *(91.79)*

13. Is a visual display appropriate to indicate non-standard traffic directions for an airport without a control tower?

Yes. A segmented circle indicating left turn or an amber flashing light somewhere on the airport (see Chapter 8, "Landings"). *(91.89)*

14. What are the basic VFR weather minimums in a control area below 10,000 ft MSL? (Control area just means controlled airspace.)

500 ft below clouds, 1,000 ft above clouds, 2,000 ft horizontal separation, and 3 miles visibility. *(91.105)*

15. What are the dimensions of the standard airport traffic areas?

Five miles radius, up to but not including 3,000 ft AGL. *(1.1)*

16. What are the basic VFR weather minimums outside controlled airspace at or below 1,200 ft above the ground?

Clear of clouds and 3 miles visibility for recreational pilots. *(91.105)*

17. Is it mandatory that pilots keep seatbelts fastened while at the controls of an aircraft?

Yes. *(91.7, 91.14)*

18. If overtaking another aircraft, in which direction should the course be altered to pass well clear of the other aircraft?

To the right. *(91.67)*

19. What are the basic VFR weather minimums in a control zone?

Ceiling 1,000 ft and visibility 3 miles. In controlled airspace, distance required from clouds is 500 ft below, 1,000 ft above, and 2,000 ft horizontally. This is also required in control zones since controlled airspace goes all the way to the surface. *(91.105)*

20. Which aircraft has the right-of-way when one aircraft is being overtaken by another?

The one being overtaken. *(91.67)*

21. What does the operation of a rotating beacon during daylight hours at an airport located within a control zone mean?

The current weather conditions are less than basic VFR. *(AIM)*

22. How can control areas and control zones and their limits be identified on sectional aeronautical charts?

A control area is "controlled airspace" which begins at 1,200 ft AGL (the blue tint on the sectional chart) except in transition areas (the magenta circle) where it begins at 700 ft AGL. Control zones (dashed lines) are controlled airspace which begin at the surface. *(Sectional aeronautical chart legend)*

23. What visual display is used to indicate that an airport runway or taxiway is closed to traffic?

An "X" at the end of the pavement that you are approaching to land or to begin taxiing on. As a practical matter, when one direction is closed, both directions are usually closed. *(AIM)*

24. What information should a pilot provide when telephoning a weather briefing facility for preflight weather information?

Planned departure time, departure point, route of flight, destination, VFR or IFR, and aircraft number. *(AIM)*

25. Assume you are crossing the flightpath of a large jet airplane that is ahead of you at the same altitude. What should you do to avoid wake turbulence?

Climb above the jet's flight path. The wake turbulence will tend to descend after the jet has passed. *(AIM)*

YOUR FIRST SOLO FLIGHT

A. You should have a good idea about when you will solo based on discussions with your flight instructor and your own evaluation of your ability to control and land your airplane.

  1. Do not hesitate to talk to your flight instructor about it. You may wish to avoid a surprise announcement that "today you solo."

B. It is customary for your flight instructor to accompany you for a few touch-and-go landings before your actual solo. If you perform well, your instructor will usually stop the airplane, get out, and instruct you on making your solo flight. This is a surprise to some students, and the reluctance and insecurity expressed by many students is normal.

C. Things to expect during your solo.

  1. A very "roomy" feeling in the cockpit.

  2. The airplane will be a little lighter. You may notice it climbs a little faster and it may tend to "float" a little on the approach and roundout.

  3. Your instructor will probably tell you to do full stop landings (taxi back each time) to give you a chance to collect your thoughts between patterns, as well as to ensure adequate runway for takeoff.

    a. Until now, if you landed a little long, your instructor used judgment to decide whether there was enough runway remaining for takeoff.

    b. Although your own judgment may normally be fine, it may be a little off due to the excitement of your first solo. By taxiing back to the beginning of the runway, runway length left for a takeoff is one less thing to be concerned with.

  4. You may feel a little hesitant or insecure, but remember, your instructor will not let you go until (s)he is sure you will not hurt yourself or the airplane. You have been performing well. Just do what you have been doing.

INSTRUCTOR SIGN-OFFS FOR SOLO FLIGHTS

A. For your instructor to sign you off for solo flight, you must have demonstrated that you are familiar with the pertinent flight rules of Part 91 of the FARs (see Appendix C). You must have received flight and ground instruction in the areas outlined in the "Pre-Solo Flight Instruction" sideheading at the beginning of this chapter. Also your instructor will give you a written test on FAR 61 and 91 and also on *POH* data pertaining to your airplane.

B. For you to legally fly solo, your instructor's signature is required in two places:

1. Your student pilot certificate (back of medical certificate).
2. Your logbook.

C. On your student pilot certificate (see the example on page 2), your instructor will put the date, his/her signature, flight instructor number, and expiration date of his/her instructor certificate (not to be confused with the expiration date of your solo privileges).

1. Also required is the logbook endorsement, which will look something like this:

   a. *"(Your name) found competent for solo flight in a C-150."* 4-10-90, CFI's signature, 324181485CFI, Exp. 2-92.

   b. *"(Your name) has received instruction from me in a (make, model), meets the requirements of FAR Part 61 for solo flight, and is competent to make safe solo flight in this aircraft."* 4-10-90, CFI's signature, 324181485CFI, Exp. 3-91.

2. Your instructor may also choose (it is not specifically required) to put in a separate endorsement about the aeronautical knowledge requirement.

   a. EXAMPLE. *"(Your name) has demonstrated that (s)he is familiar with the flight rules of FAR Part 91 which are pertinent to student solo flights."* 2-10-90, CFI's signature, 342218357CFI, Exp. 3-92.

3. The logbook endorsement for solo is only good for 90 days. After that, your instructor must re-endorse your logbook. If this is not done, you are not legal for solo flight.

4. If, for some reason, you must go to another flight instructor to re-endorse your logbook, you will have to demonstrate familiarity with the flight rules of Part 91, and the instructor will have to fly with you and go over all the items in your pre-solo training.

   a. (S)he may go over them all in an hour or two (since you have already learned them, this will just be a refresher to make certain you are safe).

   b. However, (s)he must show this instruction in your logbook before (s)he can sign it certifying that you are, in fact, "competent" to make a safe solo flight.

5. Your student pilot/medical certificate and your logbook must be in your possession during all solo flights.

SUBSEQUENT LOCAL SOLO FLIGHT

A.   After two or three "supervised" solo flights, your instructor will probably allow you to fly without going with him/her first. (S)he will probably instruct you to practice the flight maneuvers you have learned earlier in your training, or to practice landings.

B.   The following restrictions are placed on your solo privileges. A student pilot may not pilot an airplane

1.   Carrying passengers.

2.   Outside a 25 nautical mile (NM) radius area of your airport (a special cross-country endorsement permits you to fly up to 50 NM from your airport).

3.   If the logbook endorsement is more than 90 days old.

4.   For compensation or hire.

5.   In furtherance of a business.

6.   Landing at an airport other than that from which you departed, unless your instructor has specifically endorsed your logbook, saying you can practice takeoffs and landings at that other airport.

7.   Of any other make and model of airplane than what is stated on your student pilot certificate solo endorsement.

COMMON SOLO FLIGHT ERRORS

A.   Flying in conditions beyond your capability such as gusty or crosswind conditions. If you are not sure, ask your instructor or any instructor around.

B.   Not asking for clarification. If you are not sure what the tower said, tell them you are a student pilot and you do not understand.

C.   Not asking for help until the problem has been compounded. A lost student should ask for the DF Steer, to be obtained by calling a Flight Service Station (FSS), before low fuel also becomes a problem. Get help as soon as you think you might need it.

1.   *DF Steer* refers to the ability to determine an airplane's direction.

2.   Most FSSs have the capability of determining where you are based upon your radio transmissions.

D.   Continuing into deteriorating weather conditions. The 180° turn is a lifesaver and should be used when in doubt.

E.   Not being conversant with VFR and student pilots requirements.

CHAPTER TWELVE
NAVIGATION

Navigation is used to fly your airplane from one airport to another, usually over considerable distances. Air navigation is not limited to the actual guiding of an airplane from one place to another. Remember, recreational pilots are restricted to 50 nautical miles (NM) from the airport where they received their flight instruction (FAR 61.101). Navigation begins and ends on the ground. The major planning concerns of cross-country flight are preflight preparation, navigation, and weather.

This chapter covers 4 of the 34 "Tasks" in the FAA Practical Test Standards (PTSs). They are:

1. Pilotage.
2. Obtaining Weather Information.
3. Diversion.
4. Lost Procedure.

PREFLIGHT PREPARATION

A. Plan ahead.
   1. Determine the route of flight.
   2. Estimate the time en route.
   3. Determine fuel management.
   4. Plan navigation.
   5. Compute weight and balance.
   6. Check that the airplane is ready to go.
   7. Check weather.

B. Airplane airworthiness. It is your responsibility to determine that the airplane has been properly maintained and is airworthy.
   1. Check the maintenance logbooks that no maintenance or inspection is due.
   2. Carefully preflight the airplane.

C. **All necessary documents, maps, safety equipment, spare fuses, etc., should be aboard. The word ARROW will help you to remember the required documents:**

1. **A** irworthiness Certificate (see sample below).
2. **R** egistration Certificate (see sample below).
3. **R** adio station license (see sample on next page).
4. **O** perating limitations, or *FAA-Approved Airplane Flight Manual*.
5. **W** eight and balance information (also in the Flight Manual).
6. Flotation gear if the flight is to be conducted over water.

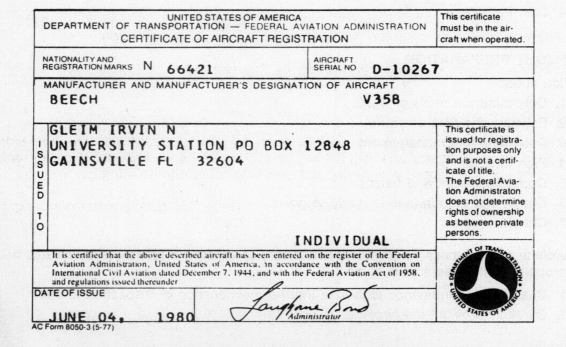

UNITED STATES OF AMERICA
DEPARTMENT OF TRANSPORTATION FEDERAL AVIATION ADMINISTRATION
STANDARD AIRWORTHINESS CERTIFICATE

1. NATIONALITY AND REGISTRATION MARKS	2. MANUFACTURER AND MODEL	3. AIRCRAFT SERIAL NUMBER	4. CATEGORY
N66421	BEECH AIRCRAFT CORP. - V35B	D-10267	UTILITY

5. AUTHORITY AND BASIS FOR ISSUANCE
This airworthiness certificate is issued pursuant to the Federal Aviation Act of 1958 and certifies that, as of the date of issuance, the aircraft to which issued has been inspected and found to conform to the type certificate therefor, to be in condition for safe operation, and has been shown to meet the requirements of the applicable comprehensive and detailed airworthiness code as provided by Annex 8 to the Convention on International Civil Aviation, except as noted herein.
Exceptions:

NONE

6. TERMS AND CONDITIONS
Unless sooner surrendered, suspended, revoked, or a termination date is otherwise established by the Administrator, this airworthiness certificate is effective as long as the maintenance, preventative maintenance, and alterations are performed in accordance with Parts 21, 43, and 91 of the Federal Aviation Regulations, as appropriate, and the aircraft is registered in the United States.

DATE OF ISSUANCE	FAA REPRESENTATIVE	DESIGNATION NUMBER
June 22, 1989	D. M. Porteous	DOA, PC#8

Any alteration, reproduction, or misuse of this certificate may be punishable by a fine not exceeding $1,000, or imprisonment not exceeding 3 years, or both. THIS CERTIFICATE MUST BE DISPLAYED IN THE AIRCRAFT IN ACCORDANCE WITH APPLICABLE FEDERAL AVIATION REGULATIONS.

FAA Form 8100-2 (7-67) FORMERLY FAA FORM 1362   U S Government Printing Office — 1978-875-526

UNITED STATES OF AMERICA
DEPARTMENT OF TRANSPORTATION — FEDERAL AVIATION ADMINISTRATION
CERTIFICATE OF AIRCRAFT REGISTRATION

This certificate must be in the aircraft when operated.

NATIONALITY AND REGISTRATION MARKS	N 66421	AIRCRAFT SERIAL NO	D-10267

MANUFACTURER AND MANUFACTURER'S DESIGNATION OF AIRCRAFT
BEECH   **V35B**

I
S GLEIM IRVIN N
S UNIVERSITY STATION PO BOX 12848
U GAINSVILLE FL   32604
E
D

T
O   INDIVIDUAL

This certificate is issued for registration purposes only and is not a certificate of title.
The Federal Aviation Administraton does not determine rights of ownership as between private persons.

It is certified that the above described aircraft has been entered on the register of the Federal Aviation Administration, United States of America, in accordance with the Convention on International Civil Aviation dated December 7, 1944, and with the Federal Aviation Act of 1958, and regulations issued thereunder.

DATE OF ISSUE	
JUNE 04, 1980	*Administrator*

AC Form 8050-3 (5-77)

SHIP/AIRCRAFT RADIO STATION LICENSE FEDERAL COMMUNICATIONS COMMISSION
WASHINGTON, D C 20554

☒ AIRCRAFT	FAA NUMBER OR FCC CONTROL NUMBER M47247	NUMBER AIRCRAFT IN FLEET	EFFECTIVE DATE 03-17-88	EXPIRATION DATE 03-17-39
☐ SHIP	NAME OF SHIP		OFFICIAL NUMBER	RADIO CALL SIGN	SELECTIVE CALLING NO
EFFECTIVE DATE	EXPIRATION DATE	ENDORSEMENT DATES		

FREQUENCIES AND CONDITIONS

PRIVATE AIRCRAFT (SECTION 87.281)
TRANSMITTERS: VHF COMM. (118-136 MHZ) EMERGENCY LOCATOR (121.5 4 243 MHZ)
TRANSPONDER (1090 MHZ)

THIS LICENSE SUBJECT TO FURTHER
CONDITIONS SET FORTH ON THE REVERSE SIDE

NOT TRANSFERABLE

(Must be posted aboard aircraft or ship)

FCC Form 559
July 1978

RICHARD E BENSON
1814 NW 23RD BLVD APT 193
GAINESVILLE   FLA
32605

D. In addition to obtaining a weather briefing, you are required to determine the runway lengths at airports of intended use and the takeoff and landing distances required by your airplane at those airports based on field altitude and weather conditions. Check for "Notices to Airmen" (NOTAMs, see page 216) affecting your route.

E. VFR rules require sufficient fuel (based on forecast wind and weather conditions) to fly to the intended destination at normal cruise speed, AND

1. Be able to continue on for 30 minutes in daytime (45 minutes at night).

F. Prior to your departure, visit your airplane and make sure it is fully fueled and that all equipment is operational.

G. Be sure to have your pilot and medical certificates in your possession.

H. Complete a flight log as explained on pages 216 and 217.

WEIGHT AND BALANCE

A. Weight and balance calculations must be reviewed prior to each flight. On local training flights without baggage and with full fuel, weight and balance should not be a problem. On cross-country flights, weight and balance data warrant more attention.

B. Operation in excess of the maximum weight or outside CG limits is extremely dangerous and prohibited.

C. See the discussion of weight and balance in Chapter 3, beginning on page 59.

NAVIGATION

A. The various means of navigation are

1. Pilotage
2. Dead reckoning
3. VOR navigation
4. ADF
5. LORAN

B. Review and make sure you have all the current navigational charts for the trip.

C. Consult Chapter 11, "Navigation Made Easy," in *PRIVATE PILOT HANDBOOK* as necessary.

D. A flight log is used to assist pilots in planning and conducting cross-country flights. The following discussion explains the flight log presented below. As a recreational pilot, you will not be making cross-country flight except under the supervision of a CFI while you are training for your private pilot certificate. Recreational pilots are restricted to within 50 NM of the airport where they received their instruction. "Navigation," as a topic, is overviewed to put the four PTSs (pilotage, weather, diversion, and lost procedures) in perspective.

1. Note that the top half is the actual "flight log." The bottom can be used for notes for weather, winds, NOTAMs, and radio frequencies.

    a. Write down all the radio frequencies you will need at each airport and for each VOR you will use for navigation. This will relieve you from frantically fumbling for them during flight and will give you added confidence.

FLIGHT LOG

		PREFLIGHT									ENROUTE					
From	To	True Course	Wind Corr.	True Head.	Var.	Mag. Head.	Dist. Log / Total	Est. GS	Time Log / Total	Est. Fuel	Act'l. Time	Act'l. GS	Dist. Next Pt.	Est. Arr'l.	Fuel Used	Fuel Remain

Weather Reports	Winds Aloft	Radio and Navigation Frequencies
Terminal Forecasts	NOTAMS	

2. The left two-thirds of the top is completed prior to your flight (after you have your winds aloft data), and the right third of the top is completed while you are en route.

3. The "from" and "to" columns are origin and destination points between which you are navigating.

   a. The most practical points are VORs. If you use VORs, you only need to calculate your estimated groundspeed, as you will automatically adjust your heading to keep your VOR CDI needle centered.

   b. However, these points may also be airports to which your flight instructor may want you to navigate without VOR for practice.

4. The true course is measured clockwise from your heading from true north, as measured by your protractor on your sectional chart.

5. Wind correction (plus or minus) is computed on the wind side of your flight computer as discussed in Chapter 12, "Flight Computers," in *PRIVATE PILOT HANDBOOK.*

6. Your true heading is your true course adjusted for wind correction.

7. Magnetic variation is the difference between true north and magnetic north. The amount of variation is identified in your geographic area by red dashed isogonic lines on your sectional charts.

8. The magnetic heading is the true heading adjusted for magnetic variation.

   a. Remember, subtract easterly variation and add westerly variation.

   b. When en route, remember that compass heading is the magnetic heading adjusted for compass error using the compass correction card. The compass correction card is found on the front of your compass. It tells you what compass heading to hold to obtain a magnetic heading.

9. The distance is measured between the two points on your sectional chart with a navigational plotter. Remember to use the side with the 1:500,000 scale for sectional charts.

10. If you are using VORs to navigate from and to (which you should), the directions of the airways are magnetic; i.e., they are adjusted for local magnetic variation.

    a. The same is true for the compass rose encircling each VOR.

    b. Thus, when using VORs, you should start with the magnetic course (unadjusted for wind) directly from the sectional chart. Then compute the wind correction angle and adjust the original magnetic heading to the adjusted magnetic heading.

11. When you compute the wind correction on your flight computer, also note your estimated groundspeed.

12. Based on the distance and groundspeed, you can determine your estimated time for this leg and the cumulative estimated time for the flight.

13. Given the estimated time en route and your planned fuel consumption, determine the fuel to be used on that leg.

14. Once en route, you should mark down the time over every checkpoint. Then you can compare your estimated groundspeed to actual groundspeed, and revise your estimated fuel (used and remaining).

E. Note that the above procedure is not mandatory and there are many possible short-cuts, even to the point of not using a flight log, which is the case with very routine flights.

1. For your training flights and your first real cross-country flights, however, you should work up a complete flight log.

2. After you gain experience, you may want to use an abbreviated flight log. A sample is reproduced below. It is the reverse side of the FAA flight plan (Form 7233-1) which is reproduced on page 222. Feel free to photocopy it for your own use.

FLIGHT LOG

DEPARTURE POINT	VOR	RADIAL	DISTANCE	TIME		GROUND SPEED
	IDENT.	TO	LEG	POINT-POINT	TAKEOFF	
	FREQ.	FROM	REMAINING	CUMULATIVE		
CHECK POINT					ETA	
					ATA	
DESTINATION						
		TOTAL				

PREFLIGHT CHECK LIST

DATE

EN ROUTE WEATHER/WEATHER ADVISORIES

DESTINATION WEATHER | **WINDS ALOFT**

ALTERNATE WEATHER

FORECASTS

NOTAMS/AIRSPACE RESTRICTIONS

PILOTAGE VS. DEAD RECKONING

A. Pilotage is the term given to navigation by known landmarks and by landmarks depicted on your sectional chart. For example, you might navigate from New Orleans, Louisiana to Jacksonville, Florida by following Interstate 10, which goes directly between them.

    1. Local flight navigation is almost entirely by pilotage, i.e., based on familiar landmarks.

    2. Practice pilotage and sectional chart interpretation by riding along in someone else's airplane on a cross-country flight and following the flight on sectional chart(s).

B. Dead reckoning navigation is based on computations involving course, wind direction and speed, airspeed, heading, groundspeed, and time enroute. The steps involved in dead reckoning are described in conjunction with the flight log discussion in the prior sideheading, "Navigation."

C. Ideally, a VFR pilot uses both pilotage and dead reckoning.

    1. This combination is required in the FAA's Practical Test Standards (PTSs).

    2. Also, radio navigation should be added to the above two, so that you use all three.

D. Radio navigation is covered extensively in Chapter 11 of *PRIVATE PILOT HANDBOOK* and other aeronautical texts.

    1. In private airplanes in the United States, the common navigation systems are

        a. VORs

        b. ADFs

        c. LORAN

    2. While you should be conversant with all three in general terms, you must be able to use the system available in the airplane in which you are training.

PILOTAGE PTS

TASK: PILOTAGE (ASEL)
PILOT OPERATION - 4
REFERENCES: AC 61-21, AC 61-23.

Objective. To determine that the applicant:

1. *Exhibits knowledge by explaining pilotage techniques and procedures.*

2. *Follows the preplanned course solely by visual reference to landmarks, with the aid of a magnetic compass.*

3. *Identifies landmarks by relating the surface features to chart symbols.*

4. *Verifies the airplane position within 3 nautical miles at all times.*

5. *Maintains the selected altitudes, ±200 feet.*

6. *Maintains the appropriate power setting for the desired airspeed.*

7. *Maintains the desired heading, ±10°.*

8. *Follows the climb, cruise, and descent checklists.*

9. *Requests in-flight weather information and uncontrolled airport trafffic advisories, as necessary, and properly operates the transponder. (Note: These requirements may be simulated in flight by the examiner when testing the applicant whose airplane IS radio or transponder equipped, and will be orally tested ONLY for the applicant whose airplane IS NOT radio or transponder equipped.)*

WEATHER

A. On all cross-country flights, the pilot is required to determine that the existing and forecasted weather conditions are appropriate for the flight (FAR 91.5).

B. As a practical matter, you are going to learn to observe weather and determine if it is "nice" enough to fly locally as a recreational pilot.

1. If marginal, you may takeoff and then decide how far you should venture from the airport if you do not land immediately.

2. Sometimes you will take off in good weather and it will deteriorate, and you will return to your airport.

C. There are several types of forecasts and reports, but the primary ones are

1. Area forecasts.
2. Terminal forecasts.
3. Hourly sequence reports.
4. Winds aloft forecasts and reports.

D. Refer to Chapter 7, "Understanding Weather," in *PRIVATE PILOT HANDBOOK*.

E. FAA Flight Service Stations (FSSs) have primary responsibility for

1. Preflight pilot briefing.
2. En route communications with VFR flights.
3. Assisting lost VFR aircraft.
4. Broadcasting aviation weather information.
5. Accepting and closing flight plans.
6. Operating the weather teletypewriter systems.
7. Taking local weather observations.
8. Issuing airport advisories.

F. You should always consult your local FSS or National Weather Service Office (NWSO) for preflight weather briefing.

1. Identify yourself as a pilot. State your airplane type and call sign, e.g., Beech Skipper 66421. Many persons calling weather service stations want information for purposes other than flying.

2. State your departure airport, intended route, desired flight altitude, destination, any probable stops, proposed departure time, and estimated time en route.

3. Advise if you intend to fly only VFR.

G. After you have your private pilot certificate, but before you have your instrument rating, you will be allowed to fly cross-country only when Visual Flight Rules (VFR) weather prevails along the route and at the destination.

1. Minimum VFR weather requires that the ceiling (height of the cloud base) be at least 1,000 ft above the surface, with at least 3 miles horizontal visibility.

a. This ceiling restriction only applies within control zones.

2. When flying below 10,000 ft MSL in controlled airspace, the VFR pilot must be able to remain at least 500 ft vertically below, 1,000 ft vertically above, and 2,000 ft horizontally from the clouds.

   a. This also applies in uncontrolled airspace above 1,200 ft AGL and below 10,000 ft MSL.

3. However, these are the absolute minimum requirements and are not recommended for pilots having limited experience. Much better weather conditions are advisable.

4. As a recreational pilot, you are required to have 3 miles visibility and always have the ground in sight.

OBTAINING WEATHER INFORMATION PTS

TASK: OBTAINING WEATHER INFORMATION (ASEL)
      PILOT OPERATION - 1
      REFERENCES: AC 00-6, AC 00-45, AC 61-21, AC 61-23, AC 61-84.

Objective. To determine that the applicant:

1. *Exhibits knowledge of aviation weather information by obtaining, reading, and analyzing -*

   a. *weather reports and forecasts.*
   b. *weather charts.*
   c. *pilot weather reports.*

   d. *SIGMETs and AIRMETs, including wind-shear reports.*
   e. *Notices to Airmen.*

2. *Makes a competent go/no-go decision based on the available weather information.*

VFR FLIGHT PLAN

A. VFR flight plans are not mandatory but are highly recommended as a safety precaution. In the event you do not reach your destination as planned, the FAA will institute a search for you. This process begins 30 minutes after you were scheduled to reach your destination.

B. Flight plans can be filed in person at FSSs, in which case you give them a completed flight plan form.

   1. Flight plans may be called in by telephone.

   2. They may be radioed in when in flight.

   3. Thus, it is wise to have a copy of the flight plan form in your airplane and at home, office, etc. to facilitate filing flight plans.

      a. You can fill out the form and read it to the FSS personnel, or you can use it as a checklist.

      b. The flight plan form (on the next page) may be photocopied for your own use. It is also available at FSSs and other FAA offices. The abbreviated flight log (page 218) is printed on the back of the FAA flight plan.

Form Approved: OMB No. 04-R0072

DEPARTMENT OF TRANSPORTATION FEDERAL AVIATION ADMINISTRATION **FLIGHT PLAN**	CIVIL AIRCRAFT PILOTS. FAR Part 91 requires you file an IFR flight plan to operate under instrument flight rules in controlled airspace. Failure to file could result in a civil penalty not to exceed $1,000 for each violation (Section 901 of the Federal Aviation Act of 1958, as amended). Filing of a VFR flight plan is recommended as a good operating practice. See also Part 99 for requirements concerning DVFR flight plans.					

1. TYPE	2. AIRCRAFT IDENTIFICATION	3. AIRCRAFT TYPE/ SPECIAL EQUIPMENT	4. TRUE AIRSPEED	5. DEPARTURE POINT	6. DEPARTURE TIME		7. CRUISING ALTITUDE
VFR					PROPOSED (Z)	ACTUAL (Z)	
IFR							
DVFR			KTS				

8. ROUTE OF FLIGHT

9. DESTINATION (Name of airport and city)	10. EST. TIME ENROUTE		11. REMARKS
	HOURS	MINUTES	

12. FUEL ON BOARD		13. ALTERNATE AIRPORT(S)	14. PILOT'S NAME, ADDRESS & TELEPHONE NUMBER & AIRCRAFT HOME BASE	15. NUMBER ABOARD
HOURS	MINUTES			

16. COLOR OF AIRCRAFT	
	CLOSE VFR FLIGHT PLAN WITH_____FSS ON ARRIVAL

FAA Form 7233-1 (5-77)

C. As illustrated above, a flight plan requires the following 16 points of information:

1. Type - VFR, IFR, DVFR (DVFR refers to defense VFR flights. They are those VFR flights into air defense identification zones which require a VFR flight plan to be filed).

2. Airplane identification.

3. Airplane type/special equipment.

4. True airspeed (kts).

5. Departure point.

6. Departure time - proposed (Z) and actual (Z).

7. Cruising altitude.

8. Route of flight.

9. Destination (name of airport and city).

10. Estimated time en route - hours and minutes.

11. Remarks.

12. Fuel on board - hours and minutes.

13. Alternate airport(s).

14. Pilot's name, address, and telephone number, and airplane home base.

15. Number aboard.

16. Color of aircraft.

D. Your FSS attendant will be glad to assist you and answer any questions. Occasionally you may have to file a flight plan without an FAA form in front of you. Give all of the data (in any order that comes to mind) and the FSS attendant will ask you for the rest.

E. CLOSE YOUR FLIGHT PLAN: REMEMBER! REMEMBER!

1. Add "Close your flight plan" to your after-landing checklist.

2. If you do not close your flight plan, the FAA will have to devote its limited and valuable resources attempting to determine if you did in fact arrive safely.

    a. If they cannot locate you or your airplane, they will contact the Civil Air Patrol (CAP) which will institute a "Search and Rescue" mission, the cost of which you may be responsible for.

3. Thus, it is particularly important to notify any FAA facility when you are late (over 30 minutes) or have diverted to an alternate route or destination.

4. While en route, you can identify yourself and your location to FSSs along your route (especially convenient if you are obtaining weather information), which will assist the FAA if they have to look for you.

DIVERSION TO AN ALTERNATE AIRPORT

A. Frequently on cross-country flights, pilots will divert from their original plan and land at another (i.e., alternate) airport. This is called "Diversion to an Alternate." Reasons include

1. Low fuel.
2. Bad weather at original destination.
3. Better weather at alternate.
4. Your own or passenger fatigue, illness, etc.
5. Airplane malfunction.
6. Alternate more convenient.
7. Changed route of flight.

B. As a practical matter, you will always be within 50 NM of your "home" airport, and "diversion" will occur infrequently. Possible causes are weather, low fuel, and mechanical difficulties.

C. Most alternates are weather induced because VFR cross-country flight is susceptible to weather changes.

1. Plan ahead with respect to weather on cross-country flights.
2. Plan to get your instrument rating.

D. Diversion is easiest when you know your present location and are aware of alternate airports.

1. As you plan your route for cross-country flight, you should consider alternates and keep them in mind as you undertake the flight.

2. As you fly cross-country, you should continuously monitor your position on sectional charts and your proximity to useful alternative airports. The FAA PTSs require you to know exactly where you are, i.e., within 3 NM.

E. Divert on a TIMELY basis. The longer you wait, the fewer the advantages or benefits of making the diversion.

1. In the event diversion to an alternate airport results from an emergency, it is important for the pilot to divert to the new course as early as possible.

   a. Consider the relative distance to all suitable alternates.
   b. Select the alternative most appropriate to the emergency at hand.
   c. Change your heading to establish the approximate course immediately.
   d. Later, wind correction, actual distance, and estimated time and fuel required can be computed.

2. Courses to alternates can be estimated with reasonable accuracy using a straight-edge and the compass roses shown at VOR stations on the sectional chart.

   a. The VOR radials and airway courses (already oriented to magnetic direction) printed on the chart can be used satisfactorily for approximation of magnetic bearings during VFR flights.
   b. Remember that the VOR radial or printed airway direction is **outbound** from the station. The course **to** the station is the reciprocal of the parallel radial or airway.
   c. Distances can be determined by using the measurements on a plotter, or by placing a finger at the appropriate place on the straight side of a piece of paper and then measuring the approximate distance on the mileage scale at the bottom of the chart.

3. If radio aids are used to divert to an alternate, the pilot should

   a. Select the appropriate facility.
   b. Tune to the proper frequency.
   c. Determine the course or radial to intercept or follow.

DIVERSION PTS

TASK: DIVERSION (ASEL)
PILOT OPERATION - 4
REFERENCES: AC 61-21, AC 61-23.

Objective. To determine that the applicant:

1. Exhibits knowledge by explaining the procedures for diverting to an alternate airport, including the recognition of conditions requiring a diversion.
2. Selects an alternate airport and route.
3. Proceeds promptly toward the alternate airport.
4. Makes a reasonable estimate of heading and fuel consumption.
5. Maintains the appropriate altitude, ±200 feet and the desired airspeed, ±10 knots.

LOST PROCEDURES

A. Nobody wants to get lost, especially in an airplane, but all pilots occasionally find themselves disoriented. The pilot should recognize disorientation quickly and implement corrective action to become reoriented.

B. Steps to avoid becoming lost.

1. Always know where you are.

2. Plan ahead and know what your next landmark will be and look for it.

   a. Similarly, anticipate the indication of your radio navigation aids.

3. Monitor your radio navigation aids and observe the expected landmarks.

4. If your radio navigation aids OR your visual observations of landmarks do not confirm your expectations, become concerned and take action.

5. As a recreational pilot, you are limited to 50 NM from the airport where you received instruction. Avoid exceeding this 50 NM limit and becoming lost by drawing a 50 NM circle around your "home" airport and studying all landmarks and their direction/distance to your airport.

   a. Always carry a sectional chart in your airplane.

   b. Be aware of available navigational aids, e.g., VOR, ADF, etc. and learn how to use them.

C. As soon as you begin to wonder where you are, remember the point where you last were confident of your location.

1. Watch your heading. Know what it is and keep it constant.

2. Do not panic. You are not "lost" yet.

3. Recompute your expected radio navigation indications and visual landmarks.

   a. Reconfirm your heading (compass and directional gyro).

   b. Confirm correct radio frequencies and settings.

   c. Review your sectional chart, noting last confirmed landmark.

4. Attempt to reconfirm present position.

D. Steps when lost.

1. Recognize the disorientation, etc. as soon as possible.

2. Recognize that only orderly, systematic procedures will help.

3. Fly the airplane. Keep a constant heading. Avoid areas of marginal visibility while keeping track of your heading.

4. Select a positive course of action and pursue it, knowing there are still other courses of action available.

5. If you have the equipment and a calm frame of mind, identify your location by tuning in several navigational aids to determine your position.

   a. If you are having trouble receiving a navigational aid, you may be slightly too low and too far away. Climb, and then recheck your reception.

6. If you are receiving a known radio aid and can identify it, fly to it.

7. If you have a very long known landmark in one direction, e.g., a sea coast, interstate highway, etc., you may wish to dead reckon to it.

8. If you are confident of your general position, you may wish to dead reckon to the general direction of your destination.

    a. Thus, even though you are unsure of your exact present position, you will proceed with the confidence that you are going in the correct direction.

9. If you are in or approaching marginal weather, and especially if weather is better behind you, you should make a 180° turn and retrace your route.

10. If you are able to reach someone on your communications radio, ask for help.

    a. There is nothing wrong with asking for assistance.

    b. DF Steer: Most FSSs have the capability of determining your location if you transmit to them.

    c. The important point is to ask for help before other problems develop, e.g., low fuel, panic, nightfall, adverse weather, etc.

    d. Remember the availability of 121.5 for emergencies.

11. Remember that marginal VFR conditions frequently contribute to a lost situation. Worse than being lost is spatial disorientation. Avoid both conditions, but the latter is worse than the former.

    a. Avoid marginal VFR cross-country weather conditions.

    b. Use a 180° turn when marginal weather conditions are encountered.

    c. Use alternate destinations.

12. If you are lost and night is approaching, declare an emergency on 121.50 MHz and land immediately on the best suitable field while still in daylight.

    a. Recreational pilots have no night training and it is illegal to fly at night.

    b. Do not wait until it is too late to find a suitable field and be forced to execute an emergency landing in inadequate light. Also, remember that it gets dark on the ground before it does at altitude. Watch the shadows as the sun begins to set.

LOST PROCEDURE PTS

TASK: LOST PROCEDURE (ASEL)
PILOT OPERATION - 4
REFERENCES: AC 61-21, AC 61-23.

Objective. *To determine that the applicant:*

1. *Exhibits knowledge by explaining lost procedures, including the following items -*

    a. *maintaining the original or an appropriate heading, identifying landmarks, and climbing, if necessary or possible.*

    b. *proceeding to and identifying the nearest concentration of prominent landmarks.*

    c. *planning a precautionary landing if deteriorating visibility and/or fuel exhaustion is imminent.*

2. *Selects the best course of action when given a lost situation.*

CHAPTER THIRTEEN
EMERGENCIES

Emergencies are threatening events and situations that you do not expect, such as equipment or engine malfunction, adverse weather, or getting lost. By definition we expect the expected and not the unexpected.

Preparation for emergencies involves anticipating the unexpected and training/planning for them. Begin by studying Section 3 of your airplane's *Pilot's Operating Handbook* (POH), "Emergency Procedures." As you fly, think about the "what ifs?" of engine failure, fire, etc.

If you are not training on a sod runway, ask your instructor to locate a sod runway and/or pasture for practice landings and takeoffs. Under your instructor's supervision, do an emergency approach and landing in a pasture.

Getting lost should not be a problem within a 50 nautical mile (NM) radius of your home base. Study your sectional chart carefully, noting all landmarks. Refer to Chapter 12, "Navigation," and see "Lost Procedures" on page 225.

Weather should not be a problem because, as a recreational pilot, you are committed to be a "fair weather pilot." Do not fly when there is any threat or forecast of bad weather (low visibility, wind, or turbulence).

TAKEOFF EMERGENCIES

A. The most common emergency you can have on takeoff is to lose engine power during the takeoff roll or during the takeoff climb.

   1. If engine power is lost during the takeoff roll and there is still enough runway to stop the airplane, pull the throttle to idle, step on the brakes, and slow the airplane to a stop.

   2. If you are just lifting off the runway and lose your engine power, try to land the airplane on the remaining runway. Immediately check your airspeed and set up approach attitude. Airspeed will tend to bleed away very fast due to drag and gravity.

      a. In a nose-up climb attitude close to the ground, you are extremely vulnerable to a stall without enough altitude to recover.

      b. After establishing approach attitude and airspeed, roundout may have to start immediately to avoid landing on your nosewheel.

3. If engine power is lost anytime during the climbout, a general rule of thumb is that if the airplane is above 500-1,000 ft AGL, you may have enough altitude to turn back and land on the runway you have just taken off from. This decision must be based on distance from airport, wind condition, and obstacles, but above all on your knowledge of the glide capability of your airplane.

    a. Watch your airspeed! Avoiding a stall is the most important consideration. Remember: control yoke forward (nose down) for more airspeed.

4. If the airplane is below 500 ft AGL, do not try to turn back. If you turn back you will probably either stall or hit the ground before you get back to the runway.

    a. The best thing to do is land the airplane straight ahead. Land in a clear area, if possible.

    b. If you have no option but to go into trees, slow the airplane to just above the stall speed (as close to the treetops as possible) to strike the trees with the slowest forward speed possible.

B. As in all emergencies, you must maintain your composure and remain in control. The peculiarity of engine power failures on takeoff is that you have so little time to attempt to correct the problem, i.e., you just have time to land.

1. However, if the problem was caused by the ignition or fuel being turned off, turn them on.

2. Here is the place to re-emphasize the need for both a thorough preflight inspection and a thorough pretakeoff check (remember your checklists!).

EQUIPMENT MALFUNCTIONS

A. When an instrument or gauge indicates abnormally, or if you recognize abnormal operation of any part of your airplane, begin by assessing the situation and possible corrective action.

1. Then choose the best corrective action, execute it, and monitor your success in dealing with the situation.

2. As appropriate, use your radio to communicate your call sign, type of airplane, location, situation, and intentions.

B. As soon as you resolve the problem, communicate your improved situation to avoid inconveniencing those who would come to your aid.

C. The real key is knowledge of your airplane. Read and study your *POH* before you fly. In an emergency, you may not have time to consult your *POH*.

D. To prepare for your practical test, research your *POH* for each malfunction contained in the PTS Task and discuss any questions or concerns with your CFI.

SYSTEMS AND EQUIPMENT MALFUNCTIONS PTS

> **TASK: SYSTEMS AND EQUIPMENT MALFUNCTIONS** *(ASEL)*
> *PILOT OPERATION - 6*
> *REFERENCES: AC 61-21; Pilot's Operating Handbook and FAA-Approved Airplane Flight Manual.*
>
> **Objective.** To determine that the applicant:
>
> 1. Exhibits knowledge, as appropriate, by explaining causes, indications, and pilot actions for various systems and equipment malfunctions.
>
> 2. Analyzes the situation and takes appropriate action for simulated emergencies such as
>
>   a. partial power loss.
>   b. rough running engine or overheat.
>   c. carburetor or induction icing.
>
>   d. loss of oil pressure.
>   e. fuel starvation.
>   f. engine compartment fire.
>   g. electrical system malfunction.
>   h. flap malfunction.
>   i. door opening in flight.
>   j. trim inoperative.
>   k. other malfunctions.

EMERGENCY LANDINGS

A. If engine power is lost, you may have to execute an emergency landing.

  1. First, trim your airplane to the maximum glide speed.

      a. Beechcraft Skipper -- 63 kts.
      b. Cessna 152 -- 60 kts.
      c. Piper Tomahawk -- 70 kts.

  2. Second, pick a landing field, road, etc. for an emergency landing site.

      a. Take into account your altitude, the wind, obstructions, landing surfaces, etc.

      b. The site should be close enough to require several turns (which will permit you to adjust your altitude). Attempting a "straight in" landing on a distant landing site leaves a high likelihood of error.

  3. Third, while keeping the airplane under full control and gliding toward your emergency landing site, perform your emergency checklist, i.e., try to restart your engine.

B. Before the actual landing, you should do everything you can to

  1. Determine why power was lost and the engine quit.
  2. Try to restart the engine.
  3. Call for help on the radio.
  4. Minimize the chances of a problem during the landing.

C. Typical emergency engine out checklist (you must refer to the flight manual for your airplane).

  1. Carburetor heat - on.
  2. Fuel selector - "on" fullest tank.
  3. Mixture - rich.

4. Establish the best glide speed. Trim to hold best glide speed. This is very important. Otherwise, the nose will almost certainly drop when attention is diverted to the other steps in the emergency process.

5. Look for a suitable landing site. Turn towards the field.

6. Throttle - try all positions and use auxiliary fuel pump if available.

7. Engine gauges - check.

8. Magnetos - try both, left, right. Attempt to restart on each.

9. Master switch - on.

10. Primer - in and locked.

11. Radio - 121.5 "Mayday, Mayday, Mayday." Report problem and position.

12. If engine will not restart, shut down.

   a. Fuel - off.
   b. Mixture - lean.
   c. Throttle - idle.
   d. Magnetos - off.
   e. Master - off (after final flap setting is established).
   f. Seatbelts and shoulder harness - tighten.
   g. Doors - unlock.
   h. Land - as slowly as possible.
   i. Brakes - apply.
   j. Evacuate.

D. In the case of a forced landing.

1. A forced landing is a soft-field touchdown without power.

2. Attempt to land into the wind, although other factors may dictate a crosswind or downwind landing.

   a. Insufficient altitude may make it inadvisable or impossible to attempt to maneuver into the wind.

   b. Ground obstacles may make landing into the wind impractical or inadvisable because they shorten the effective length of the available field.

   c. The distance from a suitable field upwind from the present position may make it impossible to reach the field from the altitude at which the engine failure occurs.

   d. The best available field may be on a hill and at such an angle to the wind that a downwind landing uphill would be preferable and safer.

   e. See the top diagram on the opposite page.

3. Choose a smooth, grassy field if possible. If you land in a cultivated field, land parallel to the furrows. See the middle diagram.

4. Plan your turn onto final approach. See the bottom diagram.

5. Use roads only if clear of BOTH traffic and electric/telephone wires.

6. Land at a stable speed and hold the control yoke full back.

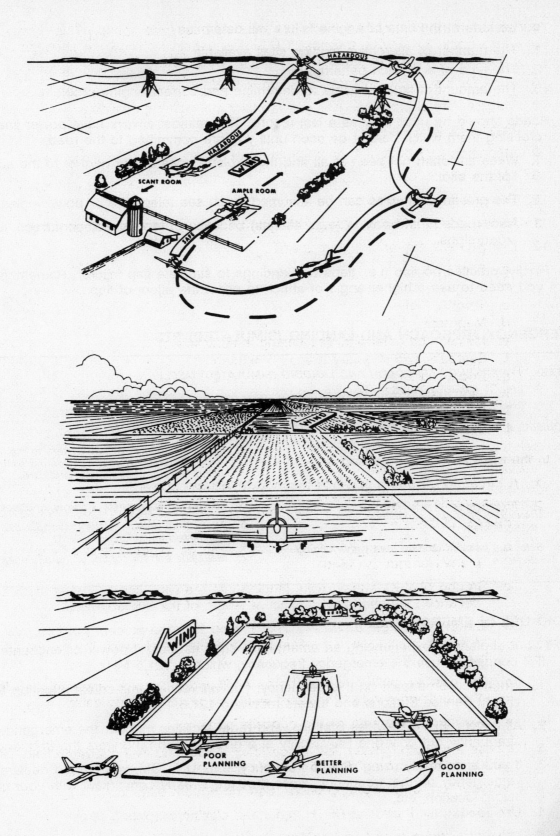

E.   Your altitude at the time of engine failure will determine

1. The number of alternative landing sites available.

2. The type of approach pattern.

3. The amount of time available to determine and correct engine problem.

F.   Roads should be used only as a last resort. They almost always have power lines crossing them which cannot be seen until you are committed to the road.

1. Wires are often not seen at all and the airplane goes out of control to the surprise of the pilot.

2. The presence of wires can be assumed if you see telephone or power poles.

3. Also, roads must be wide (e.g., 4-lanes) because of fences, adjacent trees, and road signs.

G.   Finally, practice no flap (i.e., flaps up) landings to simulate flap failure. Remember that you need to use a higher angle of attack to offset the effect of flaps.

EMERGENCY APPROACH AND LANDING (SIMULATED) PTS

> **TASK: *EMERGENCY APPROACH AND LANDING (SIMULATED)* *(ASEL)***
> *PILOT OPERATION - 6*
> *REFERENCE: AC 61-21.*
>
> ***Objective.*** *To determine that the applicant:*
>
> 1. *Exhibits knowledge by explaining approach and landing procedures to be used in various emergencies.*
>
> 2. *Establishes and maintains the recommended best-glide airspeed and configuration during simulated emergencies.*
>
> 3. *Selects a suitable landing area within gliding distance.*
>
> 4. *Plans and follows a flight pattern to the selected landing area, considering altitude, wind, terrain, obstructions, and other factors.*
>
> 5. *Follows an appropriate emergency checklist.*
>
> 6. *Attempts to determine the reason for the simulated malfunction.*
>
> 7. *Maintains correct control of the airplane.*

RADIO USE IN EMERGENCIES

A.   If your airplane is experiencing an emergency, such as loss of power or encountering IFR conditions, use the emergency frequency, which is 121.5 MHz.

1. When you broadcast on this frequency, you will receive immediate attention at the Flight Service Stations and towers receiving 121.5.

2. All towers, Flight Services Stations, and radar facilities monitor the emergency frequency but only one FAA facility at a given location monitors the frequency.

3. If you are already using a radio frequency, e.g., UNICOM, you should declare an emergency on that frequency, since they are already conversant with your call sign, location, etc.

B. A pilot in any emergency phase should do the following to obtain assistance:

1. If equipped with a radar beacon transponder and if unable to establish voice communications with an air traffic control facility, set the transponder to Code 7700.

2. Contact the controlling agency and give nature of distress and your intentions. If unable to contact controlling agencies, use 121.5.

C. Since you are within a 50 NM radius of your home base, determine which frequencies are appropriate in which areas at what altitudes.

1. Memorize them and hope you will never need them.

D. In an emergency, transmit:

1. Mayday (if appropriate).

2. Airplane identification.

3. Airplane type.

4. Location and altitude.

5. Intentions.

6. Once you have declared an emergency, issue updates to assist those coming to your aid, or let them know that assistance is NOT required.

7. Don't let the person you are talking to distract you on the radio. Aviate first, then communicate only when everything is under control.

RADIO COMMUNICATIONS (EMERGENCY) PTS

TASK: RADIO COMMUNICATIONS (ASEL)
PILOT OPERATION - 6
REFERENCES: AIM.

NOTE: For the applicant whose airplane IS NOT radio or transponder equipped, this task will be orally tested ONLY. For the applicant whose airplane IS radio or transponder equipped, this task may be simulated in flight by the examiner.

Objective. To determine that the applicant:

1. Exhibits knowledge by explaining radio communications or transponder procedures to be used in the event an emergency occurs.

2. Selects the appropriate emergency radio frequency (121.5 MHz) and/or adjusts transponder to appropriate emergency code.

3. Understands that two-way radio communications and/or radar coverage may not be available.

234

Blank Page

CHAPTER FOURTEEN
FAA PRACTICAL TEST

FAA Practical Test Standards 236
Your Practical Test 236
Preflight Preparation 237
Your Flight Maneuvers 238
Failure on the Practical Test 238
FAA-Suggested Equipment and Records Checklist 239
Recreational Pilot Certificate Application Form 240
Common Errors on the FAA Practical Test 244
Certificates and Documents PTS 244
Aeromedical Factors PTS 246
Good Luck !!! 247

This chapter consists of an overview of the FAA-designated examiner program, a checklist of equipment and records required for the FAA practical (flight) test, and the FAA forms relating to the practical test.

The FAA practical test consists of 34 Tasks as set forth in the FAA Practical Test Standards (PTSs). All 34 Tasks are listed in Appendix A with cross-references to the appropriate pages in this book (ALL 34 FAA TASKS ARE REPRODUCED IN THIS BOOK). The FAA practical test will be conducted by either an FAA inspector or an FAA-designated examiner (usually the latter).

FAA inspectors are full-time FAA employees who administer flight tests and review the paperwork generated by FAA-designated examiners. Years ago, FAA inspectors administered most flight tests, which were given at no cost. For budgetary reasons, the FAA developed a system whereby well-qualified instructors could become FAA-designated examiners and administer FAA flight tests for a fee. Most FAA practical tests are currently administered by FAA-designated examiners. FAA inspectors spend most of their time reviewing the paperwork generated by FAA-designated examiners.

As you proceed with your flight training, you and your instructor should plan ahead and schedule your practical test. Just as you inquire about doctors and barbers, you should inquire about the rigor and temperament of your FAA-designated examiner. You do not want to get stuck with someone who is unreasonable.

At least 1 week before your practical test is scheduled, you should contact one or two individuals who took a practical test with your FAA-designated examiner. Ask each person to explain the routine, length, emphasis, maneuvers, and any other peculiarities (i.e., surprises). Your instructor can probably also tell you what your FAA-designated examiner is going to require and put you in touch with one or two people who recently took a practical test with your examiner.

FAA PRACTICAL TEST STANDARDS

In previous chapters, the standards relating to 30 of the 34 Tasks were reproduced in each chapter as appropriate. The remaining two Tasks relate to the oral examination and are presented at the end of this chapter.

1. Certificates and Documents.
2. Aeromedical Factors.

YOUR PRACTICAL TEST

The practical test is your final exam. Once you complete it (successfully), your examiner will prepare a temporary pilot's certificate like the one illustrated below. Your permanent certificate will be sent to you directly from the FAA Aeronautical Center in Oklahoma City about 60 to 80 days after your flight test. At the current time, your temporary pilot certificate is valid for 120 days.

```
I. UNITED STATES OF AMERICA                               III. CERTIFICATE NO.
DEPARTMENT OF TRANSPORTATION—FEDERAL AVIATION ADMINISTRATION

  II. TEMPORARY AIRMAN CERTIFICATE

    THIS CERTIFIES THAT        IV.
                                V.

DATE OF BIRTH   HEIGHT    WEIGHT   HAIR     EYES    SEX    NATIONALITY       VI.
                      IN.

IX.   has been found to be properly qualified and is hereby authorized in accordance with
      the conditions of issuance on the reverse of this certificate to exercise the privileges of

RATINGS AND LIMITATIONS
XII.

XIII.

THIS IS ☐ AN ORIGINAL ISSUANCE ☐ A REISSUANCE     DATE OF SUPERSEDED AIRMAN CERTIFICATE
OF THIS GRADE OF CERTIFICATE

        BY DIRECTION OF THE ADMINISTRATOR          EXAMINER'S DESIGNATION NO. OR
X. DATE OF ISSUANCE   X. SIGNATURE OF EXAMINER OR   INSPECTOR'S REG. NO.
                         INSPECTOR
                                                    DATE DESIGNATION EXPIRES

FAA Form 8060-4 (4-69) Supersedes Previous Edition
```

Do not be intimidated by your examiner. His/her function is not to fail you, but rather to make sure that you can execute flight maneuvers safely.

Communicate with and talk to the examiner about what you are thinking and doing. If you make a mistake or execute a maneuver sloppily, tell the examiner what went wrong and how it should be corrected, i.e., what you would do if you were by yourself. The examiner wants you to be able to understand and correct your errors. Silence may imply that you are not aware of the error.

Think ahead!. Be prepared! Be confident! Do the best you can! (No one can ask for any more.)

Use the airplane you have been training in since you are familiar with it. If necessary, delay or reschedule your practical test. Do not get yourself into a marginal situation, i.e., with the wrong plane, bad weather, illness, etc.

During the oral examination on preflight preparation, be very attentive and show interest in the examiner. If you are not sure about something, say so and indicate where you would look it up, e.g., FARs, operating manual, etc. Ask questions of the examiner about anything you do not understand.

During the practical test YOU MUST be in control of the aircraft. If you have trouble with a maneuver, explain what you did wrong and offer to do it again. Remember: You are better than average and your examiner knows that you are a novice, not an airline transport pilot. If you feel you have executed a maneuver poorly, you may usually request to do it again with no penalty if it is done correctly the second time.

PREFLIGHT PREPARATION

The examiner may begin by asking you to plan navigating to an airport or other landmark of the examiner's choosing. You should plan the flight, including weather, fuel management, weight and balance considerations, etc. Note that it cannot be over 50 nautical miles (NM) away. The examiner will discuss the proposed flight with you, including related questions about sectional charts, weather, FARs, etc. The examiner will also ask you questions in other areas such as airplane systems and important airspeeds (e.g., V_Y, V_X, V_A, V_{NE}).

Questions about the airplane systems will include such items as the electrical system (voltage, location of the battery, what the ammeter tells you, etc.), the oil capacity, what type of oil the airplane uses, fuel grade, approximate fuel capacity, approximate range and endurance of the airplane, type and horsepower rating of the engine, and normal power settings.

In addition, the examiner will probably ask you to demonstrate the use of the airplane's operating manual or *Pilot's Operating Handbook* (POH) to determine the airplane's performance with respect to effects of temperature, pressure, altitude, wind, and gross weight. In other words, (s)he wants to see that you are familiar with the operating manual, the use of performance charts, and the location of other information about your airplane.

You will also be quizzed about the certificates and documents for the airplane: airworthiness certificate, registration, FCC radio station license, and maintenance logs. Can you determine if the annual maintenance has been done or the 100-hour inspection (if applicable), etc.? Finally, the examiner will use oral testing for certain flight demonstrations when they are impractical (e.g., equipment malfunctions, etc.) either during your oral exam or during the flight test. The oral exam will probably be 20 minutes to 1 hour in length.

YOUR FLIGHT MANEUVERS

The examiner will probably walk around the preflight with you. Do not forget the preflight. You will probably begin your practical test by executing a normal or crosswind takeoff as if you were going to fly to the airport or landmark you planned during the preflight preparation part of your practical test. The examiner will probably have you fly to your first or second checkpoint (so be sure to plan these within 10 or 15 miles away). When the examiner is satisfied that you could get to the destination, (s)he will probably have you proceed with flight maneuvers, i.e., stalls, slow flight, ground reference maneuvers, steep turns, emergency procedures, traffic patterns, landings, and takeoffs. The flight portion of your practical test will probably be 1 hour to 1½ hours in length.

FAILURE ON THE PRACTICAL TEST

About 95% of student pilots pass their FAA practical test the first time and virtually all that fail their first attempt pass the second time through. If you have a severe problem with a maneuver or have so much trouble that the examiner has to take control of the airplane to avoid or get out of a dangerous situation, the examiner will probably fail you. If so, the test will be terminated at that point.

When on the ground, the examiner will complete the Notice of Disapproval of Application, FAA Form 8060-5 which appears below. The examiner will indicate the areas necessary for re-examination.

UNITED STATES OF AMERICA
DEPARTMENT OF TRANSPORTATION—FEDERAL AVIATION ADMINISTRATION

NOTICE OF DISAPPROVAL OF APPLICATION

NOTE

PRESENT THIS FORM UPON APPLICATION FOR REEXAMINTION

NAME AND ADDRESS OF APPLICANT

CERTIFICATE OR RATING SOUGHT

On the date shown, you failed the examination indicated below:

☐ FLIGHT   ☐ ORAL   ☐ PRACTICAL

AIRCRAFT USED *(Make and Model)*	FLT. TIME RECORDED IN LOGBOOK		
	PILOT-IN-COMM. OR SOLO	INSTRUMENT	DUAL

UPON REAPPLICATION YOU WILL BE REEXAMINED ON THE FOLLOWING:

I have personally tested this applicant and deem his performance unsatisfactory for the issuance of the certificate or rating sought.

DATE OF EXAMINATION	SIGNATURE OF EXAMINER OR INSPECTOR	DESIGNATION OR OFFICE NO.

FAA Form 8060-5 (5-80)

The examiner will give you credit for the flight manuevers you successfully completed. You should indicate your intent to get with your instructor immediately to work on your deficiencies. Inquire about rescheduling the next flight test and having your flight instructor talk to the examiner about your proficiencies/problems. Many examiners have a reduced fee for a retake.

Next, promptly notify your flight instructor and schedule lessons to get you ready for the completion of your flight test. Have your flight instructor talk to the examiner. You may also wish to fly with another flight instructor prior to taking your flight test. This would give you additional confidence and also can be brought to the attention of the examiner on the second time through.

Finally, if you feel that a personality conflict developed between you and the examiner or that you have strong feelings against the examiner, you should go to another examiner for your second (and hopefully last) flight test. If you use another examiner, limit your explanation for change to the fact that you were concerned about a possible personality conflict.

Conversely, you can voluntarily terminate the examination at any point if you feel sick, get too nervous, etc. Do so by requesting voluntary termination from your examiner. (S)he will issue a letter for retake which is neither a certificate of approval nor of disapproval.

FAA-SUGGESTED EQUIPMENT AND RECORDS CHECKLIST

The following checklist should be reviewed with your instructor both 1 week before and 1 day before your scheduled flight test:

1. Acceptable airplane with dual controls
   a. Aircraft documents:
      1) Airworthiness certificate
      2) Registration certificate
      3) Operating limitations
   b. Aircraft maintenance records:
      1) Airworthiness inspections
   c. FCC station license (if applicable)
   d. Weight and balance data
2. Personal equipment
   a. Current aeronautical charts
   b. Plotter
   c. Flight plan form
   d. Flight logs (can be reverse side of flight plan; see page 218)
   e. Current *Airman's Information Manual* (AIM)

3. Personal records
    a. Pilot certificate (with current solo endorsement)
    b. Medical certificate
    c. Completed Application for an Airman Certificate and/or Rating (FAA Form 8710-1)
    d. Airman Written Test Report (AC Form 8080-2) (with instructor's endorsement, finding you competent in deficient areas)
    e. Logbook with instructor's endorsement
    f. Notice of disapproval (only if you previously failed your flight test)
    g. Examiner's fee (if applicable), which is about $100-$150 for the recreational pilot flight test

RECREATIONAL PILOT CERTIFICATE APPLICATION FORM

Prior to your FAA practical test, you and your instructor will complete the top ¾ of the front side of FAA Form 8710-1 (which appears on pages 242 and 243), and your instructor will sign the top of the back side of the form. Your instructor will provide the form and will assist in completing it, even though the form is largely self-explanatory. The FAA's instructions follow.

The bottom of the front side will be completed by the person administering your flight test (either a designated examiner or FAA inspector). (S)he will also complete the appropriate block of information on the back side after the flight test.

Whether you or your instructor fill out the Airman Certificate or Rating Application, the FAA provides a list of guidelines to keep the presentation consistent. Your examiner will appreciate receiving a form which is properly filled out, preferably typed, and correct. This also reflects well on both you and your instructor when the paperwork reaches Oklahoma City.

At the very top of FAA Form 8710, remember to check off the kind of pilot certificate you want, not the kind you already have. Until a new form is issued, you will have to check "Other" and fill in "Recreational." Also, do not forget to check "Airplane Single-Engine."

In Block E, Permanent Mailing Address, provide an address where you know you will be able to receive your certificate.

AIRMAN CERTIFICATE AND/OR RATING APPLICATION
INSTRUCTIONS FOR COMPLETING FAA FORM 8710-1 (6-86)

I. APPLICATION INFORMATION
Check appropriate block(s).

Block A. Name. Enter legal name but no more than one middle name for record purposes and do not change the name on subsequent applications unless it is done in accordance with FAR Section 61.25. If you have no middle name, enter "NMN." If you have a middle initial only, indicate "Initial only." If you are a Jr., or a 2nd or 3rd, so indicate. If you have an FAA pilot certificate, the name on the application should be the same as the name on the certificate unless you have had it changed in accordance with FAR Section 61.25.

Block B. Social Security Number. Optional: See supplemental Information Privacy Act. Do not leave blank: Enter either SSN or the words "Do not use" or "None."

Block C. Date of Birth. Check for accuracy. Enter six digits: Use numeric characters, i.e.; 07-09-25 instead of July 9, 1925. Check to see that DOB is the same as it is on the medical certificate.

Block D. Place of Birth. If you were born in the USA, enter the city and state where you were born. If the city is unknown, enter the county and state. If you were born outside the USA, enter the name of the city and country where you were born.

Block E. Permanent Mailing Address. The residence number and street, or P.O. Box number, goes in the top part of the block above the line. The city, state, and ZIP code go in the bottom part of the block below the line. Check for accuracy. Make sure the numbers are not transposed.

Block F. Nationality. Check USA if applicable. If not, enter the country where you are a citizen.

Block G. Do You Read, Speak, and Understand English? Check yes or no.

Block H. Height. Enter your height in inches. Example: 5'9" should be entered as 69 in. No fractions. Whole inches only.

Block I. Weight. Enter your weight in pounds. No fractions. Whole pounds only.

Block J. Hair. Spell out the color of your hair. If bald, enter "Bald." Color should be listed as black, red, brown, blond, or gray. If you wear a wig or toupee, enter the color of your hair under the wig or toupee.

Block K. Eyes. Spell out the color of your eyes. The color should be listed as blue, brown, black, hazel, green, or gray.

Block L. Sex. Check male or female.

Block M. Do You Now Hold or Have You Ever Held An FAA Pilot Certificate? Check yes or no. (NOTE: A student pilot certificate *is* a "Pilot Certificate.") If certificate has ever been suspended or revoked, check the appropriate box and enter the date of such action.

Block N. Grade. Enter the grade of pilot certificate (i.e., Student, Private, Commercial, or ATP). Do *NOT* enter flight instructor certificate information.

Block O. Certificate Number. Enter the number as it appears on your pilot certificate.

Block P. Date Issued. Date your pilot certificate was issued.

Block Q. Do You Now Hold A Medical Certificate? Check yes or no. If yes, complete Blocks R, S, and T.

Block R. Class of Certificate. Enter the class as shown on the medical certificate, i.e., 1st, 2nd, or 3rd class.

Block S. Date Issued. Date your medical certificate was issued.

Block T. Name of Examiner. As shown on the medical certificate.

Block U. Narcotics, Drugs, etc. Check appropriate block. This should be checked "Yes" only if you have been actually convicted. If you have been charged with a violation which has not been adjudicated, check "No."

Block V. If block "U" was checked "Yes" give the date of final conviction.

Block W. Glider or free balloon pilots should sign the medical certification in this block, if you do not hold a medical certificate. If you hold a medical certificate, be sure Blocks Q, R, S, and T are completed.

Block X. Date. Date you sign this self-certification statement.

II. Certificate Or Rating Applied For On Basis Of

Block A. Completion of Required Test.

1. AIRCRAFT TO BE USED (If flight test required) — Make and model. If more than one aircraft is to be used, indicate such.
2. TOTAL TIME IN THIS AIRCRAFT TYPE (Hrs.) — (a) Total Flight Time - In each make and model. (b) Pilot-In-Command Flight Time - In each make and model.

Block B. Military Competence Obtained In. Enter your branch of service, date rated as a military pilot, your rank or grade and service number, and the military aircraft in which you have flown 10 hours as pilot in command in the last 12 months in the boxes indicated.

Block C. Graduate of Approved Course.

1. NAME AND LOCATION OF TRAINING AGENCY. As shown on the graduation certificate. Be sure the location is entered.
2. AGENCY SCHOOL NUMBER. As shown on the graduation certificate.
3. CURRICULUM FROM WHICH GRADUATED. As shown on the graduation certificate.
4. DATE. Date of graduation from indicated course. Approved course graduate must also complete Block "A" *COMPLETION OF REQUIRED TEST.*

Block D. Holder of Foreign License Issued By.

1. COUNTRY. Country which issued the license.
2. GRADE OF LICENSE. Grade of license issued, i.e., private, commercial, etc.
3. NUMBER. Number which appears on the license.
4. RATINGS. All ratings that appear on the license.

III. Record of Pilot Time. The minimum pilot experience required by the appropriate regulation must be entered. It is recommended, however, that *ALL* pilot time be entered. If decimal points are used, be sure they are legible. Night flying must be entered when required. You should fill in the blocks that apply, and ignore the blocks that do not.

IV. Have You Failed A Test For This Certificate or Rating Within The Past 30 Days? Check appropriate block.

V. Applicant's Certification.

A. SIGNATURE. The way you normally sign your name.

B. DATE. The date you sign the application.

TYPE OR PRINT ALL ENTRIES IN INK

Form Approved OMB No: 2120-0021

Airman Certificate and/or Rating Application

U.S. Department of Transportation
Federal Aviation Administration

I Application Information

- ☐ Student
- ☐ Private
- ☐ Commercial
- ☐ Instrument
- ☐ Other _____
- ☐ Additional Aircraft Rating
- ☐ Flight Instructor
- ☐ Ground Instructor
- ☐ Airplane Single-Engine
- ☐ Airplane Multiengine
- ☐ Helicopter
- ☐ Glider
- ☐ Lighter-Than-Air
- ☐ Additional Instructor Rating
- ☐ Medical Flight Test
- ☐ Reexamination
- ☐ Reissuance of _____ Certificate
- ☐ Renewal of _____ Certificate
- ☐ Renewal of Flight Instructor Certificate
- ☐ Reinstatement of Flight Instructor Certificate

A. Name (First, Middle, Last)
B. SSN
C. Date of Birth Mo. Day Year
D. Place of Birth

E. Address
F. Nationality   Specify   ☐ USA   ☐ Other_____
G. Do you read, speak and understand English? ☐ Yes ☐No

City, State, Zip Code
H. Height   In.
I. Weight   Lbs.
J. Hair
K. Eyes
L. Sex ☐ Male ☐ Female

M. Do you now hold, or have you ever held An FAA Pilot Certificate? ☐ Yes ☐ No
If yes, has certificate ever been Suspended or Revoked ☐ Yes _____ Date ☐ No
N. Grade
O. Certificate Number
P. Date Issued

Q. Do you hold a Medical Certificate? ☐ Yes ☐ No
R. Class of Certificate
S. Date Issued
T. Name of Examiner

U. Have you ever been convicted for violation of any Federal or State statutes pertaining to narcotic drugs, Marijuana, and depressant or stimulant drugs or substances? ☐ No ☐ Yes
V. Date of Final Conviction

Glider or Free Balloon Pilots only:
Medical Statement: I have no known physical defect which makes me unable to pilot a glider or free balloon
W. Signature
X. Date

II Certificate or Rating Applied For on Basis of:

☐ A. Completion of Required Test
1. Aircraft to be used (if flight test required)
2a Total time in this aircraft   hours
2b Pilot in command   hours

☐ B. Military Competence Obtained In
1 Service
2 Date Rated
3 Rank or Grade and Service Number
4 Has flown at least 10 hours as pilot in command during the past 12 months in the following military aircraft.

☐ C. Graduate of Approved Course
1 Name and Location of Training Agency
2 Agency School Number
3 Curriculum From Which Graduated
4 Date

☐ D. Holder of Foreign License Issued By
1 Country
2 Grade of License
3 Number
4 Ratings

III Record of Pilot time (Do not write in the shaded areas.)

	Total	Instruction Rec'd	Solo	Pilot in Command	Second in Command	Cross Country Instruction Received	Cross Country Solo	Cross Country Pilot in Command	Instrument	Night Instr. Rec'd.	Night Take-off/ Landing	Night Pilot in Command	Night Takeoff/ Landing Pilot in Command	Number of Flights	Number of Aero-Tows	Number of Ground Launches	Number of Powered Launches	Number of Free Flights
Airplane																		
Rotor-Craft																		
Gliders																		
Lighter than Air																		
Instrument Ground Trainer																		

IV Have you failed a test for this certificate or rating within the past 30 days? ☐ Yes ☐ No

V Applicant's Certification
I certify that the statements made by me on this application are true.
A. Signature
B. Date

FAA Use Only

EMP	REG	D.O.	SEAL	CON	ISS	ACT	LEV	TR	S.H.	SRCH	#RTE		RATING (1)

FAA Form 8710-1 (6-86) Supersedes Previous Edition

Instructor's Recommendation
I have personally instructed the applicant and consider this person ready to take the test.

Date	Instructor's Signature	Certificate No:	Certificate Expires

Air Agency's Recommendation

The applicant has successfully completed our _____ course, and is

recommended for certification or rating without further _____ test.

Date	Agency Name and Number	Official's Signature
		Title

Designated Examiner's Report

☐ Student Pilot Certificate Issued *(Copy attached)*

☐ I have personally reviewed this applicant's pilot logbook, and certify that the individual meets the pertinent requirements of FAR 61 for the pilot certificate or rating sought.

☐ I have personally reviewed this applicant's graduation certificate, and found it to be appropriate and in order, and have returned the certificate.

☐ I have personally tested this applicant in accordance with pertinent procedures and standards, with the result indicated below.
    ☐ Approved—Temporary Certificate Issued *(Copy Attached)*
    ☐ Disapproved—Disapproval Notice Issued *(Copy Attached)*

Certificate or Rating for Which Tested	Type(s) of Aircraft Used	Registration No.(s)

Date	Examiner's Signature	Certificate No.	Designation No.	Designation Expires

Inspector's Report
I have personally tested this applicant in accordance with pertinent procedures and standards, with the result indicated below.
    ☐ Approved—Temporary Certificate Issued   ☐ Disapproved —Disapproval Notice Issued

Certificate or Rating for Which Tested	Type of Aircraft Used	Registration Number(s)

☐ Student Pilot Certificate issued   ☐ Certificate of Rating Based on   ☐ Instructor ☐ Flight ☐ Ground
☐ Examiner's Recommendation   ☐ Military Competence   ☐ Renewal ☐ Approved
    ☐ ACCEPTED ☐ REJECTED   ☐ Foreign License   ☐ Reinstatement ☐ Disapproved
☐ Examiner Recommends Retesting   ☐ Approved Course Graduate
☐ Reissue or Exchange of Pilot Certificate   ☐ Issued   **Instructor Renewal Based on**
☐ Special medical test conducted—report forwarded   ☐ Denied   ☐ Activity ☐ Training Course
    to Aeromedical Certification Branch, AAM-130   ☐ Acquaintance ☐ Test

Date	Inspector's Signature	FAA District Office

Attachments: ☐ Student Pilot Certificate (copy)   ☐ Notice of Disapproval   ☐ Answer Sheet Graded (Foreign Instrument)
☐ Report of Written Examination   ☐ Superseded Pilot Certificate(s)
☐ Temporary Pilot Certificate (copy)   ☐ Answer Sheet Graded (Military Competency)

COMMON ERRORS ON THE FAA PRACTICAL TEST

A.   Not talking to the examiner. Explain what you are doing. If you think you have made a mistake, explain the error to the examiner and ask if you should do it over.

B.   Tensing up. Relax. The examiner is not trying to be mean or to fail you. You are the pilot in command on this flight. The examiner is just observing as a passenger.

C.   Expecting help and advice from the examiner. You will be accustomed to your instructor giving help and advice. Some examiners are very suggestive. It is possible, however, that your examiner will offer none. You should know what is expected of you. Talk with others who recently took flight tests with your examiner.

D.   Thinking you have failed the flight test because the examiner is writing things down. The examiner notes things (s)he wants to go over with you on the ground. But you will be told right away if you have failed because the flight test will be terminated at that point.

E.   Doing a maneuver when you are not sure what the examiner wants. Ask for clarification, e.g., "Do you mean . . .?" Reading the examiner's mind is not a requirement of the practical test.

CERTIFICATES AND DOCUMENTS PTS

> **TASK: CERTIFICATES AND DOCUMENTS** *(ASEL)*
>   *PILOT OPERATION - 1*
>   *REFERENCES: FAR Parts 61 and 91; AC 61-21, AC 61-23; Pilot's Operating Handbook and*
>   *FAA-Approved Flight Manual.*
>
> **Objective.** *To determine that the applicant:*
>
> 1. *Exhibits knowledge by explaining the appro-priate -*
>   *a. pilot certificate privileges and limitations.*
>   *b. medical certificate and expiration.*
>   *c. personal pilot logbook or flight record.*
>
> 2. *Exhibits knowledge by locating and explaining the significance and importance of airplane -*
>   *a. airworthiness and registration certificates.*
>   *b. operating limitations, handbooks, or manuals.*
>   *c. weight and balance data.*
>   *d. maintenance requirements and appropriate records.*

1.   a.   Pilot certificates are issued without an expiration date (except student certificates, which expire after 24 calendar months). You will receive a temporary certificate at the completion of your practical test.

Recall your currency requirements to a carry passenger (3 landings in past 90 days; annual flight review) as well as the fact that you cannot receive compensation as a recreational pilot.

b.   You probably have a third-class medical certificate. It is good through the last day of the 24th month after issuance.

c. FAR 61.51 requires you to log aeronautical training and experience to meet the requirements for a certificate rating or recent flight experience. You have been maintaining a logbook that indicates the date, time of flight, places and points of departure, and aircraft used as well as the type of experience or training. You are required to carry your medical and pilot certificates. You are also required to have your logbook with you at all times while exercising your recreational pilot privileges to verify you are within 50 NM of where you received your flight instruction.

2. a. Your airplane will have to have both an airworthiness certificate and a certificate of aircraft registration. See page 214 of Chapter 12 for illustrations of both certificates.

b. The operating limitations of your airplane is in the *Pilot's Operating Handbook* (POH) or *FAA-Approved Airplane Flight Manual* (see Section 2). Some older airplanes did not have the formal *POHs* that are required by current FARs. You need to obtain your *POH*, manual, or other reprints or materials prior to beginning your flight instruction.

c. Weight and balance data are very important, and are presented and explained in Section 6 of your *POH* or included with that type of information. It is important that you understand the weight and balance calculations for the airplane you will be training in, and work through several examples to verify that you will be in the proper weight and balance given one or two persons aboard the airplane and various fuel loads. Obtain a weight and balance form for your airplane from your *POH* or CFI.

d. The maintenance requirements on aircraft which are used in commercial operations (i.e., flight training, charter, etc.) are more stringent than on Part 91, Personal Aircraft, which require maintenance only on an annual basis.

1) The basic requirement is for a check to be performed every 100 hours of use. The 100-hour limit may be exceeded by 10% or 10 hours, but the following 100-hour check must be performed within 100 hours of the original requirement. For example, if the check is performed at the 105-hour point, the next 100-hour check is due at the end of 95 hours, not 100 hours; thus, it would be due at the 200-hour point.

2) Based upon the specific make and model aircraft, further checks beyond the 100-hour check may be necessary to comply with the FARs. This additional maintenance may be required at the 50-, 150-, or 250-hour point.

3) In addition to the progressive maintenance schedule, all aircraft used in commercial operations must undergo an annual inspection on a yearly basis, as is the case with general Part 91 requirements.

4) Examine the engine logbooks and the airframe logbook of your training airplane and ask your instructor about any peculiarities.

AEROMEDICAL FACTORS PTS

TASK: AEROMEDICAL FACTORS *(ASEL)*
PILOT OPERATION - 1
REFERENCES: AC 61-21, AC 67-2; AIM.

Objective. *To determine that the applicant:*

1. Exhibits knowledge of the elements related to aeromedical factors, including the symptoms, effects, and corrective action of -

    a. hypoxia.
    b. hyperventilation.
    c. middle ear and sinus problems.
    d. spatial disorientation.
    e. motion sickness.
    f. carbon monoxide poisoning.

2. Exhibits knowledge of the effects of alcohol and drugs, and the relationship to flight safety.

3. Exhibits knowledge of nitrogen excesses during scuba dives, and how this affects a pilot during flight.

---

1.   a. *Hypoxia* is a state of oxygen deficiency in the body sufficient to impair functions of the brain and other organs. It is usually not a problem below 10,000 ft MSL. For safety reasons, oxygen should be used above that altitude (even though it is not required until above 12,500 ft MSL per Part 91).

    b. *Hyperventilation* usually results from an emotional reaction such as fear, and the rapid deep breathing of hyperventilation in turn causes insufficient carbon dioxide in the blood, as more and more carbon dioxide is blown off from rapid expirations. This, in turn, causes a condition known as respiratory alkalosis, which is an increase in the pH of the blood. This disturbance of acid-base metabolism is responsible for the symptoms of lightheadedness, tingling in the hands and feet, and carpel-pedal spasms.

    c. *Sinus and ear block:* During ascent and descent, air pressure in the sinuses equalizes with aircraft cabin pressure through small openings that connect the sinuses to the nasal passages. An upper respiratory infection (e.g., a cold or sinusitis) or nasal allergies can produce enough congestion around one or more of these small openings to slow equalization. Then, as the difference in pressure between the sinus and cabin increases, the opening may become plugged. This "sinus block" occurs most frequently during descent. Sleeping passengers should be awakened prior to descent so they can clear their ear passages by swallowing, yawning, etc.

    d. *Spatial disorientation* results from your brain obtaining false impressions from your sensory organs. This occurs when you lose visual contact with the ground and horizon and become disoriented as to airplane attitude. You correct spatial disorientation by being able to fly by instruments. Be aware of the availability of Gleim's *Instrument Pilot Flight Maneuvers and Handbook* and *Instrument Pilot FAA Written Exam.*

    e. *Motion sickness* is caused by continued stimulation of the tiny portion of the inner ear which controls the pilot's sense of balance and results in nausea. Corrective action is to open air vents, loosen clothing, keep eyes on a point outside of the airplane, avoid unnecessary head movements, and terminate the flight ASAP.

    f. *Carbon monoxide* is a colorless, odorless, and tasteless gas contained in exhaust fumes. When breathed even in minute quantities over a period of time, it can significantly reduce the ability of the blood to carry oxygen. Consequently, the effects of hypoxia occur. A pilot who detects the odor of exhaust or experiences symptoms of headache, drowsiness, or dizziness while using the heater should suspect carbon monoxide poisoning and immediately turn off the heater and open the air vents.

2. There is only one safe rule to follow with respect to combining flying and drinking -- DON'T. If you fly within 8 hours of consumption of any alcoholic beverages, or are under the influence of drugs, you are jeopardizing your life and property, and that of others, as well as violating FARs.

3. A pilot or passenger who intends to fly after scuba diving should allow the body sufficient time to rid itself of excess nitrogen absorbed during diving. If this is not done, decompression sickness due to evolved gas (bubbles in the bloodstream) can occur even at low altitudes and create a serious in-flight emergency. The recommended waiting time before flight to cabin-pressure altitudes of up to 8,000 ft is at least 4 hours after a dive which has not required controlled ascent (nondecompression diving). You should allow at least 24 hours after diving that requires controlled ascent (decompression diving). The waiting time before flight to cabin-pressure altitudes above 8,000 ft should be at least 24 hours after any scuba diving.

GOOD LUCK!!!

Pass your practical (flight) test and enjoy flying!! Thank you for using this book. Please take the time to complete the last two pages of this book and mail them to me for use in future editions. Send your name and address so I may answer your comments specifically. Also, send any suggestions you may have in the future. I look forward to hearing from you.

The issuance of a recreational pilot certificate gives you the right to exercise those privileges. It does not automatically make you a good pilot. Keep in touch with your instructor.

Continue to use this Flight Maneuvers Book to keep current and proficient for safe flight and to pass subsequent annual or biennial reviews. Finally, please recommend this book to others as appropriate.

248

Blank Page

APPENDIX A
FAA PRACTICAL TEST STANDARDS CROSS-REFERENCE TABLES

The 34 Tasks required by the FAA in the Practical Test Standards are listed below. The FAA's organization differs from this book. For example, their last area is landings, whereas in this book landings follow takeoffs and basic flight maneuvers. Since every takeoff is followed by a landing, you need to study at least normal landings as you begin your flight training.

Thus, as an organizational aid, we are presenting the FAA Tasks in FAA chronological order (your examiner will choose his/her own order) with cross-references to the chapter and page in this book. Following this list is a reverse cross-reference list of our chapters and the test standards they include.

		In This Book	
		Chapter	Page
I. PREFLIGHT PREPARATION			
A.	Certificates and Documents	14	244
B.	Obtaining Weather Information	12	221
C.	Determining Performance and Limitations	3	64
D.	Airplane Systems	3	64
E.	Aeromedical Factors	14	246
F.	Visual Inspection	4	69
G.	Cockpit Management	4	76
H.	Engine Start	4	78
I.	Taxi	5	91
J.	Pretakeoff Check	5	94
II. AIRPORT AND TRAFFIC PATTERN OPERATION			
A.	Airport and Runway Marking and Lighting	5	100
B.	Traffic Pattern Operation	8	141
C.	Postflight Procedure	5	98
D.	Radio Communications	5	87
III. NORMAL TAKEOFF AND LANDING			
A.	Normal and Crosswind Takeoff	6	108
B.	Go-Around	8	162
C.	Normal and Crosswind Landing	8	159
IV. MAXIMUM PERFORMANCE TAKEOFF AND LANDING			
A.	Short-Field Takeoff	6	110
B.	Short-Field Landing	8	166
C.	Soft-Field Takeoff	6	112
D.	Soft-Field Landing	8	163

(continued on next page)

Also, for organizational information, chapter titles 2 through 14 are listed below followed by the FAA Tasks covered in each. The page number of each Task reprint is provided.

(continued on next page)

252

Blank Page

APPENDIX B
UPGRADING TO THE PRIVATE PILOT CERTIFICATE

If you upgrade from a recreational pilot to a private pilot, you will gain the following privileges not exercisable by recreational pilots.

1. Fly anywhere in the United States and abroad as permitted.
2. Fly at night.
3. Fly in ATC controlled airspace (airport traffic areas, ARSAs, and TCAs).
4. Fly above 10,000 ft mean sea level altitude (MSL).
5. Carry more than one passenger.
6. Pilot an airplane with retractable landing gear and/or more than 180 horsepower.
7. Fly in furtherance of a business.
8. Fly in fewer than 3 miles visibility when otherwise permitted by the FARs, i.e., the day 3-mile minimum visibility (5 at night) will be lifted.
    a. And above ceilings when visible reference to the ground may be lost.
9. Add a multiengine rating to a private pilot certificate (not true for recreational).

PRIVATE PILOT UPGRADE REQUIREMENTS

A. An abbreviated FAA written test of 30 multiple-choice items emphasizing
    1. Night flight.
    2. High-altitude flight.
    3. ATC and airspace requiring ATC.
    4. Radio navigation.

> QUESTIONS COVERING THESE TOPICS ARE INCLUDED IN *PRIVATE PILOT FAA WRITTEN EXAM.*

B. An abbreviated FAA practical test emphasizing
    1. Cross-country flight planning.
    2. Flight by reference to instruments.
    3. Night flight operations.
    4. ATC communication and compliance.

C. Ground and flight instruction on the above topics followed by CFI endorsements for both the written and practical tests similar to those for the recreational certificate.

D. In training for a private pilot upgrade, if under the supervision of a CFI, you may solo an airplane:
    1. For which the pilot does not hold an appropriate category or class rating;
    2. Within airspace that requires communication with air traffic control; or
    3. Between sunset and sunrise, provided the flight or surface visibility is at least 5 statute miles.
    4. Beyond 50 nautical miles from your home airport.

E.   For each solo flight, the CFI must have provided adequate instruction, found you competent for safe flight, and so endorsed your logbook.

    1.   For cross-country flight, training and proficiency in the following areas are required (in addition to that required for solo flight).

        a.   The use of aeronautical charts for VFR navigation using pilotage and dead reckoning with the aid of a magnetic compass.

        b.   Aircraft cross-country performance, and procurement and analysis of aeronautical weather reports and forecasts, including recognition of critical weather situations and estimating visibility while in flight.

        c.   Cross-country emergency conditions including lost procedures, adverse weather conditions, and simulated precautionary off-airport approaches and landing procedures.

        d.   Traffic pattern procedures, including normal area arrival and departure, collision avoidance, and wake turbulence precautions.

        e.   Recognition of operational problems associated with the different terrain in the geographical area in which the cross-country flight is to be flown.

        f.   Proper operation of the instruments and equipment installed in the aircraft to be flown.

        g.   Short- and soft-field takeoff, approach, and landing procedures, including crosswind takeoffs and landings.

        h.   Takeoffs at best angle and rate of climb.

        i.   Control and maneuvering solely by reference to flight instruments including straight and level flight, turns, descents, climbs, and the use of radio aids and radar directives.

        j.   The use of radios for VFR navigation and for two-way communication.

        k.   For those student pilots seeking night flying privileges, night flying procedures including takeoffs, landings, go-arounds, and VFR navigation.

F.   Gleim books available:

    PRIVATE PILOT FAA WRITTEN EXAM

    PRIVATE PILOT FLIGHT MANEUVERS

    PRIVATE PILOT HANDBOOK

APPENDIX C
FEDERAL AVIATION REGULATIONS

The purpose of this appendix is to outline and explain in English the FARs relevant to recreational pilots. Note that more coverage is available in Chapter 8 of *PRIVATE PILOT HANDBOOK*, which has the same format except covers more FARs. Also in *PRIVATE PILOT HANDBOOK*, Appendix A contains a reprint of the FARs.

Only paragraphs in FAR Parts 61 and 91 and NTSB Part 830 which appear relevant to recreational pilots are covered. Note that FARs deemed of little interest and/or applicability have been omitted.

PART 61 - CERTIFICATION: PILOTS AND FLIGHT INSTRUCTORS

61.3 Requirement for Certificates, Ratings, and Authorizations

1. No person may act as a pilot-in-command or as a required flight crewmember unless (s)he has with him/her a pilot certificate issued under FAR Part 61.

2. Except in balloons and gliders, no person may act as pilot-in-command or as a required flight crewmember unless (s)he has a current medical certificate issued under FAR Part 67, "Medical Standards and Certification."

3. A person who is not an authorized flight instructor in airplanes may not give any sort of flight instruction required for solo flight in airplanes, nor may (s)he endorse a student pilot certificate or logbook for instruction or solo privileges.

4. The FAA, NTSB (National Transportation Safety Board), or any law enforcement officer can inspect a pilot's certificate, medical certificate, etc. upon request.

61.17 Temporary Certificate

1. A temporary pilot certificate is issued to a qualified applicant pending a review of his/her qualifications and the issuance of a permanent certificate.
   a. This temporary certificate is valid for a maximum of 120 days.

2. A temporary certificate expires on the date stated on the certificate or upon receipt of the permanent certificate, whichever comes first.

3. A temporary certificate also expires upon notification that the certification or rating applied for has been denied.

61.35 Written Test: Prerequisites and Passing Grades

1. An applicant for a written test must:
   a. Show that (s)he has satisfactorily completed the ground or home-study course required by Part 61.
   b. Present personal identification such as an Airman Certificate, driver's license, or other official document.
   c. Present a birth certificate showing that the age requirements of Part 61 are met or will be met within 2 years of taking the test.

2. The minimum passing grade for the test specified by the FAA is printed on the test booklets.

61.37 Written Tests: Cheating or Other Unauthorized Conduct

1. No person may:
   a. Copy or intentionally remove a written test.
   b. Give to another or receive from another a copy of the test.
   c. Give help to another or receive help from another while taking the test.
   d. Take the test on behalf of another.
   e. Use any material as an aid during the test.
   f. Intentionally cause, assist, or participate in any act contrary to this part.

2. Any person caught in any of these acts is ineligible to take the test or receive any certificates or ratings for a period of 1 year.

3. This is also grounds to suspend or revoke any certificate or ratings already possessed.

4. Note: You are permitted to take and use a flight computer, plotter, and calculator (you must erase all memory before you start your test).

61.39 Prerequisites for Flight Tests

1. To be eligible for a flight test, the applicant must have:
   a. Passed any required written tests within the preceding 24 months.
   b. Have the required instruction and aeronautical experience as prescribed in Part 61.
   c. Have a current and appropriate medical certificate for the rating sought.

d. Meet the minimum age requirements as given in Part 61. (This does not pertain to the ATP flight test.)

e. Have a written statement from a CFI certifying that (s)he has given the applicant flight instruction in preparation for the flight test, within the preceding 60 days, and finds the applicant competent to pass the test and have satisfactory knowledge of the areas shown to be deficient on the written test. (This does not pertain to the ATP flight test.)

61.41 Flight Instruction Received from Flight Instructors Not Certificated by the FAA

1. Flight instruction may be credited toward the requirements for a pilot certificate or rating issued under Part 61 if it was received from:

a. An Armed Forces instructor teaching in a program to train military pilots.

b. A flight instructor who is authorized to give instruction by the International Civil Aviation Organization (ICAO) and the flight instruction is given outside the United States.

61.43 Flight Tests: General Procedures

1. The ability to pass the flight test for a new certificate or rating is judged by the ability to:

a. Execute procedures and maneuvers within the aircraft's performance capabilities and limitations.

b. Execute emergency procedures and maneuvers appropriate to the aircraft.

c. Pilot the aircraft with smoothness and accuracy.

d. Exercise judgment.

e. Apply aeronautical knowledge.

f. Show that (s)he is master of the aircraft and the outcome of any maneuver is never seriously in doubt.

2. If the applicant fails any of the required pilot operations, the entire checkride is failed.

3. The examiner or applicant may discontinue the flight test at any time when the failure of a pilot operation has caused the failure of the checkride.

61.45 Flight Tests: Required Aircraft and Equipment

1. An applicant for a certificate or rating must furnish for each flight test an appropriate U.S. registered aircraft that has a current airworthiness certificate.

2. Aircraft furnished for the flight test must have:

a. The equipment for each pilot operation required by the flight test.

b. No operating limitations that will preclude the performance of a required pilot operation.

c. Pilot seats with adequate outside visibility for each pilot to operate the aircraft safely.

d. Flight and power controls which are all accessible and easily controlled by both pilots.

e. For testing of flight by reference to instruments only, the applicant must provide a satisfactory view-limiting device.

61.47 Flight Tests: Status of FAA Inspectors and Other Authorized Flight Examiners

1. An FAA inspector or a designated examiner conducts the flight test for certificates and ratings for the purpose of observing the applicant's ability to perform the required maneuvers.

2. The examiner is not the pilot-in-command unless he acts in that capacity in order to perform the flight test. This determination must be made prior to starting the checkride.

3. The applicant and the examiner are not considered a passenger of one another and are thereby not responsible for the passenger-carrying provisions of the FARs.

61.49 Retesting After Failure

1. An applicant for a written or flight test may not apply for retesting until 30 days have passed since the failure.

2. In the case of a first-time failure, the applicant may apply sooner than 30 days if a written statement is presented from a CFI stating that the CFI has given additional instruction and finds the applicant competent to pass the test.

61.51 Pilot Logbooks

1. All the aeronautical training and experience used to meet the requirements for a certificate or rating must be shown by a reliable record.

2. All flight time used to meet the recent flight requirements must also be logged in a reliable record (e.g., instrument currency).

3. All other time need not be logged at the discretion of the pilot.

4. Each logbook entry shall include:

   a. Date.
   b. Total time of flight.
   c. Points of departure and arrival.
   d. Type and identification of aircraft.
   e. Type of pilot time (e.g, PIC, SIC, solo, dual, etc.).
   f. Conditions of flight (e.g., day, night, actual instrument, or simulated instrument).

5. Types of flight time:

   a. *Solo* is when you are the sole occupant of an aircraft you are training in before certification.
   b. *PIC* is when you are the sole manipulator of the controls in an aircraft you are rated in, or you are the PIC during a flight in which an SIC is required.
   c. *SIC time* is when you are acting as a second-in-command on an aircraft requiring more than one pilot by the type certificate or FARs.
   d. *Instrument time* is when the aircraft is operated solely by reference to instruments under actual or simulated conditions.
   e. All time logged as flight instruction, instrument flight instruction, pilot ground trainer instruction, or ground instruction must be certified by an appropriately rated and certificated instructor giving the instruction.

6. A pilot must present his/her logbook upon reasonable request by the FAA, or a member of the NTSB, or a local or state law enforcement officer.

61.53 Operations During Medical Deficiency

1. A pilot with a known medical deficiency, or increase thereof, may not act as pilot-in-command if the condition would render him/her unable to meet the requirements of his/her medical certificate.

61.56 Flight Review

1. Flight review encompasses a review of Part 91, general operating and flight rules, and those maneuvers necessary, in the opinion of the CFI, to demonstrate safe exercise of the pilot certificate.

2. In order to act as pilot-in-command, you must have completed a flight review since the beginning of the preceding 24th calendar month and have a logbook endorsement stating the satisfactory completion of the flight review.

3. Recreational pilots and non-instrument rated private pilots with less than 400 hours of flight time must have annual flight reviews consisting of at least 1 hour of ground instruction and 1 hour of flight instruction.

4. A new rating or certificate based on a practical or simulator flight test takes the place of a flight review.

61.57 Recent Flight Experience: Pilot-in-Command

1. In order to carry passengers, three takeoffs and landings are required within the preceding 90 days, as the sole manipulator of the controls in the same category and class of aircraft. If a type rating is required, it must be the same type of aircraft.

2. For night currency, three takeoffs and landings to a full stop at night are required within the preceding 90 days.

3. For instrument currency, within the past 6 months, you must have at least 6 hours of actual or simulated instrument time, 3 of which were in the same category of aircraft involved, including 6 instrument approaches; or have passed an instrument competency check.

61.59 Falsification, Reproduction, or Alteration of Applications, Certificates, Logbooks, Reports, or Records

1. No person may make or cause to be made any
    a. Fraudulent or intentionally false statement on an FAA application.
    b. Fraudulent or intentionally false entry in a logbook, report, etc.
    c. Reproduction for fraudulent purposes of any certificate or rating.
    d. Alteration of any certificate or rating.
2. The commission of such an act is the basis for suspending or revoking any certificate or rating.

61.60 Change of Address

1. A pilot or flight instructor must notify the FAA • Airman Certification Branch • Box 25082 • Oklahoma City, OK 73125, of a change of permanent mailing address within 30 days after moving. Otherwise, his/her certificate is not valid.

61.69 Glider Towing: Experience and Instruction Requirements

1. The pilot must have a current pilot certificate (not a student pilot or recreational certificate).
2. A glider flight instructor must have endorsed the logbook certifying the pilot has received appropriate instruction and is competent.
3. The pilot must have made and entered in the logbook at least three flights as sole manipulator of the controls of an aircraft while accompanied by an appropriately qualified glider tow pilot
    a. Towing a glider, or
    b. Simulating glider tow flights and at least three flights in a glider towed by an aircraft.
4. A private pilot must have 100 hours of pilot flight time in powered aircraft or 200 hours of total flight time in powered or other aircraft.
5. Within the preceding 12 months, the pilot must have made at least
    a. Three actual or simulated glider tows accompanied by a qualified tow pilot, or
    b. Three flights as pilot-in-command of a glider towed by an aircraft.

Subpart (C) - Student and Recreational Pilots

61.83 Eligibility Requirements: General

1. To be eligible for a student pilot's certificate, a person must:
    a. Be at least 16 years old.
    b. Be able to read, speak, and understand the English language.
    c. Hold at least a current third-class medical certificate issued under FAR Part 67.

61.85 Application

1. An application for a student pilot certificate is made on a form and in a manner approved by the FAA.
2. It is submitted to a designated aviation medical examiner when applying for an FAA medical certificate, or to an FAA inspector or designated examiner when it is accompanied by a current FAA medical certificate.

61.87 Requirements for Solo Flight

1. A student pilot may not operate an aircraft in solo flight until (s)he has complied with the requirements of this section.
2. (S)he must have demonstrated to a CFI that (s)he is knowledgeable about FAR Part 91 and the flight and operational characteristics of the make and model of the airplane to be soloed in.
    a. This will be confirmed by a written test administered by the CFI.

3. Before students are allowed to solo, they must receive flight instruction in the following 15 flight maneuvers:

(a) Flight preparation procedures, including preflight inspections, powerplant operation, and aircraft systems;

(b) Taxiing or surface operations, including runups;

(c) Takeoffs and landings, including normal and crosswind;

(d) Straight-and-level flight, shallow, medium, and steep banked turns in both directions;

(e) Climbs and climbing turns;

(f) Airport traffic patterns including entry and departure procedures, and collision and wake turbulence avoidance;

(g) Descents with and without turns using high and low drag configurations;

(h) Flight at various airspeeds from cruising to minimum controllable airspeed;

(i) Emergency procedures and equipment malfunctions;

(j) Ground reference maneuvers;

(k) Approaches to the landing area with engine power at idle and with partial power;

(l) Slips to a landing;

(m) Go-arounds from final approach and from the landing flare in various flight configurations including turns;

(n) Forced landing procedures initiated on takeoff, during initial climb, cruise, descent, and in the landing pattern; and

(o) Stall entries from various flight attitudes and power combinations with recovery initiated at the first indication of a stall, and recovery from a full stall.

---

4. Student pilots may not fly solo without a CFI logbook endorsement indicating:
    a. Flight instruction in the make and model of the plane to be used for solo flight.
    b. Proficiency in the above maneuvers.
    c. Competency for safe solo flight in that make and model.

61.89 General Limitations

1. A student pilot may **not** act as a pilot-in-command of an aircraft:
    a. Carrying passengers.
    b. Carrying property for compensation or hire.
    c. In return for compensation or hire.
    d. In furtherance of a business.
    e. On an international flight.
    f. If visibility is below 3 miles in day or below 5 miles in night.
    g. Above overcast, i.e., without visual reference to the surface.
    h. In violation to any CFI-imposed limitations in the pilot log book.

2. A student pilot may not act as a crewmember on an aircraft requiring more than one pilot.

61.93 Cross-Country Flight Requirements

1. A student pilot may not operate an aircraft in solo cross-country unless properly authorized by an instructor.

2. A student may not make a solo landing (except in an emergency) other than the one from which (s)he is authorized to depart.
    a. A CFI may, however, authorize a student to practice solo takeoffs and landings at an airport within 25 NM of the base airport after
        1) Determining adequate pilot proficiency by the student pilot.
        2) Flying with the student pilot.
        3) Endorsing the student pilot's logbook.

3. A student must receive training from a CFI in the following areas before being authorized to conduct solo cross-country flights:
    a. Use of aeronautical charts, pilotage, and elementary dead-reckoning using the magnetic compass.
    b. Recognition of critical weather situations, estimating visibility, and the procurement and use of weather charts and forecasts.
    c. Cross-country emergency procedures.
    d. Traffic patterns and arrival procedures, including collision and wake turbulence avoidance.
    e. Recognition of problems caused by peculiar terrain features, if applicable.
    f. Proper operation of instruments and equipment.
    g. Short- and soft-field procedures as well as crosswind takeoffs and landings.
    h. Takeoffs at best rate and best angle of climb.

   i. Control of an airplane by reference to flight instruments.

   j. The use of radio VFR navigation and two-way communication.

   k. For night privileges: takeoffs, landings, go-arounds, and VFR night navigation.

4. A CFI logbook endorsement is required for each cross-country flight with any CFI-imposed conditions listed in the endorsement.

5. An endorsement can be made for repeated solo cross-country flight to an airport less than 50 NM after dual cross-country flight in both directions.

61.95 Operations in a Terminal Control Area or at Airports Located Within a Terminal Control Area

1. In order for a student pilot to solo in a Terminal Control Area or at a specific airport within a TCA, the student must have:
   a. Received both ground and flight instruction concerning TCA operations, and the flight instruction must have been given in the TCA or at the specific airport in the TCA where the student will be operating.
   b. A current 90-day logbook endorsement from the instructor who gave the training which says that the student has received the required training and has been found competent to operate in that specific TCA or at that specific airport within the TCA.

61.96 Eligibility Requirements: Recreational Pilots

1. Be at least 17 years of age.
2. Be able to read, speak, and understand English.
3. Hold at least a current third-class medical certificate.
4. Pass a written test (see FAR 61.97).
5. Pass an oral and flight test (see FAR 61.98).
6. Comply with applicable FARs.

61.97 Aeronautical Knowledge

1. Recreational pilot applicants must receive ground instruction from an authorized instructor, or show satisfactory completion of a course of instruction or home study.
2. The following topics are required:
   a. FARs, NTSB 830, *AIM,* and ACs.
   b. Use of aeronautical charts for VFR navigation using piloting with the aid of a magnetic compass.
   c. Recognition of critical weather situations.
      1) Procurement and use of aeronautical weather reports and forecasts.
   d. Safe and efficient operation of aircraft including collision and wake turbulence avoidance.
   e. Effects of density altitude on takeoff and climb performance.
   f. Weight and balance computation.
   g. Principles of aerodynamics, powerplants, and aircraft systems.

61.98 Flight Proficiency

1. Recreational pilot applicants must receive flight instruction from a CFI and have the CFI sign-off in his/her logbook.
2. The following topics are required:
   a. Preflight operations, including weight and balance.
   b. Airport and traffic pattern operations, including collision and wake turbulence avoidance.
   c. Flight maneuvering by reference to ground objects.
   d. Pilotage with the aid of magnetic compass.
   e. Flight at critically slow airspeeds, and the recognition of and recovery from imminent and full stalls entered from straight flight and from turns.
   f. Emergency operations, including simulated aircraft and equipment malfunctions.
   g. Maximum performance takeoffs and landings.
   h. Normal and crosswind takeoffs and landings.

61.99 Airplane Rating: Aeronautical Experience

1. Recreational pilot applicants for an airplane rating must have had at least a total of 30 hours of flight instruction and solo flight time including:
    a. 15 hours of flight instruction from a CFI.
        1) 2 hours away from the airport, including at least three landings at another airport that is located more than 25 NM from the airport of departure (pilots based on small islands have different mileage requirements).
        2) 2 hours in airplanes in preparation for the recreational pilot flight test within the 60-day period before the test.
    b. 15 hours of solo flight time in airplanes.

61.101 Recreational Pilot Privileges and Limitations

1. A recreational pilot may
    a. Not carry more than one passenger.
    b. Share the operating expenses of the flight with the passenger.
    c. Act as pilot-in-command within 50 NM of an airport at which the pilot has received ground and flight instruction.
    d. Land at an airport within 50 NM of the departure airport.
2. Recreational pilots must carry a logbook with an endorsement attesting to the required instructions.
3. A recreational pilot may not act as pilot-in-command of an aircraft:
    a. That is certificated:
        1) For more than four occupants.
        2) With more than one powerplant.
        3) With a powerplant of more than 180 horsepower.
        4) With retractable landing gear.
    b. That is classified as a glider, airship, or balloon.
    c. That is carrying a passenger or property for compensation or hire.
    d. For compensation or hire.
    e. In furtherance of a business.
    f. Between sunset and sunrise.
    g. In airspace in which communication with ATC is required.
    h. At an altitude of more than 10,000 ft MSL or 2,000 ft AGL, whichever is higher.
    i. When the flight or surface visibility is less than 3 statute miles.
    j. Without visual reference to the surface.
    k. On a flight outside the United States.
    l. To demonstrate that aircraft in flight to a prospective buyer.
    m. That is used in a passenger-carrying airlift and sponsored by a charitable organization.
    n. That is towing any object.
4. A recreational pilot may not act as a required pilot flight crewmember on any aircraft for which more than one pilot is required.
5. A recreational pilot who has less than 400 flight hours and who has not logged pilot-in-command time within the preceding 180 days may not act as pilot-in-command until receiving flight instruction and logbook endorsement for competency.
6. The recreational pilot certificate carries the notation "Holder does not meet ICAO requirements."
7. To obtain additional certificates or ratings, a recreational pilot may solo under CFI supervision
    a. For which the pilot does not hold an appropriate category or class rating.
    b. Within airspace that requires communication with ATC.
    c. Between sunset and sunrise, provided visibility is at least 5 statute miles.
    d. In order to fly solo, the recreational pilot must meet the appropriate aeronautical knowledge and flight training requirements of FAR 61.87 and carry his/her logbook with an appropriate CFI endorsement for each flight.
        1) The appropriate endorsement is required for each flight in excess of 50 NM from the home airport and the recreational pilot must comply with Para 61.93.

PART 91 - GENERAL OPERATING AND FLIGHT RULES

91.3 Responsibility and Authority of the Pilot-in-Command

1. The pilot-in-command of an aircraft is directly responsible for, and is the final authority as to, the operation of that aircraft.

2. Thus, in emergencies, a pilot may deviate from the FARs to the extent needed to maintain the safety of the airplane and passengers.

3. A written report shall be filed with the FAA upon request. *(IF Requested) No 24 hr. deadline*

91.5 Preflight Action

1. Pilots are required to familiarize themselves with all available information concerning the flight prior to every flight, and specifically to determine:
   a. For any flight, runway lengths at airports of intended use and the airplane's takeoff and landing requirements.
   b. For flights not in the vicinity of an airport,
      1) Weather reports and forecasts,
      2) Fuel requirements,
      3) Alternatives available if the planned flight cannot be completed, and
      4) Any known traffic delays.

91.9 Careless or Reckless Operation

1. No person may operate an aircraft in a careless or reckless manner so as to endanger the life or property of another.

91.11 Alcohol or Drugs

1. No person may act as a crewmember of a civil aircraft when:
   a. They are under the influence of drugs or alcohol.
   b. They have consumed alcoholic beverages within 8 hours prior to the flight.
   c. They have a blood alcohol level of .04 percent by weight or more.

2. No person who appears to be under the influence of drugs or alcohol (except those under medical care) may be carried aboard an aircraft.

91.12 Carriage of Narcotic Drugs, Marihuana, and Depressant or Stimulant Drugs or Substances

1. No person may operate within the United States with knowledge that any of these substances are aboard. This does not apply to flights that are authorized by the federal government or a state government or agency.

91.13 Dropping Objects

1. Dropping objects from an airplane is not prohibited provided the pilot takes reasonable precautions to avoid injury or damage to persons or property.

91.14 Use of Safety Belts and Shoulder Harnesses

1. No pilot may takeoff without first briefing the passengers on how to use the seatbelts.

2. He must also notify them to fasten their seatbelts before each takeoff and landing.

91.22 Fuel Requirements for Flight under VFR

1. No person may fly Day VFR unless there is enough fuel to fly to the destination and then at least 30 minutes beyond that.

2. No person may fly Night VFR unless there is enough fuel to fly to the destination and at least 45 minutes beyond that.

91.24 ATC Transponder and Altitude Reporting Equipment and Use

1. Mode C is required in all TCAs and in the positive control area.
2. As of July 1, 1989, all aircraft certified with an engine-driven electrical system must have the appropriate transponder equipment (Mode C)
   a. Within 30 nautical miles of the primary airport of a TCA from the surface up to 10,000 feet MSL.
   b. Above 10,000 feet MSL and below the floor of the positive control area, excluding airspace at or below 2,500 feet AGL.
3. As of December 30, 1990, all aircraft must have Mode C transponder equipment
   a. Within ARSAs and when above the lateral limits of the ARSA.
   b. Within 10 nautical miles of specified airports (except below 1,200 ft AGL outside of the airport traffic area).

91.27 Civil Aircraft: Certifications Required

1. You may not operate a civil aircraft unless it has in it:
   a. An appropriate and current airworthiness certificate which is posted near the aircraft entrance for passengers and crew to see.
   b. A registration certificate issued to the aircraft owner.

91.29 Civil Aircraft Airworthiness

1. No person may operate an aircraft that is not in an airworthy condition.
2. The pilot-in-command is responsible for determining whether the aircraft is fit for safe flight.

91.30 Inoperative Instruments and Equipment

1. No person may take off in an aircraft with inoperable instruments or equipment installed unless:
   a. An approved minimum equipment list (MEL) exists for that specific aircraft. Note that the MEL is a list of equipment that does NOT have to be operable.
      1) This includes the different flight limitations placed upon the aircraft when that equipment is inoperative, e.g., you cannot fly at night if the landing light is out.
   b. The aircraft has within it a letter of authorization, issued by the FAA FSDO in the area where the operator is based, authorizing operation of the aircraft under the minimum equipment list. The MEL and authorization letter constitute an STC (supplemental type certificate) for the aircraft.
   c. The approved MEL must:
      1) Be prepared in accordance with specified limitations.
      2) Provide how the aircraft is to be operated with the instruments and equipment in an inoperable condition.
   d. The aircraft records available to the pilot must include an entry describing the inoperable instruments and equipment.
   e. The aircraft must be operated under all applicable conditions and limitations contained in the MEL.
2. The following instruments and equipment may NOT be included in an MEL:
   a. Instruments and equipment that are specifically or otherwise required by the airworthiness requirements under which the aircraft is type-certificated and which are essential to the safe operation of the aircraft.
   b. Instruments and equipment required by an Airworthiness Directive.
   c. Instruments and equipment required for operations by the FARs.
3. Persons with MELs per FARs 121, 125, or 135 shall use them.
4. Except for those with MELs described above, a person may take off with inoperative equipment and NO MEL if:
   a. An FAA Master MEL has not been developed by the FAA and the inoperative equipment is not required by the aircraft manufacturer's equipment list, any other FARs, ADs, etc.
   b. If an FAA Master MEL (MMEL) exists, and the inoperative equipment is not required by the MMEL, the aircraft manufacturer's equipment list, any other FARs, ADs, etc.
   c. The inoperative equipment is removed, or deactivated and placarded "inoperative."

d. The pilot or an appropriate maintenance person determines that the inoperative equipment does not constitute a hazard.

e. Then the aircraft is deemed to be in a "properly altered condition" by the FAA.

5. Special flight permits (from the FAA) are possible under FAR 21 when the above requirements cannot be met.

6. Author's note: This 12/88 revision applies the MEL concept to all aircraft but provides an "out" for Part 91 operations if an FAA Master MEL has not been developed for a particular type of aircraft **or** the equipment is not required by the Master MEL, the aircraft manufacturer's equipment list, FARs, ADs, etc.

91.31 Civil Aircraft Flight Manual, Marking, and Placard Requirements

1. No person may operate an aircraft that has an approved flight manual unless it is aboard the aircraft.

2. No person may operate contrary to any limitations specified in that manual.

91.52 Emergency Locator Transmitters

1. ELT batteries must be replaced after one cumulative hour of use or after 50% of their useful life expires.

2. Airplanes may be operated for training purposes within 50 miles of the originating airport without an ELT.

3. The expiration date for batteries used in an ELT must be legibly marked on the outside of the transmitter.

91.57 Aviation Safety Reporting Program; Prohibition Against Use of Reports for Enforcement Purposes

1. A pilot who believes that he has been involved in a violation of the FARs or a situation which is contrary to safety may submit a report to NASA without fear of action by the FAA. These reports are used to research and improve aviation safety. The pilot may file an unlimited number of reports. Immunity to an FAA action against a pilot may be gained on one occasion only.

91.65 Operating Near Other Aircraft

1. No person may operate an aircraft so as to create a collision hazard with other aircraft.

2. Formation flights are not permitted except by arrangement with the pilot-in-command of each aircraft.

3. Aircraft may not carry passengers for hire in formation flights.

4. No person may operate an aircraft in accordance with a clearance or instruction issued by ATC for another aircraft.

91.67 Right-of-Way Rules; Except Water Operations

1. When weather permits, all pilots shall maintain vigilence for other aircraft so as to see and avoid them. When another has the right-of-way, one must always give way to the other aircraft and pass well clear of it.

2. Aircraft in distress have the right-of-way over all other air traffic.

3. When aircraft of the same category are converging at approximately the same altitude, except head-on or nearly so, the aircraft to the other's right has the right-of-way. If aircraft are of different categories,

a. A balloon has the right-of-way over all other aircraft.
b. A glider has the right-of-way over airships, airplanes, and rotorcraft.
c. An airship has the right-of-way over an airplane or rotorcraft.

However, an aircraft towing or refueling other aircraft has the right-of-way over all other engine-driven aircraft.

4. If approaching head-on, each aircraft shall alter course to the right.

5. An aircraft overtaking another shall alter course to the right to pass well clear. The aircraft being overtaken has the right-of-way.

6. Aircraft on final approach to land or landing have the right-of-way over all other aircraft in flight or on the surface. If two or more aircraft are landing, the lower altitude aircraft has the right-of-way but shall not take advantage of this rule to cut in front of another approaching to land.

91.70 Aircraft Speed

1. You may not operate an airplane at an airspeed greater than 250 knots if you are under 10,000 feet MSL.

2. When operating in an Airport Traffic Area, you are limited to 156 knots in a reciprocating engine aircraft or 200 knots if operating a turbine-powered aircraft, unless required by ATC.

3. You may not operate under a TCA or in a VFR corridor through a TCA at an airspeed greater than 200 knots.

4. If your minimum safe speed in your airplane is faster than the speed normally allowed, you may operate at that minimum safe speed.

91.71 Aerobatic Flight

1. Aerobatic flight is not permitted
   a. Over any congested area of a city, town, or settlement.
   b. Over an open-air assembly of persons.
   c. Within a control zone or federal airway.
   d. Below 1,500 feet AGL.
   e. In less than three miles visibility.

2. Aerobatic flight means an intentional maneuver involving an abrupt change in an aircraft's attitude, or an abnormal attitude or acceleration not necessary for normal flight.

91.79 Minimum Safe Altitudes; General

1. Except for takeoff and landing, the following altitudes are required:
   a. You must have sufficient altitude for an emergency landing without undue hazard to persons or property on the surface if a power unit fails.
   b. Over congested areas of a city, town, or settlement, or over an open-air assembly of persons, you must have 1,000 feet of clearance over the highest obstacle within 2,000 feet radius of the airplane.
   c. Over other areas, you must remain at least 500 feet from any persons or property.

91.81 Altimeter Settings

1. All aircraft shall maintain a cruising altitude or flight level by reference to an altimeter that has been set, when operating,
   a. Below 18,000 feet MSL, to,
      1) The current reported altimeter setting of a station along the route and within 100 nautical miles of the aircraft.
      2) An appropriate available station.
      3) The elevation of the departure airport or an appropriate altimeter setting available before departure, or,
   b. At or above 18,000 feet MSL, to, 29.92 " Hg.

91.88 Airport Radar Service Areas

1. You must maintain two-way radio contact with ATC while operating in an ARSA.

2. If you depart a satellite airport, you should establish two-way radio contact with ATC as soon as is practical.

3. As of December 30, 1990, you will be required to have an operating radar transponder with altitude encoding within all ARSAs as well as above the ARSAs.

91.89 Operation at Airports Without Control Towers

1. All turns of an airplane approaching to land shall be to the left unless the airport displays approved light signals or visual markings indicating turns to the right.

2. Helicopters shall avoid the flow of fixed-wing aircraft.

3. Departing aircraft shall comply with FAA traffic patterns for that airport.

91.90 *Terminal Control Areas*

1. You must have an ATC clearance to operate in a TCA.

2. Pilots operating large turbine-powered airplanes to or from the primary airport in the TCA must observe the designated floors while within the lateral limits of the TCA airspace.

3. If it is necessary to conduct training operations within the TCA, procedures established for these flights within the TCA will be followed.

4. In order to land at an airport within the TCA or even operate within the TCA, you must:
   a. Be at least a private pilot; or
   b. Be a student pilot who has been instructed and authorized to operate in that specific TCA by a flight instructor (a specific logbook CFI signoff is required).

5. However, there are certain TCAs which require the pilot to hold at least a private pilot certificate to operate there. These are very busy areas such as Atlanta and Chicago.

6. The equipment aboard your aircraft must include an operative VOR receiver, two-way radio communications, and a radar transponder with altitude encoding.

91.95 *Restricted and Prohibited Areas*

1. One may not operate an aircraft within a restricted area contrary to the restrictions imposed or within a prohibited area, unless the pilot has the permission of the using or controlling agency.

2. Each person conducting an approved operation within a restricted area, which creates the same hazard as that for which the area was designated, may deviate from the rules of this subpart that are incompatible with the operation.

91.105 *Basic VFR Weather Minimums*

1. Except as provided in 91.107 (Special VFR, which is not applicable to recreational pilots), certain minimum distances for flight visibility and distances from clouds are required.

2. Weather Minimums Within Controlled Airspace
   a. When 1,200 feet or less above the surface (AGL).
      1) 3 statute miles visibility.
      2) Distance from clouds
         a) 500 feet below.
         b) 1,000 feet above.
         c) 2,000 feet horizontal.
      3) Memory aid: Be higher (1,000 feet) above than lower (500 feet) below.
   b. When above 1,200 feet AGL and below 10,000 feet MSL.
      1) 3 statute miles visibility.
      2) Distance from clouds
         a) 500 feet below.
         b) 1,000 feet above.
         c) 2,000 feet horizontal.
   c. When above 1,200 feet AGL and at or above 10,000 feet MSL.
      1) 5 statute miles visibility.
      2) Distance from clouds
         a) 1,000 feet above and below.
         b) 1 statute mile horizontal.
   d. Except with a special VFR clearance, no one may operate an aircraft under VFR, in a control zone, and beneath the cloud ceiling if the ceiling is less than 1,000 feet AGL.

3. Weather Minimums Outside Controlled Airspace
   a. When 1,200 feet or less above the surface (AGL).
      1) 1 statute mile visibility.
      2) Clear of clouds.
   b. When above 1,200 feet AGL and below 10,000 feet MSL.
      1) 1 statute mile visibility.
      2) Distance from clouds
         a) 500 feet below.
         b) 1,000 feet above.
         c) 2,000 feet horizontal.
   c. When above 1,200 feet AGL and at or above 10,000 feet MSL.
      1) 5 statute miles visibility.
      2) Distance from clouds
         a) 1,000 feet above and below.
         b) 1 statute mile horizontal.
   d. Memory aid: VFR weather minimums for controlled and uncontrolled airspace are the same except that uncontrolled airspace calls only for
      1) 1 statute mile visibility if under 10,000 feet MSL.
      2) Being clear of clouds below 1,200 feet AGL.

4. Except with a special VFR clearance, no one may land, take off, or enter a traffic pattern within a control zone unless ground visibility is at least three statute miles. If ground visibility is not reported, flight visibility must be at least three statute miles.

91.109 VFR Cruising Altitude or Flight Level

1. All VFR aircraft above 3,000 feet AGL and below 18,000 feet MSL in level cruising flight shall maintain specified altitudes.
   a. The altitude prescribed is based upon the magnetic course (not magnetic heading) and is in terms of mean sea level (MSL).
   b. For magnetic courses of 0° to 179°, use odd thousand foot MSL altitudes plus 500 feet; e.g., 3,500, 5,500, or 7,500 if the course is easterly.
   c. For magnetic courses of 180° to 359°, use even thousand foot MSL altitudes plus 500 feet; e.g., 4,500, 6,500, or 8,500 if the course is westerly.
   d. Memory aid: The "E" in Even does not indicate east; i.e., easterly headings for 0° through 179°, use odd rather than even.

91.163 General

1. The owner or operator of an aircraft is primarily responsible for maintaining the aircraft in an airworthy condition.
2. No person may perform work on aircraft in a manner contrary to this subpart.
3. No person may operate an aircraft contrary to any airworthiness limitations specified by the manufacturer. This includes following the required replacement time, inspection intervals, and related procedures.

91.165 Maintenance Required

1. Each owner or operator shall have the aircraft inspected as prescribed in 91.169, 91.171, and 91.172.
2. Between inspections, any discrepancies shall be dealt with in accordance with FAR Part 43 (Maintenance, Preventive Maintenance, Rebuilding, and Alteration).

91.167 Operation After Maintenance, Preventive Maintenance, Rebuilding, or Alteration

1. No person may operate an aircraft that has undergone any maintenance, preventative maintenance, rebuilding, or alteration unless:
   a. It has been approved for return to service by a person authorized by FAR 43.7.
   b. The logbook entry required by FARs 43.9 and 43.11 has been made.
2. No person may operate an aircraft that has significantly been altered or rebuilt, to the extent that it changes its flight characteristics, until it has been test-flown by an appropriately-rated pilot with at least a Private Pilot certificate.

91.169 Inspections

1. Annual inspections are good through the last day of the 12th calendar month after the previous annual inspection.
2. For commercial operations, an inspection is required every 100 hours.
   a. The 100 hours may not be exceeded by more than 10 hours if necessary to reach a place at which an inspection can be performed.
   b. The next inspection, however, is due 200 hours from the prior inspection; e.g., if the inspection is done at 105 hours, the next inspection is due in 95 hours.
   c. If you have an inspection done prior to 100 hours, you cannot add the time remaining to 100 hours to the next inspection.

91.170 Changes to Aircraft Inspection Programs

1. Whenever the FAA determines that a change is required in the approved aircraft inspection program to maintain safety, the owner or operator shall, after notification, make the required changes.
2. The owner or operator may petition against this change within 30 days of receiving the notice of the change.

91.171 Altimeter System and Altitude Reporting Equipment Tests and Inspections

1. No person may operate in controlled airspace under IFR unless:
   a. Within the preceding 24 calendar months each static pressure system, each altimeter instrument, and each automatic pressure altitude reporting system has been tested and found to comply with Appendices E and F of Part 43.
   b. The tests can be performed by the aircraft manufacturer or a certified repair shop.

91.172 ATC Transponder Tests and Inspections

1. No person may use an ATC Transponder unless it has been tested within the last 24 calendar months and found to comply with Appendix F of FAR Part 43.
2. The test must be done by a certified repair shop.

91.173 Maintenance Records

1. Each owner or operator shall keep the following records:
   a. Alteration or rebuilding records
   b. 100-hour inspections
   c. Annual inspections
   d. Progressive and other required inspections
2. The records must be kept for each aircraft (airframe), engine, propeller, and appliance.
3. Each record shall include a description of the work performed, the date of completion, and the signature and certificate number of the person performing the work.

91.174 Transfer of Maintenance Records

1. Any owner or operator who sells as U.S. registered aircraft must, at the time of the sale, transfer to the new owner the following records:
   a. Records of maintenance, preventative maintenance, and alteration.
   b. Records of all 100-hour, annual, progressive, and other required inspections.

91.175 *Rebuilt Engine Maintenance Records*

1. The owner or operator may use a new maintenance record for an aircraft engine rebuilt by the manufacturer or a shop approved by the manufacturer.

2. Each shop that grants zero time to an engine shall enter in the new record:
    a. A signed statement of the date it was rebuilt.
    b. Each change made as required by an Airworthiness Directive.
    c. Each change made in compliance with a Manufacturer's Service Bulletin.

3. A rebuilt engine is one that is completely disassembled, inspected, repaired, reassembled, tested, and approved to the same tolerances as new.

NATIONAL TRANSPORTATION SAFETY BOARD (NTSB) PART 830

The National Transportation Safety Board is part of the U.S. Department of Transportation (similar to the Federal Aviation Administration). The NTSB is responsible for investigating transportation accidents. Like the FAA, it issues rules.

PART 830 - RULES PERTAINING TO THE NOTIFICATION AND REPORTING OF AIRCRAFT ACCIDENTS OR INCIDENTS AND OVERDUE AIRCRAFT, AND PRESERVATION OF AIRCRAFT WRECKAGE, MAIL, CARGO, AND RECORDS

830.1 *Applicability*

1. This part concerns reporting accidents, incidents, and certain other occurrences involving U.S. civil aircraft and preservation of the wreckage, mail, cargo, and records.

830.2 *Definitions*

1. *Aircraft accident* -- An occurrence that takes place between the time any person boards an aircraft with the intention of flight until such time as all such persons have disembarked, and in which
    a. Any person suffers death or serious injury as a result of being in or upon the aircraft or by direct contact with the aircraft or anything attached thereto, or
    b. The aircraft receives substantial damage.

2. *Fatal injury* -- An injury resulting in death within 30 days of the accident.

3. *Incident* -- An occurrence other than an accident, associated with the operation of an aircraft, that affects or could affect the safety of operations.

4. *Operator* -- Means any person who causes or authorizes the operation of an aircraft, such as the owner, lessee, or bailee of an aircraft.

5. *Serious injury* -- Means any injury that
    a. Requires hospitalization for more than 48 hours, commencing within seven days from the date the injury was received.
    b. Results in a fracture of any bone (except simple fractures of fingers, toes, or nose).
    c. Causes severe hemorrhages, nerve, muscle, or tendon damage.
    d. Involves injury to any internal organ.
    e. Involves second- or third-degree burns, or any burns affecting more than five percent of the body surface.

6. *Substantial damage* -- Damage or failure that adversely affects the structural strength, performance, or flight characteristics of the aircraft, and that would normally require major repair or replacement of the affected component.
    a. Engine failure, damage limited to an engine, bent fairings or cowling, dented skin, small punctured holes in the skin or fabric, ground damage to rotor or propeller blades, damage to landing gear, wheels, tires, flaps, engine accessories, brakes, or wingtips are not considered to be "substantial damage."

830.5 Immediate Notification

1. The nearest NTSB office must be notified immediately when an aircraft is overdue and believed to be involved in an accident, when an accident occurs, or when any of the following incidents occurs:
    a. Flight control system malfunction or failure.
    b. Inability of any required flight crewmember to perform normal flight duties as a result of injury or illness.
    c. Failure of structural components of a turbine engine excluding compressor and turbine blades and vanes.
    d. In-flight fire.
    e. Aircraft collide in flight.

830.6 Information to Be Given In Notification

1. The operator shall file a report on the prescribed form within 10 days after an accident (seven days if an overdue aircraft is missing). A report on an incident for which notification is required shall be filed only upon request.
2. Name of owner, and operator of the aircraft.
3. Name of the pilot-in-command.
4. Date and time of the accident.
5. Last point of departure and point of intended landing of the aircraft.
6. Position of the aircraft with reference to some easily defined geographical point.
7. Number of persons aboard, number killed, and number seriously injured.
8. Nature of the accident, the weather, and the extent of damage to the aircraft, so far as is known.
9. A description of any explosives, radioactive materials, or other dangerous articles carried.

830.10 Preservation of Aircraft Wreckage, Mail, Cargo, and Records

1. The operator of an aircraft is reponsible for preserving any aircraft wreckage, cargo, mail, and all records until the Board takes custody.
2. The wreckage may only be disturbed to
    a. Remove persons injured or trapped.
    b. Protect the wreckage from further damage.
    c. Protect the public from injury.
3. When it is necessary to disturb or move aircraft wreckage or mail or cargo, sketches, descriptive notes, and photographs shall be made if possible of the accident locale, including original position and condition of the wreckage and any significant impact marks.
4. The operator of an aircraft involved in an accident or incident shall retain all records and reports, including all internal documents and memoranda dealing with the event, until authorized by the NTSB to the contrary.

830.15 Reports and Statements to Be Filed

1. The operator shall file a report on the prescribed form within 10 days after an accident (seven days if an overdue aircraft is missing). A report on an incident for which notification is required shall be filed only upon request.
2. Each crewmember shall, as soon as physically able, attach a statement concerning the facts, conditions, and circumstances relating to the accident or incident.
3. The report shall be filed at the nearest NTSB office.

INSTRUCTOR CERTIFICATION FORM
FLIGHT TEST

Date: _____

Name: _____

    I certify that I have given the above individual the flight instruction required by FAR Part 61 within the preceding 60 days, including a review of the subject areas found to be deficient on his/her airman's written test, and find his/her performance satisfactory to apply for a recreational pilot certificate.

Signed: _____

CFI Number: _____ Expiration Date: _____

INSTRUCTOR CERTIFICATION FORM
WRITTEN TEST

Date: _____

Name: _____

    I certify that I have reviewed the above individual's completion of the *RECREATIONAL PILOT FAA WRITTEN EXAM* home-study course by Irvin N. Gleim for the FAA Recreational Pilot written test (covering the topics specified in FAR 61.97). I find that (s)he has satisfactorily completed the course and find him/her competent to pass the recreational pilot (airplane) written test.

Signed: _____

CFI Number: _____ Expiration Date: _____

AUTHOR'S RECOMMENDATION

The Experimental Aircraft Association, Inc. is a very successful and effective nonprofit organization that represents and serves those of us interested in flying, in general, and in sport aviation, in particular. I personally invite you to enjoy becoming a member:

> $30 for a one-year membership
> $18 per year for individuals under 19 years old
> Family membership available for an extra $10 per year.

Membership includes the monthly magazine *Sport Aviation*.

> *Write to:*   Experimental Aircraft Association, Inc.
> Wittman Airfield
> Oshkosh, WI   54903

> *or call:*   (414) 426-4800
> (800) 322-2412   (in Wisconsin: 1-800-236-4800)

The annual EEA Oshkosh Fly-In is an unbelievable aviation spectacular with over 10,000 airplanes at one airport! Virtually everything aviation-oriented you can imagine! Plan to spend at least one day (not everything can be seen in a day) in Oshkosh (100 miles northwest of Milwaukee).

> *Convention dates:*   1990 - July 27 through August 3
> 1991 - July 26 through August 1
> 1992 - July 31 through August 6

274

WRITTEN EXAM BOOKS
available from
AVIATION PUBLICATIONS, Inc.

RECREATIONAL PILOT FAA WRITTEN EXAM ($9.95)

The newest certificate offered by the FAA. The FAA's written test consists of 50 questions out of the 445 questions in our book.

PRIVATE PILOT FAA WRITTEN EXAM ($9.95)

The FAA's written test consists of 50 questions out of the 673 questions in our book.

INSTRUMENT PILOT FAA WRITTEN EXAM ($14.95)

The FAA's written test consists of 60 questions out of the 834 questions in our book. Also, those people who wish to become an instrument-rated flight instructor (CFII) or an instrument ground instructor (IGI) must take the FAA's written test of 50 questions from this book.

COMMERCIAL PILOT FAA WRITTEN EXAM ($14.95)

The FAA's written test will consist of 100 questions out of the 575 questions in our book.

FUNDAMENTALS OF INSTRUCTING FAA WRITTEN EXAM ($9.95)

The FAA's written test consists of 50 questions out of the 182 questions in our book. This is required of any person to become a flight instructor or ground instructor. The test only needs to be taken once, so if someone is already a flight instructor and wants to become a ground instructor, taking the FOI test a second time is not required. Conversely, a ground instructor who wants to become a flight instructor does not have to take the FOI test again.

FLIGHT/GROUND INSTRUCTOR FAA WRITTEN EXAM ($14.95)

The FAA's written test consists of 100 questions out of the 834 questions in our book. To be used for the Certificated Flight Instructor (CFI) written test and those who aspire to the Advanced Ground Instructor (AGI) rating for airplanes. Note that this book also covers what is known as the Basic Ground Instructor (BGI) rating. However, the BGI is not useful because it does not give the holder full authority to sign off private pilots to take their written test. In other words, this book should be used for the AGI rating.

FLIGHT MANEUVER AND REFERENCE BOOKS
available from
AVIATION PUBLICATIONS, Inc.

RECREATIONAL PILOT FLIGHT MANEUVERS ($11.95)

Contains, in outline format, pertinent information necessary to be a skilled recreational pilot. An excellent reference book to begin your flight training endeavors with.

PRIVATE PILOT HANDBOOK ($11.95)

A complete private pilot ground school text in outline format with many diagrams for ease in understanding. To make it more useful and save user's time, it has a very complete, detailed index. It contains a special section on biennial flight reviews.

PRIVATE PILOT FLIGHT MANEUVERS ($9.95)

A complete guide for airplane flight training leading to the private pilot certificate. Covers the flight maneuvers in outline format with numerous diagrams. It includes a reprint of the new FAA Practical Test Standards, with outlines of the maneuvers to be performed on the FAA airplane flight test (including acceptable performance limits).

INSTRUMENT PILOT FLIGHT MANEUVERS & HANDBOOK ($17.95)

A comprehensive explanation with illustrations of flight by reference to instruments, IFR charts and navigation, instrument approaches, IFR cross-country, and includes complete discussion of the current FAA Practical Test Standards for the instrument rating-airplane.

MULTIENGINE AND SEAPLANE FLIGHT MANEUVERS & HANDBOOK ($14.95)

Provides separate and comprehensive explanation of each rating. Emphasis is placed on how each airplane is different from single-engine airplanes. Flight and ground operation is explained, illustrated, and analyzed in terms of the FAA Practical Test Standards. This book is extremely helpful as a reference book as well as a training text.

COMMERCIAL PILOT AND FLIGHT INSTRUCTOR FLIGHT MANEUVERS & HANDBOOK ($14.95)

Separate and complete coverage of the commercial certificate and flight instructor certificate. It begins with an explanation of the requirements and recommended steps to obtain each certificate. All flight maneuvers are explained, illustrated, and analyzed in terms of the current FAA Practical Test Standards. It is an excellent reference text for professional pilots.

MAIL TO:

Aviation Publications, Inc.
P.O. Box 12848
University Station
Gainesville, FL   32604

OR CALL: **(904) 375-0772**

Books Currently Available

RECREATIONAL PILOT FAA WRITTEN EXAM . . . . First (1989-1991) Edition	$ 9.95	$_____
PRIVATE PILOT FAA WRITTEN EXAM . . . . Fourth (1988-1990) Edition	9.95	_____
INSTRUMENT PILOT FAA WRITTEN EXAM . . . . Second (1988-1990) Edition	14.95	_____
COMMERCIAL PILOT FAA WRITTEN EXAM . . . . Second (1988-1990) Edition	14.95	_____
FUNDAMENTALS OF INSTRUCTING FAA WRITTEN EXAM . . . . . Third (1989-1991) Edition	9.95	_____
FLIGHT/GROUND INSTRUCTOR FAA WRITTEN EXAM . . . . Third (1989-1991) Edition	14.95	_____

RECREATIONAL PILOT FLIGHT MANEUVERS (First Edition)	$11.95	_____
PRIVATE PILOT HANDBOOK (Third Edition)	11.95	_____
PRIVATE PILOT FLIGHT MANEUVERS (Second Edition)	9.95	_____
INSTRUMENT PILOT FLIGHT MANEUVERS & HANDBOOK (First Edition)	17.95	_____
MULTIENGINE AND SEAPLANE FLIGHT MANEUVERS & HANDBOOK (First Edition)	14.95	_____
COMMERCIAL PILOT AND FLIGHT INSTRUCTOR FLIGHT MANEUVERS & HANDBOOK (First Edition) . .	14.95	_____

Florida residents add 6% sales tax . . . .   6% Tax   _____

Please call or write for additional charges for out-of-the-U.S. shipments

                                                                                                                    TOTAL $_____

1. We process and ship orders within one day of receipt of your order. We generally ship via UPS for the Eastern U.S. and U.S. mail for the Western U.S.

2. Please PHOTOCOPY this order form for friends and others.

3. No CODs. All orders from individuals must be prepaid and are protected by our unequivocal refund policy.
    Library and company orders may be on account.
    Shipping charges will be added to telephone orders and to orders not prepaid.

Name _____

Mailing Address _____

Street Address (for UPS) _____

City _____ State _____ Zip _____

☐ MasterCard   ☐ VISA   ☐ Check or Money Order Enclosed

MasterCard/VISA No.

__ __ __ __ - __ __ __ __ - __ __ __ __ - __ __ __ __

Expiration Date *(month/year)* ____/____

Signature _____

Aviation Publications GUARANTEES
AN IMMEDIATE, COMPLETE REFUND
ON ALL MAIL ORDERS
IF A RESALABLE TEXT IS RETURNED IN 30 DAYS

INDEX

Please forward your suggestions, corrections, and comments concerning typographical errors, etc. to **Irvin N. Gleim • c/o Aviation Publications, Inc. • P.O. Box 12848 • University Station • Gainesville, Florida • 32604.** Please include your name and address so we can properly thank you for your interest.

1. _____

2. _____

3. _____

4. _____

5. _____

Name: _____

Address: _____

_____

City/State/Zip: _____

Telephone: (_____) _____